DISCLAIMER

The information in this book is based on the author's experiences and research. It is not professional financial advice. The strategies described have worked for some people. They may not work for you. Your financial situation is unique. Consult qualified professionals for advice specific to your circumstances.

The author and publisher are not liable for any losses or damages related to the use of this information. All investments and business ventures carry risk. Past results do not guarantee future performance. Income examples in this book represent best-case scenarios, not typical results.

This book discusses general principles. Laws and regulations vary by location. Verify all information against your local requirements.

If you have mental health concerns related to financial stress, seek professional help.

INCOME DISCLOSURE

Most readers who apply these principles see modest improvements in their financial situation. Some see no improvement. A small percentage achieve significant results. Success depends on factors including but not limited to: starting point, consistency, local economic conditions, personal skills, and market timing.

The average reader who applies these principles may see little to no financial improvement. Success requires factors beyond just following this book, including but not limited to: market timing, geographic location, existing skills, available time, and economic conditions.

Income figures mentioned in case studies and examples represent actual results achieved by specific individuals but are not typical. Individual results vary based on effort, market conditions, and numerous other factors.

1

Table of Contents:

INTRODUCTION:

YOU'RE NOT CRAZY.

Your parents bought a house on one income.

You can't afford groceries on two.

You're not crazy.

That sick certainty when you check your bank balance before buying toothpaste? That moment when you realize your "good job" pays less than your dad made in 1985—adjusted for inflation? The suffocating math that says even if you save every penny for twenty years, you'll never afford the neighborhood you grew up in?

You're not crazy. You're correct.

The game is rigged. And everyone's pretending it's not.

The raise that felt like victory until rent went up more. The promotion that somehow left you broker. The budget spreadsheet documenting your perfect management of inevitable decline.

Rent eats 50% of your income—whether you're in San Francisco or São Paulo. You choose between gas and groceries in Mumbai and Miami alike. Your phone bill costs what your parents' entire monthly expenses did. A coffee costs an hour's wage. A house costs a lifetime you don't have.

You work harder than your parents. Longer hours. Better educated. More productive. Yet they vacationed. You can't afford sick days. They saved. You survive. They retired. You'll work forever.

The math broke while you were following the rules.

I know because I was you.

$9 an hour hauling concrete in July heat. Coming home too exhausted to shower. Sleeping in work clothes. Waking up to do it again. Doing the math: After rent, I had $287 a month. For everything else. Forever.

The success books said "work harder." I was already working too many hours.

The finance blogs said "save more." Save what?

The motivational speakers said "believe in yourself." My confidence didn't pay bills.

So I did something different. I stopped managing my poverty perfectly and started building my way out messily.

Construction to new job: $9 to $18 an hour.

New job to specialized skill: $18 to $45 an hour.

Employee to business owner: $45/hour to $20,000/month.

Lost it all. Built it back bigger. No trust fund. No connections. No magic.

Just different math. The kind they don't teach because it threatens their game.

The principles I learned in those valleys—crawling from $9 to $90 an hour—are the same ones that work whether you're in Manhattan or Mumbai, whether you're 20 or 60, whether you're starting from zero or starting over.

But I'm getting ahead of myself. First, you need to understand why everything changed...

Here's the beautiful, terrifying truth: You're not failing at the game. The game changed, and nobody sent you the new rulebook. You're playing checkers while the economy plays chess. With your money. With your future. With your life.

But physics has laws. Even broken physics.

Once you understand the real rules—not the fantasy they're still teaching—you can stop managing decline and start building wealth. Stop budgeting poverty and start creating abundance. Stop playing their rigged game and start building your own.

This book contains those laws. The real physics. The builder's path.

Not magic. Math. The kind that works in Delhi and Detroit. In good economies and bad. Whether you're 25 or 65. Whether you're starting from zero or starting over.

The math that broke can be rebuilt. But not by budgeting better.

By building different.

Ready to stop being crazy and start being free?

The Three Economic Eras

Picture Sunday dinner. The table your grandmother inherited, now yours. Three generations passing the potatoes. Same family. Same values. Same work ethic.

Completely different economic physics.

Grandpa's telling that story again—how he bought the house in '72 on his factory wages. Single income. Grandma stayed home with four kids. Summer vacations to the lake. Two cars in the garage. College funds growing. Retirement secured.

He's not bragging. He's confused why you're struggling.

Era 1: The Golden Ratio (Your Grandparents)

The physics were beautiful. Mathematical poetry.

Wages climbed 5% yearly. Predictable as sunrise.
Costs crept up 2%. Manageable as seasons.
The gap? Pure prosperity.

Detroit, 1965: Assembly line worker. High school diploma. Buys 3-bedroom house at 25. Supports family of six. Retires with pension.

Delhi, 1962: Government clerk. Basic education. Purchases family home. Educates all children. Builds generational wealth.

London, 1958: Post office worker. Single income. Owns row house. Annual holidays. Children attend university.

São Paulo, 1967: Bank teller. One salary. Apartment purchased. Kids in private school. Beach house for summers.

Same physics worldwide. Work hard $\rightarrow$ Live well. The equation balanced.

5

Your grandparents weren't financial geniuses. They just lived when the math worked.

Era 2: The Squeeze (Your Parents)

Watch your mother's face tighten when Grandpa talks. She remembers.

The physics shifted. Subtle at first.

Wages grew 3% yearly. Still climbing, but slower.
Costs accelerated to 3%. The race was on.
The gap? Vanished.

Suddenly, Mom needed to work too. Not for extras—for existence.

Detroit, 1985: Same factory. Now needs spouse's income for smaller house. Vacations become staycations.

Delhi, 1988: Same government job. Wife takes teaching position. Together they match what father earned alone.

London, 1990: Same postal route. Partner works retail. Combined, they maintain middle class.

São Paulo, 1992: Same bank. Both parents working. Apartment smaller than parents'. No beach house.

Remember your exhausted parents? Racing on a treadmill that kept speeding up? They weren't lazy. They were trapped between eras.

Your parents worked twice as hard to stay in place. The equation strained.

Era 3: The Divergence (You)

Now you. Scrolling housing listings during dinner. Pretending you're not.

The physics broke. Shattered. Exploded.

Wages barely limp upward yearly. If you're lucky.
Costs sprint upward.
The gap? A widening abyss.

Two incomes. Smaller apartment than your childhood home. No savings. Vacation means visiting parents. Retirement is a bitter joke. Kids? Can't afford them.

Detroit, 2024: Grandson of factory worker. College degree. Two tech jobs. Can't afford grandpa's neighborhood.

Delhi, 2024: Granddaughter of clerk. MBA. Husband's an engineer. Rent eats 60% of combined income.

London, 2024: Postal worker's kid. Both partners in finance. Priced out of parents' row house by millions.

São Paulo, 2024: Bank teller's daughter. Dual income lawyers. Live in apartment half the size of childhood home.

The math isn't slightly off. It's catastrophically broken.

Your grandfather bought a house at 25 on one income.

Your parents needed two incomes at 30.

You can't afford that same house at 35 with two incomes and a side hustle.

Each year the gap widens. Like a wound that won't heal. Like a river cutting deeper into rock.

5% wage growth vs 2% costs = prosperity
3% wages vs 3% costs = survival
2% wages vs 7% costs = drowning in slow motion

Same table. Same work ethic. Same Sunday dinner.

Your grandfather built wealth accidentally.

Your parents maintained position desperately.

You're falling behind mathematically.

Three generations. Three physics. Same table.

The game changed, and nobody told you the new rules.

Worse-they're still teaching the old rules. Save more. Budget better. Skip lattes. As if you could budget your way out of broken physics.

You can't.

But you can build your way out.

Once you see the physics clearly, you can stop trying to win the old game and start playing a different one entirely.

Angela's Discovery

11 PM. Kitchen table. Kids finally asleep.

Angela spreads the bills across scratched wood like tarot cards predicting doom. The laptop glows with her budget spreadsheet-a masterpiece of financial management. Every dollar tracked. Every penny assigned. Every expense justified.

Still $200 short.

Always $200 short.

She's manager at McDonald's. Forty-seven hours this week because corporate caps her under fifty to avoid benefits. The calculator confirms what she already knows: even with next week's check, she'll fall further behind. The rent increase notification sits unopened. She already knows.

"I did everything right," she tells her reflection in the laptop screen. "No Starbucks. No subscriptions. No nothing. Still drowning."

The spreadsheet stares back. Perfect columns documenting perfect failure.

She'd followed every rule. Tracked every expense. Cut everything cuttable. Her budget was a work of art-if the art form was "managing decline."

Two weeks later. Different kind of table. Medical lab. Annual blood work she'd postponed twice because who has $50 for preventive care?

The phlebotomist makes small talk while finding a vein. Young woman, about Angela's age. Scrubs that fit. Nails done. Energy that doesn't scream "exhausted."

"Long shift?" Angela asks.

"Just eight hours. Three twelve-hour days, then four off. Love this schedule."

Angela's manager brain kicks in. "What's the hourly for-" She stops. Rude to ask.

The woman laughs. "Everyone asks. Twenty-eight an hour, thirty-two with shift differential. Plus benefits. Not bad for a year of training, right?"

The needle slides in. Angela watches her blood fill the vial. Dark red. Same color as her budget spreadsheet cells.

Twenty-eight dollars. An hour.

She makes fifteen-fifty. After six years.

Same city. Same hours. One skill difference.

The math hits like cold water. This woman makes in one day what Angela makes in two. Not because she works harder. Not because she budgets better. Because she plays a different game entirely.

That night, Angela stares at her spreadsheet again. But now she sees it differently. Like those optical illusions-once you see the second image, you can't unsee it.

She wasn't failing at the game.

She was playing the only game she'd been taught.

Budget. Cut. Manage. Shrink. Accept. Survive.

But somewhere, other people were playing build. Learn. Expand. Grow. Create. Thrive.

Same city. Same economy. Different physics.

She closes the budget spreadsheet. Opens Google. Types: "Phlebotomy certification programs near me."

Today, Angela runs Mobile Medical Services. Corporate contracts with companies too busy to send workers to labs. That phlebotomist who drew her blood? Now works for her.

Same Angela. Same city. Same 24 hours in her day.

Completely different physics.

Her kitchen table still has scratches. But now they're from grandkids doing homework while she helps them build lemonade stand spreadsheets- the kind that track growth, not decline. The bills still come. She pays them in minutes, not tears.

She still budgets. But budgeting is now her defense, not her entire strategy. Building is her offense. One maintains. One multiplies.

"I thought I needed to manage money better," she says now, training her newest hire. "Turns out I needed to make money differently."

The old game: How can I need less?
The new game: How can I create more?
One has a floor. One has no ceiling.

This book teaches those physics.

The same physics Angela discovered watching her blood drain into a vial. The physics that transform kitchen table tears into conference table decisions. The physics available to anyone willing to see the second image in the optical illusion of modern economics.

You've been playing the only game you were taught.

There's another game entirely.

Ready to learn?

The Two Neighbors

Maple Street. Every town has one. Identical houses built in the '80s. Driveways with the same cracks. Dreams deferred by the same bills.

Watch these two front doors. Number 42 and 46. Same square footage. Same mortgage terms. Completely different futures unfolding.

House 42: Sarah, the Perfect Manager

Sunday morning. Sarah's at the kitchen table with her color-coded binder. Red tabs for bills. Green for coupons. Yellow for meal plans. She's been up since 5 AM, planning the week's assault on expenses.

The grocery spreadsheet is a masterpiece. Three stores mapped for best prices. Coupons matched to sales. Every meal planned. Every penny allocated. Total savings: $47.83. Time invested: four hours.

She's cancelled Netflix. Negotiated insurance down $12/month. Switched to generic everything. Her Facebook group cheers: "You're so disciplined!" Her budget is Instagram-worthy. Financial gurus would weep with joy.

Her vision board hangs in the closet. The house three streets over-the one with the bigger yard. "2025 GOAL!" written in hopeful Sharpie.

House 46: Marcus, the Messy Builder

Same Sunday. Marcus is in the garage, laptop balanced on a paint can. He's trying to understand YouTube ads for the lawn care service he started. Already spent $50 wrong. Clicks wrong buttons. Wastes money.

His neighbor's lawns look decent, not perfect. His budget? What budget? He bought good equipment instead of tracking every penny. His wife's still got Netflix. They order pizza when he's too tired to cook.

But he's noticing things. Mrs. Chen needs weekly service. The Johnsons want organic treatment. That apartment complex has nobody maintaining their grounds...

Year One

Sarah saved $2,847 through extreme couponing. Her binder has its own binder. She's exhausted but proud. Still in the same house. The dream house sold to someone else.

Marcus made every mistake possible. Undercharged clients. Forgot to invoice. Bought wrong equipment. But he's got twelve regular lawns. Hired a high school kid. Learning QuickBooks badly.

Year Two

Sarah's system is legendary. She teaches coupon classes at the library. Tracks every penny in four apps. Her cost per meal is $1.47. She hasn't eaten at a restaurant in 18 months. The stress headaches started.

Marcus added pressure washing. Same clients wanted it. Watched YouTube University. Bought used equipment. His wife handles the books now-she's better with numbers. Twenty-five regular clients.

Year Three

Sarah's burned out but can't stop. The spreadsheets own her now. She saved another $3,200 but her car needs transmission work. That's $3,000. The treadmill of perfect management. Maple Street feels like a prison.

Marcus incorporated. Tax benefits he barely understands. Hired two more kids. Added Christmas lights installation because why not? Some attorney client asked. Now doing whole neighborhoods. Mistakes everywhere. Growth anyway.

Year Four

Sarah's at her table. Same scratched surface. Same red binder. Same perfect tracking of the same insufficient income. Her vision board's in the trash. The houses she wants cost 40% more now. Her savings buy 40% less. The math is perfect. The outcome is brutal.

Marcus bought a truck. Used, but reliable. His crews run routes while he quotes new jobs. Added commercial contracts. The apartment complex alone pays five grand monthly. He's terrible at operations. Good at solving problems.

Year Five

Sunday morning. Maple Street. Two moving trucks.

Sarah's helping her sister pack. Another foreclosure on the street. Her binder documents five years of perfect management. Every penny tracked. Every sacrifice recorded. Still renting the same life, just more efficiently. The exhaustion shows in her eyes.

Marcus is loading boxes too. Into the house three streets over. The one with the bigger yard. The one from Sarah's old vision board. His business runs itself mostly. He still makes mistakes. But mistakes at a higher level.

Sarah waves from her window. Same window. Same view. Same future.

Marcus waves back from his truck. New view. New possibilities. New physics.

One managed decline perfectly.
One built growth imperfectly.
One tracked every penny escaping.
One created new pennies flowing.
One played defense flawlessly.
One played offense chaotically.
Guess who won?

Not because Marcus was smarter. Not because he worked harder. But because he played a different game with different rules. Rules Sarah never learned. Rules they don't teach in coupon classes.

The tragedy? Sarah did everything right-for the wrong game. She optimized a broken system instead of building a better one. She managed scarcity instead of creating abundance.

The hope? Marcus was no genius. Made every mistake. Still won. Because building imperfectly beats managing perfectly in broken physics.

The difference? Four laws that change everything.

Laws that work on Maple Street or Main Street. In boom times or bust. Whether you're Sarah with your perfect binder or Marcus with your messy garage.

Four laws that separate those who document decline from those who create growth.

Ready to learn what Marcus stumbled onto?

The Builder's Compound Curve

THE JOURNEY EVERY BUILDER TAKES:

THE BUILDER'S COMPOUND CURVE

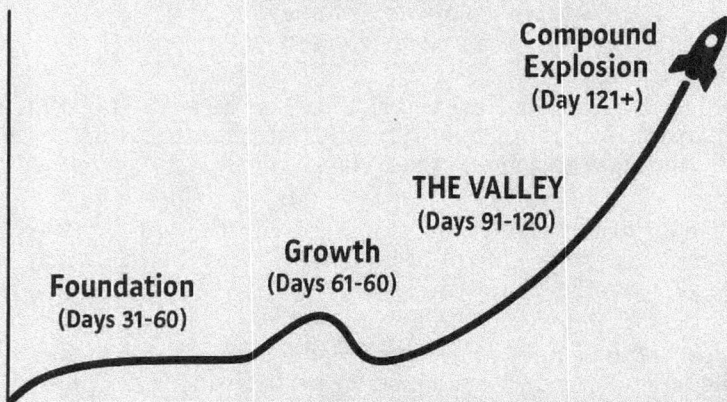

Compound
Explosion
(Day 121+)

THE VALLEY
(Days 91-120)

Growth
(Days 61-60)

Foundation
(Days 31-60)

THIS IS YOUR ROADMAP. SCREENSHOT IT NOW.

YOU'LL NEED IT AROUND DAY 75 WHEN YOU WANT TO QUIT.

EVERY BUILDER WHO MADE IT THROUGH HAS THIS EXACT CURVE

THE VALLEY IS NOT YOUR ENEMY. IT'S YOUR LAUNCHING PAD.

This is your roadmap. Screenshot it. You'll need it around day 75.

Look at that curve. Really look at it.

See that dip between days 61-90? That's not failure. That's physics. Every rocket needs a launchpad. Every jump requires a crouch. Every breakthrough demands a valley.

What This Map Really Shows:

Days 1-30: Foundation (Invisible Progress)
You're planting seeds underground. Nothing visible yet. Your spouse thinks you're wasting time. You wonder if they're right. They're not. Roots are growing where nobody can see.

Days 31-60: Growth (First Green Shoots)
Tiny visible progress. One person notices. You made $50. Or lost 5 pounds. Or wrote 10 pages. Still small, but movement. Hope tastes real for the first time.

Days 61-90: THE VALLEY (The Sacred Test)
Everything stalls. Progress reverses. Doubts scream. Family "worries about you." This is where 90% quit. This is also where 100% of success stories are born. The Valley isn't your enemy-it's your cocoon.

Days 91-120: Breakthrough (The Physics Shift)
Suddenly, connections. What felt impossible becomes inevitable. Skills compound. Network activates. Results accelerate. You can't explain it, but everything's different. The same actions now yield 10X results.

Day 121+: Compound Explosion (New Reality)
Not linear growth-exponential. Each day builds on the last 120. Opportunities find you. Problems you couldn't solve become simple. Income multiplies. Impact scales. You look back at Day 1 You with compassion and amazement.

The Valley Truth Nobody Tells You:

The Valley isn't where dreams go to die.

The Valley is where dreamers become builders.

Every entrepreneur hit it. Every athlete. Every artist. Every person whose life you admire spent days 61-90 wanting to quit.

The only difference between failure and success stories?

Success stories kept showing up on day 76.

Valley Survival Kit:
Day 65: "This isn't working" → Normal
Day 72: "Maybe I should quit" → Expected
Day 78: "One more week" → The turning point
Day 85: "Something feels different" → Physics shifting
Day 92: "Holy shit, it's working" → Welcome to your new life

Why This Curve Is Sacred:

It's not a suggestion. It's a law. Like gravity.

You can't skip the Valley any more than you can skip Wednesday to get to Thursday. But knowing it's coming transforms it from an ambush to an appointment.

When you hit day 70 and want to quit, you'll remember: "Oh, this is that part. The map showed me this. Everyone feels this. I just need to keep walking."

Screenshot this curve now.

Print it. Frame it. Tattoo it on your brain.

Because around day 75, when your inner critic is screaming and your outer world is silent, you'll need to see that you're not lost-you're exactly where every successful builder has been.

The Valley isn't your grave. It's your graduation.

The compound explosion isn't a maybe. It's a mathematical certainty for those who keep building.

Your only job? Show up tomorrow.

Then show up again.

Especially on days 61-90.

This curve has predicted every success story in history.

Now it's predicting yours.

Welcome to the journey, Builder.

See you on the other side of the Valley.

What This Book Promises

Not magic. Math.

Not schemes. Systems.

Not overnight. Over time.

Not lucky breaks. Learnable laws.

Not motivational fluff. Mechanical physics.

Not another hustle. Another approach entirely.

You'll discover:

Why traditional financial advice now guarantees decline
That "safe" savings account losing 5% yearly to inflation. The stable job that's automated next Tuesday. The retirement plan requiring you to live to 147. Every "smart" move designed for an economy that died in 2008. You'll see why following good advice from the wrong era is like using a map of ancient Rome to navigate modern Tokyo.

Four timeless laws that create wealth in any economy
The same laws that built fortunes during the Great Depression and the Great Recession. That work whether inflation's at 2% or 20%. Whether you're in Silicon Valley or a village without running water. Laws so simple your teenager understands them, so powerful they transform physics. (Warning: Once you see them, you can't unsee how much opportunity you've been walking past daily.)

A daily practice that compounds into transformation
Fifteen minutes. One small action. Invisible at first, like drops wearing away stone. Then sudden breakthrough-like stone splitting open. The CFO who started with YouTube videos at 5 AM. The janitor learning code on lunch breaks, now running IT. Not morning routines for millionaires. Morning physics for builders. The exact sequence that turns time into money, globally.

How ordinary people escape extraordinary traps
The Mumbai teacher making $300/month who now earns $3,000 teaching online. The Memphis mechanic whose repair videos fund his shop expansion. The grandmother in Ghana whose cooking channel pays her grandkids' college. Same constraints you face. Same doubts you have. Different outcomes because they learned what this book teaches: Your ZIP code isn't your destiny.

Your exact path from surviving to thriving
Not generic advice. Your situation, solved. Whether you're the overwhelmed parent juggling two jobs, the recent graduate facing a dead job market, the mid-career professional watching your industry vanish, or the retiree whose fixed income isn't fixed enough. Specific blueprints for specific physics. Chapter 8 will hand you your personal escape route.

Plus hidden treasures you don't expect:

- Why the Valley everyone quits in is actually where fortunes are forged
- How to make geography irrelevant to your income
- The multiplication method that turns one skill into ten income streams

- Why your "disadvantages" are probably your biggest assets in disguise
- The community of builders waiting to support your journey

But mostly, you'll discover this:

The game isn't rigged against you. You've been playing the wrong game entirely. Like trying to win chess using checkers rules. Frustrating. Futile. Fixable.

In the next 14 chapters, you'll learn the real rules. The ones that work from Nairobi to New York. From your current bank balance to your future freedom.

Not because you're special. Because the physics are.

Not through extraordinary effort. Through ordinary actions compounded.

Not by becoming someone else. By becoming who you were before the world taught you to manage decline instead of build growth.

One warning: This book will ruin your excuses. All of them. You'll see builders everywhere-people with worse situations creating better outcomes. You'll realize the only thing between your current reality and your possible future is knowing what they know.

Which, by page 247, you will.

Ready to learn what school never taught, what your boss won't tell you, and what the economy doesn't want you to know?

Your old life ends on the next page.

Your new one begins with Chapter 1.

Your First Win Starts Here

Before you read another page, do this:

Seriously. Put the book down for three minutes. Your future self will thank you.

The 3-Minute Subscription Audit:

Step 1: Grab your phone right now. Open your banking app.

Step 2: Search transactions for these keywords: "recurring," "subscription," "monthly," or just scroll through last month.

Step 3: Find the zombie subscriptions. That meditation app from January's motivation. The streaming service you meant to cancel after that one show. The premium version of something you use the free version of.

Cancel one. Right now. Before you talk yourself out of it.

Average person finds $47/month they didn't even know they were spending.

That's not a typo. Forty-seven dollars. Every month. Automatically drained. For services you forgot existed.

Let's do the math that matters:

$47 x 12 months = $564/year

That's a plane ticket to see family. That's a month of groceries. That's the online course that changes your career. That's seed money for your first builder experiment.

But here's what really just happened:

You didn't just save money. You took builder action. You found hidden value in three minutes. You changed your financial physics without anyone's permission, without a perfect plan, without waiting until Monday.

That feeling? That tiny rush of victory? That's building.

And you haven't even finished the introduction.

Make It Multiply:

Post your savings right now:

"Just found $[amount]/month I was wasting. My #FirstBuilderWin @BuildDontBudget"

Watch what happens. Your cousin finds $30. Your coworker finds $65. Your friend finds $120. You didn't just save money-you started a chain reaction.

That's the builder's way. Your small action inspires ten more. Ten inspire a hundred. Suddenly thousands are finding money they didn't know they were losing.

The Hidden Lesson:

You just proved something critical: There's money hidden in your current life. Not tomorrow's life. Not your perfect future life. Your messy, imperfect, right-now life.

If three minutes found $564/year, what could the four laws in this book find?

If one cancelled subscription created this feeling, what could daily builder actions create?

If you can win before finishing the introduction, what's possible by the final page?

Ready to find more?

Turn the page. But remember this moment. The moment you stopped reading about change and created it. The moment you shifted from consumer to builder. The moment you found $564 you didn't know you had.

Your first builder victory is complete.

Your next one starts with Chapter 1.

P.S. - Seriously, post your win. Tag a friend who needs to find their zombie subscriptions. Watch the movement begin. Building is better together.

Your First Builder Victory Just Helped Someone Else

You just found $564 you didn't know you had. Felt good, right?

Now imagine someone scrolling Amazon at 2 AM, drowning in financial advice books, seeing this one but unsure because it only has 12 reviews. They almost scroll past. Almost miss their first builder win. Almost stay stuck managing decline.

Your review changes that.

The 60-Second Multiplier Effect:

You found hidden money. Now help someone else find theirs.

Right now, while that victory feeling is fresh:

1. Go to where you bought this book
2. Leave an honest review
3. Share what just happened (that first win)
4. Help another builder find their path

That person who's about to scroll past? They're one review away from finding $564 they don't know they're losing. One review away from joining the builders. One review away from their transformation.

Your review is their permission slip.

Do it now. Before you turn the page. Make your first builder win multiply.

#FirstBuilderWin #PayItForward

P.S. - Builders help builders. Always. That's the code.

Join the Revolution

This isn't just a book. It's a movement of people who refuse to manage decline.

People who got tired of perfecting their poverty. Who stopped color-coding their scarcity. Who realized that the best-organized sinking ship still sinks.

Right now-this very second-someone in Mumbai is canceling their zombie subscription from your #FirstBuilderWin post. Someone in Memphis is setting their alarm 30 minutes earlier for tomorrow. Someone in Manchester is googling "skills that pay more than my job."

They're not waiting for Monday. Not waiting for perfect conditions. Not waiting for permission.

They're building. Right now. While others sleep, scroll, or settle.

By tomorrow, you'll be comparing notes with builders worldwide.

The teacher in Thailand sharing what worked. The mechanic in Mexico posting his breakthrough. The parent in Poland celebrating their first client. Your struggles aren't unique-but neither are your possibilities.

The physics work everywhere. The community exists everywhere. The support flows 24/7 across every timezone. While you sleep in Seattle, builders in Singapore cheer your progress. While you work in Warsaw, builders in Washington strategize your next move.

You're not alone anymore. You never have to be.

Here's the uncomfortable truth:

Every day you wait, the gap widens. Inflation doesn't pause for your preparation. Technology doesn't slow for your comfort. The economy doesn't care about your hesitation.

But here's the beautiful counter-truth:

Every day you build, you compound. Every skill you learn multiplies. Every connection you make creates possibilities. Every small action adds to an unstoppable momentum.

The question isn't whether you can do this. Thousands with worse situations already are.

The question is: When will you start?

Picture yourself one year from today.

Version A: Still reading books about other people's transformations. Still managing decline with prettier spreadsheets. Still waiting for the "right time" that never comes. Still wondering what if.

Version B: Writing your own transformation story. Teaching others what worked. Building instead of budgeting. Living instead of surviving. Creating the life that Version A dreams about.

The only difference between Version A and Version B?

Version B turned this page.

Will you be telling your story of transformation next year, or still reading about others'?

Will you be the builder who inspires your family, or the dreamer who quotes this book at dinner parties?

Will you be posting #BuilderVictory updates, or lurking in feeds watching others level up?

The movement is happening with or without you. The revolution doesn't wait. The physics keep compounding for those who understand them.

But you're here. Book in hand. Subscription already cancelled. First victory already won.

You're not a reader anymore. You're a builder who happens to be reading.

Welcome to your tribe. Welcome to your transformation. Welcome to the thousands worldwide who chose building over budgeting, growth over management, physics over fantasy.

Turn the page.

Your old life is over.

Your builder's life begins now.

PART ONE: YOUR NEW FINANCIAL REALITY.

Why Everything Changed While You Weren't Looking

CHAPTER 1: When the Math Broke.

"You're not failing at the game. The game changed, and nobody told you the new rules."

The Day Everything Changed (And Nobody Told You)

There wasn't a press conference. No breaking news alert. No emergency broadcast interrupting your show.

But somewhere between when you were playing as a child without a care, and today, the fundamental mathematics of survival changed.

Nobody sent a memo. Nobody updated the textbooks. Nobody told your parents their advice had expired.

The old equation was beautiful in its simplicity:

Work Hard + Save Carefully = Security

Work your forty hours. Bank your 10%. Watch it grow. Buy the house. Fund the retirement. Live the life. The math worked for generations. Clockwork reliable.

The new equation is brutal in its honesty:

Work Hard + Save Carefully = Slow Decline

Same effort. Opposite outcome.

Picture two rivers that flowed side by side for a century. Income and costs. Moving together. Same speed, same direction. Your grandparents walked between them easily. Your parents had to jog.

Then the rivers diverged.

One racing. One crawling.

Costs sprint. Income limps.

The gap widening with each passing year.

And you're drowning in between.

That promotion you celebrated? 5% raise. Felt like victory until you opened the rent renewal. 8% increase. You got promoted into poverty. The math is that broken.

That savings account your dad insisted on? Earning 0.5% while inflation eats 6%. You're literally paying the bank to make your money disappear. Twenty thousand saved is eighteen thousand in purchasing power next year. Seventeen thousand the year after.

Saving money now means losing money slowly.

This isn't a rough patch. Not a phase. Not a correction.

This is the new physics.

Your parents' map shows roads that no longer exist. Their compass points to true north in a world where north moved. They're not wrong about the destination. They're using navigation from a different century.

"Just work harder" assumes work pays fairly.

"Just save more" assumes saved money holds value.

"Just be patient" assumes time is on your side.

All three assumptions died while you were following the rules.

The contract changed, but nobody told you. The game board flipped, but you're still moving pieces. The economy evolved into something alien while you were doing everything right.

That sick feeling in your stomach when bills arrive? That's not failure. That's the rational response to irrational physics. That panic at 3 AM when you run the numbers again? You're not crazy. You're correct.

The math broke.

And until you learn the new equations-the real equations that govern this alien economy-you'll keep playing checkers while the world plays something else entirely with your future.

But here's what changes everything: Once you see the new rules, you can't unsee them. Once you understand the actual physics, you can stop fighting gravity and start using it.

The old game is over. You lost because it ended, not because you played badly.

Time to learn the new game.

The one where builders win and budgeters just document their decline.

The one where understanding physics matters more than following rules.

The one that's actually being played, whether you know it or not.

The Tale of Two Merchants (Ancient Wisdom, Modern Application)

From the markets of ancient Damascus to the streets of modern Detroit:

Dawn broke over dusty hills as two merchants crested the final ridge. Below them, the great city sprawled-their destination for twenty years. But where the eastern gate should welcome caravans, military banners snapped in desert wind.

War had closed their route.

The merchants sat on their camels, staring at their blocked future. Same sunrise. Same city. Same goods packed for trade. Everything the same except the one thing that mattered-the path forward had vanished.

The First Merchant

His face went from confusion to fury. "This is MY route!" he shouted at the indifferent walls. Twenty-three years perfecting every detail. Every stop memorized. Every customer relationship cultivated. Every margin calculated.

He knew which guard preferred dates to figs for bribes. Which innkeeper's daughter made the strongest tea. Where to water camels at noon for shade. The precise haggling dance with the spice dealer's wife.

Perfection, now worthless.

He made camp at the blocked gates. Set up his tent facing the closed road, as if his glare could reopen it. Each morning, he counted his remaining goods. Rationed his dates. Calculated how long he could wait.

"Temporary," he muttered, organizing his silks for the thousandth time. "Wars end. Routes reopen. The world returns to normal."

His goods grew dusty. His camels grew thin. His money dwindled. But he waited. Managed his decline with mathematical precision. Forty dates became thirty. Thirty became twenty. Each day stretching his supplies, shrinking his life.

The Second Merchant

He sat quietly for an hour, mourning the familiar path. Then curiosity stirred. If traders couldn't enter from the east, what did the city now lack?

He rode to the western gate. Found taverns. Asked questions.

"Salt," the innkeeper sighed. "The eastern routes brought salt. Now? We pay three times the price, when we find it at all."

"The mines," a drunk soldier mumbled. "Two days north. Salt everywhere. But no one trades there. Wrong side of the city."

That evening, while the first merchant counted his shrinking supplies, the second was already moving. North to mines nobody visited. West to cities nobody supplied. Creating paths where none existed.

One Month Later

The first merchant had eaten half his trade goods. His perfect rationing system documented each loss. His tent still faced east, waiting.

The second merchant returned. Dust-covered. Exhausted. Leading twelve camels loaded with salt. The city paid double normal prices. He'd found not just salt, but wheat the north needed, wool the west wanted. New routes. New relationships. New possibilities.

One Year Later

Morning at the eastern gate. The first merchant sat with his final bolts of silk, selling at massive losses to anyone passing. His perfection had preserved him for a year. A year of decline. A year of diminishing. A year of waiting for yesterday to return.

His tent was patched with unsold fabric. His ledgers documented a masterpiece of managed failure.

Down the western road came a caravan. The second merchant now employed five others. Three established routes. New goods, new cities, new opportunities. He stopped, recognizing his old companion.

"The route never reopened," the first merchant said, looking at his last three bolts of silk.

"No," the second replied gently. "It didn't."

They sat in silence. Same men who'd crested that ridge together. Same skills. Same starting resources. One had preserved. One had built. One managed what was. One created what could be.

The blockage wasn't personal. The war didn't choose favorites. It was simply change.

Change that revealed who would adapt and who would await.

The Universal Truth

One merchant asked: "How can I preserve what I have until normal returns?" One merchant asked: "What does this new reality need?"

One merchant perfected rationing.

One merchant practiced exploring.

One merchant managed decline.

One built alternatives.

One survived a year.

One thrived forever.

Your economic "trade route" is blocked. The path your parents traveled, the one that worked for generations, has a wall across it. Not temporary. Not personal. Just closed.

You can set up camp at the gates. Count your remaining resources. Perfect your rationing. Wait for normal to return.

Or you can turn your camel around. Find who needs what. Build new paths. Create different value.

The first merchant wasn't wrong. He was playing last century's game with last century's rules. Perfectly. Pointlessly.

The second merchant wasn't lucky. He was playing this century's game with this century's physics.

Will you wait at the gates or find new paths?

The city doesn't care. The economy doesn't pause. But your future depends entirely on which merchant you become.

The gates you're watching won't reopen.

The paths you build are already there.

Choose.

The Four Tides of Modern Life

Think of these not as enemies but as forces of nature. Like gravity. Like erosion. Like entropy. Neither good nor evil. Simply physics.

But if you don't understand physics, you can't fly planes. And if you don't understand these tides, you can't navigate modern life.

Tide #1: The Current of Obsolescence

Remember travel agents? Film developers? Typists?

Masters of their craft. Decades of expertise. Comfortable incomes. Respected positions.

Vanished. Not over generations. Over lunch breaks.

The travel agent who booked honeymoons for thirty years, replaced by Expedia in thirty months. The film developer whose darkroom precision meant nothing when phones became cameras. The typist who achieved 120 words per minute, made obsolete by voice recognition.

All experts in vanished worlds.

The acceleration is breathtaking. Your grandfather learned blacksmithing and died a blacksmith. Your father learned accounting and retired an accountant. You? You'll learn five careers and still might not make it to retirement.

Skills that lasted 30-year careers now expire in 3 years. 5 if you're lucky.

Universal Truth: From scribes resisting printing presses to taxi drivers fighting Uber, the pattern never changes. Those who adapt to new tools thrive. Those who resist them perish. This isn't Western or Eastern. It's physics.

Global Proof:

Lagos: Phone repairman who fixed Nokia buttons for a decade. Fought smartphones. Shop empty. His neighbor learned smartphone repair. Line out the door.

London: Investment banker who mastered traditional models. Ignored fintech. Laid off at 45. His junior who understood blockchain? Running a startup worth millions.

Mumbai: Accountant calculating by hand, proud of speed. Refused software. Clients vanished. His daughter learned QuickBooks in a weekend. Manages his former clients.

The Key Insight: Resistance guarantees extinction. Adaptation guarantees opportunity. The current doesn't care about your expertise in yesterday's world.

Tide #2: The Current of Erosion

Put $100 in your drawer. Come back in five years. You still have $100. But it only buys $77 worth of stuff.

You didn't lose money. You lost purchasing power. The silent theft that robs everyone, everywhere, always.

What bought a week's groceries five years ago now buys three days. What covered rent last year leaves you short this year. Your money sits still while the world moves forward, and the gap is your loss.

This isn't American inflation or European inflation. It's human inflation. Ask anyone in Buenos Aires who watched savings evaporate. Ask anyone in Harare who measured inflation hourly. Ask anyone in Istanbul who learned that money has an expiration date.

Global Reality Check:

Argentina: Middle class became poor without changing anything

Zimbabwe: Millionaires became paupers holding the same bills

Turkey: Lifetime savings became coffee money in months

USA/UK/EU: Slow motion version of the same film

Universal Truth: Money sitting still is money dying. Slowly in stable countries. Quickly in unstable ones. But dying everywhere, always.

Your savings account paying 0.5% while inflation runs 6%? That's not saving. That's documented decay.

Tide #3: The Current of Stagnation

The 20-year veteran watching the new hire's salary offer. Higher than what loyalty earned. The rage. The betrayal. The mathematics.

Old promise: Stay loyal, get rewarded.

New reality: Stay put, get passed.

This isn't one bad company. This is the new physics from Silicon Valley to Shenzhen. The employee who changes companies every 3 years earns 50% more than the one who stays for 10. Not because jumping is virtuous. Because movement now creates value.

The Universal Pattern:

Tokyo: Salaryman dedication once meant security. Now means stagnation.

Toronto: Government worker pensions once meant wealth. Now mean poverty.

Berlin: Company loyalty once meant advancement. Now means replacement.

São Paulo: Same desk, same dedication, same declining purchasing power.

Your parents' stability was an asset. Your stability is a liability.

The Painful Truth: Staying loyal now often means staying poor. Not because companies are evil. Because value accumulates through movement, not maintenance.

Tide #4: The Current of Complexity

Count your monthly bills. Go ahead. Every recurring charge. Every subscription. Every fee.

Your grandparents had five: Rent. Electric. Phone. Gas. Maybe car payment.

You have fifty. Minimum.

Rent. Electric. Gas. Water. Trash. Internet. Cell phone. Phone insurance. Car payment. Car insurance. Health insurance. Dental. Vision. Netflix. Spotify. Amazon Prime. Cloud storage. Gym. LinkedIn Premium. Software subscriptions. App subscriptions. Bank fees. Credit card fees.

Death by a thousand small cuts. Each seems insignificant. Together they're suffocating.

Global Drain Count:

Mumbai resident: 12 subscriptions average

Mexico City: 15 subscriptions average

Manhattan: 18 subscriptions average

London: 20 subscriptions average

Every culture. Every economy. Same multiplication of complexity.

Your grandmother managed five bills with a pencil. You need spreadsheets for fifty and still miss some. It's not that you're worse at managing. It's that the game became exponentially more complex.

The Trap: Even perfect budgeting can't overcome this complexity. Like trying to bail out a boat with fifty holes using a teaspoon. Exhausting. Futile. Guaranteed to fail.

These are the four tides reshaping every life on every continent:

Not temporary disruptions. Permanent physics. Not targeting you personally. Affecting everyone universally.

You can rage at tides. You can ignore tides. You can pretend tides don't exist.

Or you can understand tides and use them.

The obsolescence that destroys old skills? It creates demand for new ones.

The erosion eating saved money? It rewards invested money.

The stagnation punishing loyalty? It prizes strategic movement.

The complexity overwhelming budgets? It births simplification opportunities.

Every tide that takes also gives. But only to those who understand the physics.

Understand these tides or be swept away by them.

The choice isn't whether to face them. You will. The choice is whether to harness them or be crushed by them.

Which will you choose?

The tides don't care. But your future does.

Understanding the New Physics

The rules didn't just change. They inverted. What once guaranteed success now ensures decline. Like gravity reversing while you were mid-jump.

What Used to Work (Everywhere):

Work   hard   →   Get   ahead
Your grandfather clocked in at the factory. Eight hours. Good effort. Each year, life got measurably better. The house got bigger. The car got newer. The vacation got longer. Work equaled progress. Effort equaled elevation.

Watch old photos. Each year showing visible improvement. The math was clean: Input work, output prosperity.

Save   money   →   Build   wealth
The miracle of compound interest. Save $100, earn 5%, have $105. While bread cost 2% more. You won. Money grew faster than costs. Time was your friend. The patient got rich slowly but surely.

Banks paid real interest. 5%, 6%, sometimes more. Inflation ran 2%, maybe 3%. The gap meant growth. Your savings doubled every decade while costs crawled up slowly.

Stay   loyal   →   Get   rewarded
The company man. Twenty-five years, same desk. Each year brought raises, bonuses, security. Retirement came with pension, gold watch, dignity. Loyalty paid. Literally.

From Detroit autoworkers to Japanese salarymen, the contract was sacred: Give us your career, we'll give you your life.

Budget   well   →   Create   security
Five bills. Predictable amounts. Manageable increases. Budget carefully, save the excess, build your future. The math worked because the variables were stable.

Your grandmother's envelope system actually created wealth. Income grew faster than her five expenses. The surplus meant security.

What Happens Now (Everywhere):

Work   perfectly   →   Fall   behind   slowly
You're more educated than your grandfather. More productive. Better tools. Longer hours. Yet each year, purchasing power shrinks. The promotion feels like running in place. The raise is a mirage that evaporates at the grocery store.

Excellence no longer guarantees elevation. It merely slows your descent.

Save money → Watch it shrink

Modern miracle in reverse. Save $100 at 0.5% interest. Have $100.50 next year. While everything costs 6% more. You lost $5.50 by saving. The patient now get poor slowly but surely.

The Math:
Bank pays: 0.5% (if you're lucky)
Inflation takes: 6% (if you're lucky)
Net loss: -5.5% annually
Your $10,000 saved = $9,450 in purchasing power

Time became your enemy. Compound interest became compound decay.

Stay loyal → Earn less than newcomers

The 15-year veteran training the new hire. Who earns 20% more. For the same job. The loyalty tax is real, universal, and devastating.

Global Proof:

Berlin: Loyal programmer, €50k. New hire, €65k. Same skill.

Mumbai: Dedicated manager, ₹8 lakh. Fresh MBA, ₹12 lakh. Same role.

Seattle: Senior developer, $120k. New bootcamp grad, $140k. Same team.

Singapore: Veteran analyst, S$60k. Job hopper, S$85k. Same desk.

Movement pays. Stillness costs. Loyalty means volunteering for poverty.

Budget perfectly → Document your decline

Fifty bills. Unpredictable increases. Unmanageable complexity. Budget perfectly, track every penny, still fall behind. Your spreadsheet becomes a detailed diary of descent.

You can't budget your way out of a physics problem any more than you can diet your way out of aging.

The Universal Pattern:

London teacher: Perfect budgeting, 20% purchasing power loss in 5 years

Lagos nurse: Every expense tracked, still can't afford her childhood neighborhood

Phoenix plumber: Detailed spreadsheets showing steady decline despite steady work

Seoul office worker: Budgeting apps documenting the impossibility of homeownership

Same story. Different currencies. Universal physics.

This isn't Western. It's worldwide. Physics doesn't check passports.

The rules changed in:

- New York and New Delhi
- London and Lagos
- Tokyo and Toronto
- Sydney and São Paulo

Different speeds, same direction. Different currencies, same erosion. Different cultures, same broken math.

Your Turkish friend watching savings evaporate? Same physics, accelerated timeline.

Your Canadian cousin priced out of housing? Same physics, different asset.

Your Mexican neighbor working two jobs? Same physics, different grind.

We're all in the same storm. Just different boats.

The Liberation in Understanding:

Here's what changes everything: Once you see the new physics, you can work with them instead of against them.

Like ancient sailors who learned wind patterns. The wind didn't become friendly. But understanding it meant traveling thousands of miles instead of rowing hundreds.

New Physics Navigation:

- Work creates value → Build systems that multiply value

- Saving means shrinking → Invest in things that grow
- Loyalty costs money → Strategic movement creates wealth
- Budgeting manages decline → Building creates abundance

The old rules broke. Mourning them won't fix them. Following them guarantees failure.

But new physics means new possibilities. Different rules create different games. And builders who understand the actual game being played can't lose to budgeters still playing last century's version.

You can't change physics. But you can use physics.

The question is: Will you keep following the old rules harder, or learn the new ones faster?

The physics don't care. But your future is shaped entirely by your answer.

Ready to learn what actually works?

Global Proof Points

Four continents. Four currencies. Four lives. Same physics. Same transformation.

Maria in São Paulo: The Teacher Who Refused to Shrink

Twenty years shaping young minds. Twenty years of perfect budgeting. Twenty years watching her life get smaller.

Maria kept meticulous records. 2004: Starting salary bought 1,000 items at the market. 2024: Same salary-after all the raises-bought 600 items. The math was irrefutable. Two decades of excellence rewarded with 40% less life.

The breaking point came during a Sunday drive. She passed her childhood neighborhood-modest houses where teachers once lived. The "For Sale" sign made her pull over. The price made her cry. Three teacher salaries couldn't afford one small house where one teacher's salary once bought dignity.

"I realized I was managing my way to poverty," she says. "Perfect budgeting of a shrinking pie."

That night, she posted in a teaching forum: "Anyone need Portuguese lessons?"

A startup founder in San Francisco responded. Then a diplomat in Dubai. Then executives across Asia preparing for Brazilian operations. Same skill she'd used for twenty years. Different delivery. Different currency.

Today, Maria teaches from her apartment overlooking Ibirapuera Park- the dream apartment she bought with global income. Morning classes for Silicon Valley. Evening sessions for London. Recording lessons that sell while she sleeps.

"I stopped managing decline and started building growth. Same Maria. Same 24 hours. Completely different trajectory."

Chen in Shanghai: The Supervisor Who Stopped Saving and Started Building

Chen did everything his father taught him. Work hard at the factory. Save 40% of income. Watch it grow. Build security.

For fifteen years, it worked. Supervisor salary. Careful saving. Growing account balance. Then the math turned cruel. Inflation at 8%. Savings interest at 2%. The harder he saved, the poorer he became. Like filling a bucket with holes that grew larger each year.

"My savings account showed bigger numbers buying smaller life," he reflects. "I was drowning in my own discipline."

The revelation came during a factory upgrade. Watching German engineers install automation systems. Making notes. Asking questions. Realizing: The machines replacing workers could be managed by workers who understood them.

Nights studying industrial IoT. Weekends learning predictive maintenance. Not through expensive courses-through YouTube, forums, documentation. The internet university that never closes.

First consulting project: His own factory. Reduced downtime 30%. Word spread. Factories in Vietnam needed help. Then Thailand. Then Indonesia. Each project building reputation and capability.

Now Chen advises factories across Asia. Earns in euros, dollars, yuan- whatever clients prefer. His savings still exist, but they're irrelevant. His skills compound faster than any interest rate.

"Savings account was a leaking bucket. Skills were a flowing spring. I chose the spring."

Kwame in Nairobi: The Teller Who Counted Different Value

Six years behind bulletproof glass. Counting other people's money. Tracking every shilling of his own. Budget spreadsheets that would make accountants weep. Still sinking.

Rent up 15% yearly. Transport costs doubled. Food prices climbing like they had wings. His teller salary crawling forward like it had chains. The gap widening into a chasm.

But Kwame noticed something else through that glass. Customers struggling with M-Pesa. Elderly afraid of mobile money. Small business owners losing money to failed transactions. Everyone fumbling with the financial revolution in their phones.

"I was counting money that was losing value. Meanwhile, people needed help with money that could multiply value."

Started helping after hours. One grandmother. Then her friends. Then their families. Word spread like only word spreads in Nairobi-faster than light. Soon running weekend workshops in church halls.

The transformation was mathematical. Bank teller: 40,000 shillings monthly. Mobile money trainer: 200,000 shillings from multiple clients. Then banks started calling. Telcos needed trainers. NGOs required financial inclusion programs.

Today, Kwame's company trains entire institutions. His former bank is now a client. The bulletproof glass that once trapped him now protects the trainers he employs.

"I was counting money that was losing value. Now I create value that counts."

Dmitri in Moscow: The Engineer Who Built Currency Independence

Dmitri had survived the '98 crisis. Knew to save carefully. Budget precisely. Prepare for storms. His spreadsheets tracked every ruble. His preparations were perfect.

Then 2014. Ruble lost 40% overnight. His perfect preparations perfectly useless. Years of disciplined saving evaporated between breakfast and lunch.

The mathematical precision of his budgeting mocked by the mathematical brutality of currency collapse.

"Like measuring precisely while the ruler shrinks," he says. "Perfect technique. Worthless outcome."

But engineers solve problems. And Dmitri saw the problem clearly: His value was trapped in one currency, one geography, one system. The internet offered escape routes.

Started with technical English. Then Python tutorials. Then contributing to open-source projects. Building reputation in spaces where Moscow meant nothing but code quality meant everything. The global engineering community that judges by Git commits, not geography.

First remote contract: Berlin startup. Paid in euros. Second: Canadian company. Paid in dollars. Now manages distributed teams for multiple companies. Lives in Moscow's costs. Earns in the world's currencies.

His ruble salary from local work? Still there. Pin money now. His global earnings? Building the life currency crashes can't touch.

"Currency failed me. Capability saved me. Now I'm currency-agnostic."

Same problem. Same solution. Different continents.

Maria's Brazilian real lost purchasing power steadily.

Chen's Chinese yuan savings betrayed mathematical promises.

Kwame's Kenyan shilling couldn't keep pace with life.

Dmitri's Russian ruble crashed catastrophically.

Different speeds. Same direction: Down.

But all four discovered the same physics:

- Skills compound. Savings shrink.
- Value creation beats expense management.
- Global reach trumps local limits.
- Building beats budgeting. Always.

They didn't move countries. They moved their value creation online.

They didn't change currencies. They changed capabilities.

They didn't manage better. They built different.

The physics are universal.

Your currency might be dollars or dinars. Your city might be Melbourne or Mumbai. Your profession might be teaching or technology.

The problem remains constant: Perfect budgeting of shrinking resources leads to perfectly managed decline.

The solution remains constant: Build value that transcends borders, currencies, and conventional limits.

Four people proved it. Thousands more are proving it daily.

The only question: When will you start your proof?

Your Chapter 1 Challenge (With Immediate Win)

Before you move to Chapter 2, you must do this.

Not tomorrow. Not after coffee. Right now. This challenge separates readers from builders, and you're about to become a builder.

The Reality Audit

Step 1: The Numbers That Matter

Grab your phone. Open calculator. We're doing math that matters.

Your income growth over the last 5 years: _____% *(If you made $40k in 2019 and $46k now, that's 15% growth)*

Your cost growth over the last 5 years: _____% *(Rent, food, gas, insurance-if they totaled $3k monthly then and $4k now, that's 33% growth)*

The gap: _____%

This is your Decline Rate. The speed at which you're falling behind despite doing everything right.

Most people discover they're losing 2-5% annually. Working harder to live smaller. Now you have proof.

Step 2: Your Instant Win

Put this book down. Open your banking app RIGHT NOW.

Search for recurring charges. Or just scroll last month's transactions. Find the zombie subscriptions-the ones you forgot existed. That meditation app from New Year's. The premium version of something you use the free version of. The streaming service you meant to cancel after that one show.

Find one. Cancel it. Now.

Average results:

- Time invested: 3 minutes
- Money found: $19-47/month
- Yearly impact: $228-564
- Feeling: Priceless

You just made more money in 3 minutes than your savings account will make all year.

Step 3: Start the Movement

Success without sharing is just personal. Success shared becomes a movement.

Post right now:

"Just found $[amount]/month I was wasting. My #FirstBuilderWin"

Then share this challenge with one person. Text them. Call them. Send them this exact audit. When they find their zombie subscription and save money too, something magical happens:

You've stopped being a consumer and started being a builder.

You built awareness. You built savings. You built momentum. You built inspiration for someone else.

The Identity Shift

Look what just happened.

Five minutes ago, you were reading about broken math. Feeling like a victim of forces beyond your control. Nodding along with problems.

Now? You've taken action. Found money. Started change. Inspired others.

You're no longer just reading about building. You're building.

That feeling? That tiny rush of control? That's what builders feel every day.

Welcome to the builders.

Tomorrow, you'll do it again.

Different action. Same feeling. Small wins compound into transformed lives.

That's how movements start-one person finding $27/month and telling a friend.

That's how lives change-one small action that proves bigger actions are possible.

Your Decline Rate is real. But now you know something else is real too:

Your ability to build your way out.

Chapter 2 will show you why managing decline-even perfectly-guarantees failure. But first, go cancel that subscription. Find that money. Start that movement.

The builders are waiting for your #FirstBuilderWin post.

The Choice at the Gate

The math broke.

Now you know.

You've seen the numbers. Felt the physics. Recognized your reflection in Maria and Chen, in the merchant at the blocked gate, in the perfect budgeter documenting decline.

The comfortable lie is dead: Work hard and get ahead. Save money and build wealth. Budget well and create security.

The uncomfortable truth is alive: The rules inverted while you were playing. The same actions that created prosperity now guarantee poverty. Your parents' roadmap leads off a cliff.

Question is: What will you do?

You've seen the problem. Chapter 2 reveals why budgeting harder makes it worse.

Why your perfect spreadsheet is actually a detailed map of your descent. Why managing money better when the physics are broken is like organizing deck chairs on the Titanic-helpful, but insufficient.

But first-did you do the challenge?

Did you find that forgotten subscription? That zombie charge draining your account while you slept?

If not, stop. Go back. Do it now. This book only works for builders, not browsers. The difference between knowing and doing is the difference between the two merchants-one still waiting at the gate, one building an empire.

Check #FirstBuilderWin right now.

See others finding their zombie subscriptions. $23 here. $47 there. Someone just found $120/month they forgot about. Each post a small victory. Together, a revolution against the broken math.

Your post could inspire someone else to start. Their success could inspire ten more. This is how movements begin-not with manifestos, but with small actions that prove change is possible.

That queasy feeling in your stomach?

That vertigo sensation like the ground shifted?

That's your old worldview dying.

Good. It was killing you slowly.

The fairy tale that hard work alone equals success. The myth that saving builds wealth. The lie that budgeting creates security. All dying. Making room for physics that actually work.

You can mourn the old rules. You can rage at their passing. You can pretend they still apply.

Or you can learn the new ones.

The merchants at the blocked gate are still waiting.

Still counting their dwindling supplies. Still managing their decline with mathematical precision. Still believing normal will return if they just wait long enough.

The builders already found new routes. New customers. New possibilities. They're not smarter. Not luckier. They just accepted reality faster and adapted to it.

Which are you?

The answer isn't in your words. It's in your actions. Did you find that subscription? Did you take the first builder action? Did you start something, however small?

Because Chapter 2 is for builders only. For those ready to see why their perfect budgeting is perfectly useless. For those willing to learn a completely different game.

The gate is blocked. It's not reopening.

But infinite paths exist for those willing to build them.

Which are you?

Turn the page to find out.

CHAPTER 2: The Truth About Budgeting.

Why Managing Perfectly Still Means Losing

"Budgeting in a broken economy is like organizing deck chairs on the Titanic. Helpful, but insufficient."
The Sacred Cow Nobody Questions

Open any financial blog. Download any money app. Walk into any bookstore's finance section. The gospel never changes:

"Track every penny!"

"Cut all waste!"

"Live below your means!"

"Budget your way to wealth!"

From New York financial advisors to New Delhi money coaches, from London seminars to Lagos workshops-the prescription remains identical. Track more. Cut more. Shrink more. Manage better.

The advice spans continents because it seems like universal truth. Mathematical law. Common sense.

And they're not wrong.

They're just solving yesterday's problem with yesterday's tools.

It's like using a map from 1950 to navigate 2025. The streets have changed, but you're still turning where the map says turn. Getting more lost with each perfectly followed direction.

It's bringing a knife to a gunfight-excellent knife, wrong battle.

It's bailing water from a boat with no bottom-perfect technique, futile outcome.

Here's the painful truth no guru mentions:

Perfect budgeting in a broken system just helps you document your decline more accurately.

Meet Sarah, the accountant. Her spreadsheets are art. Every expense categorized, analyzed, optimized. Spending tracked to the penny for five years. Her budgeting apps send her gold stars. Her financial discipline is legendary.

She can't afford kids.

The math-her perfectly tracked math-shows that daycare would break them. The spreadsheet that documents every penny also documents why she'll never use the second bedroom.

Meet James, the teacher. His budgeting system wins praise in online forums. Six apps syncing data. Automated alerts. Spending predictions. AI-powered insights. He teaches in Riverside Heights.

He can't afford to live in Riverside Heights.

His students' parents bought homes there on one income twenty years ago. He can't qualify for a studio apartment there on his teacher's salary plus his wife's nurse wages. His budgeting apps precisely calculate how far he falls short each month.

The Brutal Math of Perfect Budgeting:
Income: $5,000/month
Perfect budgeting saves: 10% ($500)
Inflation eats: 6% of purchasing power
Real loss: $300 of value monthly

You saved $500 but lost $300 in purchasing power.
Net gain: $200 in declining money.
Congratulations, you're getting poorer more slowly.

That's what perfect budgeting achieves now-slower drowning.

What if the problem isn't how well you budget, but that budgeting alone can't solve a physics problem?

What if tracking every penny when pennies lose value daily is like counting sand while the tide comes in?

What if cutting expenses to the bone when bones aren't enough is missing the point entirely?

What if the solution isn't managing better but building different?

Your grandparents could budget their way to prosperity because their income grew faster than their costs. One paddle, rowing downstream.

You're budgeting against a current that's stronger than your rowing. Two paddles, rushing upstream.

Different physics require different strategies.

The tragedy isn't that you're bad at budgeting. The tragedy is that you're excellent at a game that no longer rewards excellence.

Time to learn a different game entirely.

A Tale of Two Approaches (Global Edition)

The Perfect Manager: Lisa in London

Lisa's credentials could wallpaper her Shoreditch flat-share: MBA from London School of Economics. Chartered Financial Analyst. Started budgeting at 16 when other teens were buying PlayStation games. She approached personal finance like defusing a bomb-methodically, precisely, perfectly.

Her spreadsheets are symphonies. Twenty-seven categories of expenses. Five-year trending analyses. Predictive modeling for inflation. Color-coded by priority: red for essential, amber for negotiable, green for cuttable. She's eliminated all greens. Most ambers are gone too.

The optimizations border on Olympic:

Coffee shops: Eliminated (saves £150/month)

Subscriptions: None except phone (saves £89/month)

Entertainment: Library books and free museums only

Transport: Cycles in all weather (saves £156/month)

Food: Meal prep Sundays, batch cooking, discount shopping

She saves 12% of her income. After tax. In London. That's like holding your breath underwater for ten minutes-theoretically possible, practically superhuman.

48

Five years of this discipline. Five years of tracking every penny. Five years of optimization and she's further from buying a flat than when she started.

The numbers mock her:
2019: Needed £50,000 deposit for Zone 3 flat
2024: Needs £75,000 for same flat
Saved: £15,000 (extraordinary achievement)
Purchasing power lost: £20,000 (ordinary inflation)

Her spreadsheets perfectly document her declining purchasing power. Each cell precisely calculated. Each formula flawlessly executed. Each result proving that perfection isn't enough.

"I did everything right," she says, staring at the numbers that confirm she'll need another decade to afford what her parents bought in their twenties. "Why am I losing?"

The Imperfect Builder: Priya in Pune

Priya would make budgeting gurus weep. Her financial habits are everything Lisa eliminated:

Yoga membership: ₹2000/month ("It keeps me sane")

Daily chai: ₹50 at the street vendor ("I solve problems while sipping")

Auto-rickshaws when tired: ₹200 here and there ("Time is money")

Eating out with friends: Occasional indulgence

She doesn't track every rupee. Sometimes overspends. Her Excel skills are basic at best.

But Priya does track something else: learning hours. Two hours daily, religious as prayer:

5-6 AM: Online coding tutorials

6-7 AM: Building projects

Weekends: Tech meetups and hackathons

Lunch breaks: Technical documentation

Her GitHub profile grew while Lisa's savings crawled. Her network expanded while Lisa's expenses shrank. Her skills compounded while Lisa's money didn't.

The transformation took eighteen months:

Month 1-6: JavaScript basics, building toy projects

Month 7-12: React framework, real applications

Month 13-15: Contributing to open source

Month 16: First freelance client (US startup)

Month 18: Full-time remote role, Silicon Valley rates

Now earning $5,000 monthly while living in Pune. Same cost of living. San Francisco salary.

The beautiful irony: Lisa reached out to Priya through LinkedIn. Saw her transformation. Wanted to learn how.

Now Priya teaches Lisa to code. The perfect budgeter learning from the imperfect builder. The person who tracked every penny learning from someone who invests every hour.

"I focused on growing the pie," Priya explains during their video call, "not cutting smaller slices."

The Mathematical Truth:

Lisa's Approach:

Income: £4,000/month (static)
Savings: 12% (£480)
Inflation: 6% (£240 lost in purchasing power)
Net progress: £240/month (declining value)
Time to goal: Never (gap widens faster than savings)

Priya's Approach:

Starting income: ₹40,000/month
Investment: 2 hours daily in skills
Result: $5,000/month (₹400,000)

One managed decline perfectly.

One built growth messily.

One tracked every penny leaving.

One created new pennies flowing.

One mastered the old game.

One learned the new rules.

Guess who can afford the flat?

Actually, Priya could buy Lisa's dream flat in cash now. But she's looking at property in Goa instead. Beach view. Remote work. Builder's lifestyle.

Lisa still has her spreadsheets. Still tracks perfectly. Still falls behind precisely.

The tragedy? Lisa's discipline is extraordinary. Her execution flawless. Her system perfect. She's just playing the wrong game with the wrong tools for the wrong era.

The hope? Lisa's now learning to code. Applying her discipline to building instead of budgeting. Using her analytical skills to create rather than cut.

Because once you see the difference between managing decline and building growth, you can't unsee it.

Which one are you right now?

Which one will you be tomorrow?

The Mathematical Floor (Universal Truth)

Here's what nobody admits about budgeting, whether in Paris or Pretoria:

It has a floor. A mathematical bottom. A point where you can't cut anymore without ceasing to exist.

Every budgeting guru preaches "cut more, save more" as if you could infinitely shrink. As if human needs compress to zero. As if you could budget your way to not requiring shelter, food, or basic dignity.

Let's talk about the floor nobody mentions.

The Unbreakable Minimums:

Shelter: Can only go so low before homeless

You can downsize from house to apartment. Apartment to room. Room to shared room. Shared room to couch. Couch to car. Car to... what?

The floor exists. Hard. Cold. Real.

Food: Can only cut so much before malnourished

You can switch from restaurants to cooking. Cooking to meal prep. Meal prep to rice and beans. Rice and beans to... malnutrition?

Your body requires minimum calories. Minimum nutrients. Physics doesn't care about your budget.

Transport: Must reach work somehow

You can sell the car, take the bus. Skip the bus, ride a bike. Sell the bike, walk. But if work is 20 miles away? If there's no safe walking route? If weather makes walking impossible?

The floor: You either reach work or lose work.

Health: Can't skip forever without catastrophe

You can cancel gym membership. Skip dental cleanings. Ignore that persistent cough. Delay the check-up. Until the tooth abscess. Until pneumonia. Until the emergency room.

Prevention costs little. Emergencies cost everything.

Global Examples of the Floor:

Tokyo: Capsule hotel ¥2,500/night. Below that, 24-hour manga cafe ¥1,500. Below that, train station benches. Below that, cardboard cities under bridges. The salary man to homeless pipeline is three budget cuts wide.

Mumbai: Shared room in chawl ₹3,000/month. Below that, slum dwelling ₹1,000. Below that, pavement dwelling. Below that, railway station platforms. Each step down harder to climb back from.

New York: Room share in deep Queens $800. Below that, illegal basement $500. Below that, shelter system. Below that, subway grates in winter. The city of dreams has floors made of concrete.

São Paulo: Small favela dwelling R$400. Below that, shared favela room R$200. Below that, under highway overpasses. Below that, cardboard collectors who never stop walking. Even the favela has floors beneath floors.

London: Bed in shared room £600. Below that, night buses £2.40 to ride in circles. Below that, shop doorways. Below that, Thames embankments. The financial capital has workers sleeping in its ATM lobbies.

The Brutal Truth:

You'll hit the floor. Everyone does. Then what?

You can't budget below zero.

You can't optimize homelessness.

You can't spreadsheet your way out of mathematical impossibility.

Your budgeting app can't help when there's nothing left to cut. Your expense tracking can't create money from void. Your financial discipline can't bend physics.

The floor is real. Hard. Unforgiving. And closer than you think.

That perfect budgeter managing decline? They're not approaching wealth. They're approaching the floor. Slowly if they're lucky. Quickly if they're not. But approaching it with mathematical certainty.

The Floor's Cruelest Feature:

It's sticky. Once you hit it, escape becomes exponentially harder.

No address? Can't get hired.

No phone? Can't get called.

No shower? Can't interview.

No nutrition? Can't think clearly.

No health? Can't work.

The floor isn't just where you stop falling. It's where gravity reverses, pulling you down harder.

Every city has its floor. Every economy has its bottom. Every human has their breaking point.

And budgeting alone guarantees you'll find yours.

What if, instead of managing how far you fall, you learned how to rise?

What if the energy you spend calculating the perfect descent could build wings instead?

What if the floor isn't your destiny but your launching pad?

Because here's what else is true: While budgeting has a floor, building has no ceiling.

You can only cut expenses to zero. You can grow income to infinity.

You can only shrink so small. You can expand without limit.

You can only fall so far. You can rise forever.

The floor is real. But so is the sky.

Which direction are you moving?

The Beautiful Truth About Building

Where budgeting has limits, building has none.

Every floor has a ceiling above it. Every limit has an expanse beyond it. Every ending has a beginning waiting.

Let's flip the equation.

Skills: No Ceiling Exists

Budgeting limit: You can only cut so much

Eventually you hit zero. Can't spend negative money. Can't reduce below nothing. Mathematics has boundaries.

Building truth: No ceiling exists on what you can learn

Learn Excel. Then Python. Then machine learning. Then teaching others. Then creating systems. Each skill multiplies the others. Compound knowledge has no upper limit.

Example: Nigerian coder started with free YouTube tutorials. No computer-used internet cafe. Month 1: HTML basics. Month 6: Full websites. Month 12: React applications. Month 18: Remote job, $100k salary. Same person. Same 24 hours. Infinite expansion.

Value: Scales Without Borders

Budgeting limit: You can only save what you earn

Make $3,000, save 20% maximum = $600. Physics won't let you save $3,001 from $3,000. Impossible.

Building truth: Value creation scales infinitely

Create once, impact millions. Write once, read forever. Solve once, replicate endlessly. Digital leverage breaks physical limits.

Example: Indonesian teacher reached 30 students in her classroom. Started recording lessons. Now reaches 10,000 students across Southeast Asia. Same teaching. 333x impact. Monthly income went from $400 to $15,000. Value has no borders.

Problems: Never Run Out

Budgeting limit: Your expenses are finite

Count them. List them. You'll reach the end. Only so many bills to cut. Only so many subscriptions to cancel. The list ends.

Building truth: World's problems are infinite

Every solution creates new problems to solve. Every innovation needs optimization. Every human need creates opportunity. Problems multiply faster than solutions.

Example: Solved email? Now we need spam filters. Solved spam? Now we need priority systems. Solved priority? Now we need AI assistants. Each solution births ten opportunities. Builders never lack work.

Solutions: Create New Worlds

Budgeting limit: You can only optimize existing systems

Make the car more efficient. Make the budget tighter. Make the process faster. But you're still playing within the rules.

Building truth: You can create new systems entirely

Don't like the game? Build a new one. System broken? Create alternative. Rules unfair? Write new ones.

Example: Uber didn't optimize taxi dispatch systems. It eliminated dispatch. Airbnb didn't make hotels cheaper. It turned homes into hotels. Builders don't optimize broken systems. They obsolete them.

The Multiplication Effect

Watch what happens when builders build:

- Skills multiply: Coding + design = valuable apps
- Value multiplies: One solution × thousand users = massive impact
- Income multiplies: Local salary → global rates
- Opportunities multiply: Each success opens three doors
- Impact multiplies: Help one → they help ten → exponential growth

Meanwhile, budgeters subtract:

- Cut this expense -$50
- Eliminate that cost -$30
- Reduce consumption -$100
- Until nothing remains to cut.

The Mindset Shift

Budgeters ask: "How can I need less?"

Builders ask: "How can I create more?"

Budgeters ask: "What can I cut?"

Builders ask: "What can I add?"

Budgeters ask: "How do I save?"

Builders ask: "How do I scale?"

One question shrinks your life. One expands it.

One leads to the floor. One leads to the sky.

One manages decline. One creates abundance.

The Physics of Possibility
Budgeting operates in subtraction: Income - Expenses = Savings
Building operates in multiplication: Skills × Problems × Scale = Unlimited

You can only subtract to zero.

You can multiply to infinity.

You can only shrink so small.

You can grow beyond measurement.

You can only fall to the floor.

You can rise past the clouds.

The floor has a bottom. The sky has no top.

Which direction would you rather focus on?

The energy you spend calculating your descent could be building your ascent. The perfectionism you apply to shrinking could be applied to growing. The discipline you use to manage less could create more.

Same effort. Different direction. Opposite outcomes.

The floor will always be there if you need it. But why visit when you could fly?

The builders are already airborne. They started where you are. They faced what you face. They simply chose up instead of down.

Your wings are waiting.

Ready to build them?

The Two-Part Strategy

You need both. Not because it's nice. Because it's physics.

Like breathing in AND out. Like a heart that contracts AND expands. Like a championship team that plays defense AND offense.

Focusing on only one guarantees loss.

Part 1: Budget (Defense)

Essential everywhere. Non-negotiable. The foundation without which everything crumbles.

Awareness: Can't fix what you don't see You're bleeding money somewhere. Everyone is. Maybe it's the subscription you forgot. Maybe it's the convenience tax you never calculated. Maybe it's the small leaks that compound into hemorrhages. Budgeting shows you where.

Leak-stopping: Why earn more to waste more? What good is doubling your income if your expenses triple? What victory is earning $10,000 more if you waste $15,000 more? Budgeting stops you from inflating your lifestyle faster than your income.

Reality check: Live in truth, not fantasy That dream vacation? Your budget says 18 months. That business idea? Your budget says need $5,000 capital. That retirement plan? Your budget says never at current rate. Truth hurts. Fantasy kills.

Foundation: Can't build on quicksand Try constructing a building on soup. Try growing a garden in the ocean. Try building wealth while drowning in chaos. Budgeting creates solid ground. Not exciting. Absolutely essential.

Without budgeting, you're blind in any currency.

But...

Part 2: Build (Offense)

Essential everywhere budgeting fails. Which is everywhere now.

When costs outpace income: Build new income streams Your 2% raise versus 7% inflation means you're losing 5% yearly. No amount of budgeting fixes that math. Only building does. New skills. New value. New physics.

When skills become obsolete: Build new capabilities Your industry is dying. Your role is automating. Your expertise is expiring. Can't budget your way out of obsolescence. Can only build your way into relevance.

When industries transform: Build transformation skills Taxi drivers didn't need better budgets when Uber arrived. They needed new skills. Travel agents didn't need expense tracking when Expedia launched. They needed new careers. Build or be buried.

When paths close: Build new paths The promotion that will never come. The pension that won't exist. The ladder that ends at a cliff. When forward is blocked, build sideways. Build up. Build around. But build.

Without building, you're dying slowly in any economy.
The Integration

Here's what champions do:

Morning Reality: 30 Minutes Total

5 minutes: Check spending, spot leaks, stay aware (defense)

25 minutes: Learn new skill, apply knowledge, create value (offense)

Weekly Practice:

Sunday: 30-minute budget review (defense)

Monday-Saturday: 3 hours building (offense)

Monthly Results:

Budget shows you saved $200 (defense)

Building earned you extra $500 (offense)

Combined: $700 ahead instead of behind
The Sports Truth

Watch any championship team. Defense wins games, but only if you score. The best defense with zero offense loses 0-3. The best offense with no defense loses 45-48.

Champions play both. Always.

The 90s Chicago Bulls: Legendary defense AND Jordan's offense. Barcelona's golden era: Pressing defense AND Messi's magic. New England Patriots dynasty: Bend-don't-break defense AND Brady's clutch drives.

Your financial game is no different.

Budget (Defense) prevents:

- Wasting money on forgotten subscriptions
- Lifestyle inflation eating raises
- Living in denial about reality
- Building on unstable foundation

Build (Offense) creates:

- New income sources
- Valuable capabilities
- Growing opportunities
- Expanding possibilities

One maintains. One multiplies.

One preserves. One produces.

One manages. One manufactures.

Use both or lose everything.

The Daily Championship Formula

Morning Defense (5 minutes): "Where am I leaking?" Check. Plug. Move on.

Morning Offense (25 minutes): "What am I building?" Learn. Apply. Grow.

Evening Review (2 minutes): "Did I play both sides today?"

That's it. 32 minutes daily. Defense and offense. Awareness and growth. Managing and building.

The person who only budgets documents their perfect decline.

The person who only builds creates chaos without foundation.

The person who does both creates sustainable transformation.

Budget to stop the bleeding.

Build to create new life.

Both. Always. No exceptions.

Because in this economy, playing only defense means losing slowly. Playing only offense means losing quickly.

Playing both means winning inevitably.

Which game are you playing?

The Morning That Changes Everything (24 Time Zones, Same Truth)

6 AM - The Global Dawn of Builders

Right now, as you read this, someone somewhere is waking at 6 AM to build their future. The sun never sets on ambition. The dawn never stops arriving for those ready to meet it.

Follow the sun as builders rise:

6 AM in Sydney - Sarah's alarm vibrates. Kids still sleeping. Coffee brewing. Laptop open. Python tutorial loading. Today's lesson: automation scripts. By 7 AM, she'll have built something that saves her company hours. By next year, she'll be the automation consultant, not the administrator.

6 AM in Mumbai - Rajesh silences his phone before it wakes his parents. Earbuds in. English pronunciation app open. Practicing presentation skills. Each morning, his accent softens, his confidence grows. Six months from now, he'll lead client calls for American companies.

6 AM in London - James rolls out of bed in his studio flat. Sketch app launching. Today: redesigning a local restaurant's menu. Free work now, portfolio piece forever. The side projects at dawn become the main income by December.

6 AM in São Paulo - Carolina opens LinkedIn before her eyes fully open. Connection requests to ten industry leaders. Personalized messages, not templates. Building relationships while others sleep. Her network becomes her net worth within months.

6 AM in Lagos - Kola's ring light clicks on. Camera rolling. Today's video: "Nigerian Business English Mistakes to Avoid." His 50 viewers will become 50,000. His teaching at dawn becomes his empire by dusk.

Same sunrise. Different continents. Same commitment. Different skills. Same trajectory: UP.

Each building while their city sleeps. Each investing in tomorrow while living today. Each choosing growth over comfort, creation over consumption, possibility over predictability.

Meanwhile, budgeters worldwide wake to the same ritual:

6 AM Anywhere - Phone grabbed. Banking app opened. Balance checked.

The number is lower than hoped: Anxiety floods in. Where did it go? Scroll through transactions. Find the culprit. Promise to cut it.

Open budgeting app: Seven notifications about overspending. Adjust categories. Move money from entertainment to groceries. Feel the squeeze.

Cut something else: Cancel the gym (again). Skip lunch with friends (again). Delay the dentist (again). Document the decline.

Feel virtuous but stuck: "I'm being so responsible." Yet further from goals than yesterday. Perfect management of shrinking resources.

Plan to repeat tomorrow: Same wake time. Same check. Same cuts. Same trajectory: DOWN.

The Brutal Comparison:

Builders at 6 AM:

- Creating value
- Learning skills
- Expanding possibilities
- Investing in growth
- Building assets

Budgeters at 6 AM:

- Checking decline
- Feeling anxiety
- Cutting life smaller
- Managing scarcity
- Documenting descent

One group is playing defense against decline.

One group is building toward growth.

Both woke at 6 AM.

Both have 24 hours.

Both face the same economy.

Only one group will be in a different place next year.

Next Year's 6 AM:

Sydney Sarah: Leading automation team, salary doubled

Mumbai Rajesh: Managing global accounts, earning in dollars

London James: Running design agency, choosing clients

São Paulo Carolina: C-suite network, executive opportunities

Lagos Kola: Educational empire, impacting thousands

Budgeters worldwide: Same alarm. Same anxiety. Same app. Same decline. Perfect spreadsheets showing why they can't afford their dreams. Smaller life, perfectly managed.

The Morning Truth:

Every sunrise is an invitation. Every dawn is a door. Every 6 AM is a choice:

Will you check your decline or build your ascent?

Will you document problems or create solutions?

Will you manage less or manufacture more?

The sun doesn't care. It rises anyway.

But here's the profound difference:

The sun rises on builders and budgeters alike.
But only builders rise with it.

Tomorrow at 6 AM, the sun will rise again. Builders worldwide will rise to meet it. Budgeters worldwide will wake to manage their descent.

Which sunrise will be yours?

The alarm is already set.

The choice remains unmade.

The sun is waiting.

Your Chapter 2 Challenge (Quick Win + Share)

Theory is nice. Proof is better. Here's your 7-day experiment that will change how you see money forever:

Not next month. Not Monday. Starting right now.

The 7-Day Build vs Budget Test

Days 1-3: Budget Focus (The Old Way)

- Track every penny obsessively
- Use any app-Mint, YNAB, Excel, notebook, whatever
- Cut one expense each day (subscription, habit, anything)
- Before bed: Write one sentence about how you feel

What you'll likely experience:

- Day 1: "I'm in control!"
- Day 2: "This is tedious..."
- Day 3: "I saved $50 but feel... smaller?"

Days 4-7: Build Focus (The New Way)

- Basic tracking only (5 minutes max-don't abandon awareness)
- Spend 15 minutes learning ONE skill (YouTube, article, course-pick one)
- Apply immediately (even badly)
- Before bed: Write one sentence about how you feel

What you'll likely experience:

- Day 4: "This feels different..."
- Day 5: "I created something!"
- Day 6: "Why didn't I start sooner?"
- Day 7: "I want to keep going"

DO NOT DO THIS ALONE. Here's why:

Solo experiments die in darkness. Group experiments thrive in light.

Right now, before you turn the page:

1. Message 3 friends: "I'm doing a 7-day money mindset experiment. You in?"
2. Create a WhatsApp/Telegram group
3. Name it "7-Day Build Test"
4. Everyone starts TODAY
5. Daily check-ins required (just one sentence)

Sample day 1 check-in: "Day 1: Tracked everything. Found $12 in forgotten subscriptions. Feeling weirdly powerful. 💪"

Sample day 5 check-in: "Day 5: Learned basic Excel formulas. Automated my expense report. Boss noticed. Feel like Neo in the Matrix. 🕶️"

Why This Works:

Social proof = 73% higher completion rate
When Sarah posts her Day 3 results, you won't quit on Day 2.

Peer accountability = No quiet quitting
When everyone's checking in, ghosting feels worse than continuing.

Shared insights = Faster learning
Mark finds a great Python tutorial. Everyone benefits. Group intelligence > solo struggle.

Group energy = Unstoppable momentum
One person's breakthrough becomes everyone's possibility.

By Day 7, your entire group will discover:

Days 1-3 (Budget Focus):

- Felt controlled but constrained
- Saved money but felt smaller
- Perfect tracking of limited resources
- Proud but... uninspired?

Days 4-7 (Build Focus):

- Felt uncertain but expanding
- Invested time but felt bigger
- Imperfect creation of new possibilities
- Messy but... alive?

The verdict: Building creates energy. Budgeting just counts what's left.

The Instant Share

Stop reading. Pick up your phone. Post this right now:

"Starting the #7DayBuildTest with [tag 3 friends]. Testing budgeting vs building mindset for 7 days. Who else wants in? 🚀"

Watch what happens:

- Your friends respond (FOMO is real)
- Their friends ask "What's that?"
- Suddenly you have 10 people experimenting
- Everyone sharing discoveries
- Momentum building
- Mindsets shifting

The Hidden Magic:

You're not just testing a concept. You're:

- Building your first accountability network
- Creating your first value (organizing the experiment)
- Teaching others (leadership practice)
- Starting a movement (even if small)

That's four builder actions disguised as one experiment.

Seven days from now, you'll never see money the same way.

Neither will your friends.

You'll have proof-not theory-that building beats budgeting. You'll have a group that gets it. You'll have momentum that continues past Day 7.

Most importantly, you'll have started. Not tomorrow. Not perfectly. But now.

That's how movements begin.

One person decides to test the truth. Brings three friends. They bring three each. Suddenly dozens are discovering what you're about to prove:

Building > Budgeting. Always.

Your group is waiting. Your experiment starts now. Your old financial worldview has seven days left.

Post the message. Start the timer. Change your life.

See you on Day 7 with your results.

#7DayBuildTest starts... NOW.

The Choice Is Made

Let's be crystal clear about what you just learned:

- Budgeting is organizing deck chairs on the Titanic-helpful but insufficient when the ship is sinking
- There's a mathematical floor to cutting-you can only shrink to zero
- There's no ceiling to building-you can grow to infinity
- You need both defense AND offense-champions play the complete game
- Builders worldwide are rising while budgeters are sinking-same sunrise, different trajectories

This isn't opinion. It's physics. As real as gravity. As universal as sunrise.

The Identity Bridge

You started this chapter as someone who believed budgeting better was the answer. More tracking. Tighter control. Smaller life.

You're ending it as someone who knows building is the solution. More creating. Expanded possibilities. Bigger future.

That's not just information. That's transformation.

The person who started Chapter 2 would have downloaded another budgeting app tonight. The person finishing it is messaging friends about the 7-Day Experiment. Same person. Different physics. Different future.

The Challenge Check

Stop. Right now. Answer honestly:

- Have you started the 7-Day Experiment?
- Have you recruited your three friends?
- Have you created the group chat?
- Have you posted #7DayBuildTest?

If not, stop reading. Do it now.

Books don't change lives. Actions do. And your first builder action is creating that experiment group. Not tomorrow. Not after you finish the book. Now.

Still reading without acting? Then you're still a budgeter-consuming information instead of creating transformation. Prove me wrong. Take the action. Then continue.

You now see why budgeting alone fails.

The math is broken. The floor is real. The ceiling doesn't exist for builders.

But what exactly should you build? What are these mysterious "skills" everyone keeps mentioning? How do you know which value to create first?

You understand building beats budgeting. But building what? How? When? Where do you even start when every guru screams different advice?

Chapter 3 reveals the Builder's Path-the four types of value everyone can create.

Not just for entrepreneurs. Not just for the privileged. Not just for the young or tech-savvy.

Four universal types of building available to anyone who can fog a mirror and set an alarm. Whether you're a single parent in Singapore or a retiree in Rio, a student in Stockholm or a worker in Warsaw-these four paths exist for you.

You'll discover:

- Why your current problem is probably your biggest asset
- How to identify which type of builder you naturally are
- The exact steps from consumer to creator
- Why starting messy beats planning perfectly
- Real stories of builders who started with less than you have

The budgeters are still cutting.

Right now, someone's canceling their third streaming service. Feeling virtuous about saving $15 while losing $500 in purchasing power. Organizing their decline with military precision.

The builders are already creating.

Right now, someone's learning their first line of code. Recording their first video. Making their first connection. Building their first solution. Messy. Imperfect. Unstoppable.

Both woke up today with the same 24 hours.

Only one will wake up tomorrow with new possibilities.

Which will you be tomorrow morning?

Your alarm clock is about to become your answer.

When it rings, you'll either:

- Reach for your budgeting app to check your decline, or
- Reach for your laptop to build your future

The choice is binary. The results are exponential. The time is now.

Chapter 3 awaits. But only for builders.

Are you one?

Your next action answers.

CHAPTER 3: The Builder's Path

A Different Way to Think About Everything

"Budgeters ask 'How can I need less?' Builders ask 'How can I create more?' One question shrinks your life. One expands it."

The Ancient Choice

Since the first human picked up a stone, two paths have existed.

One group polished the stone, preserved it, protected it from weather. Made it last as long as possible. Rationed its use. Managed its decline.

The other group asked: What if we attach this to a stick? What if we sharpen it? What if we trade it? What if we teach others to make better ones?

Both groups held the same stone. One managed what was. One created what could be.

This choice echoes through every era, every culture, every life. Including yours.

The Path of the Maintainer

Honorable. Necessary. Vital to civilization.

Maintainers preserve what exists. The librarian protecting ancient texts. The accountant ensuring accurate records. The administrator keeping systems running. Without them, chaos.

They polish, perfect, and protect. They manage resources carefully. They make things last. They prevent waste. They create stability.

In stable times, Maintainers are heroes. They're why Rome's aqueducts lasted centuries. Why family businesses survive generations. Why traditions pass parent to child.

But when the ground shifts...

The Path of the Builder

Uncomfortable. Uncertain. Essential to evolution.

Builders create what's missing. The inventor trying new combinations. The entrepreneur seeing unmet needs. The artist imagining different worlds. Without them, stagnation.

They experiment, expand, and evolve. They see resources as seeds. They make things grow. They risk waste for reward. They create possibility.

In changing times, Builders are saviors. They're why we have wheels instead of dragging things. Why we have medicines instead of prayers alone. Why we have futures instead of just pasts.

When the ground shifts, the paths diverge.

Maintainers polish the brass on a sinking ship. It gleams beautifully as it descends.

Builders build lifeboats. They're ugly, untested, but they float.

Maintainers perfect the candle as electricity arrives.

Builders wire the first bulbs badly but bring light.

Maintainers optimize the horse carriage for maximum efficiency.

Builders build sputtering automobiles that break down but point forward.

Modern Manifestation

The Blockbuster Executive (Maintainer):

2008. Perfecting DVD distribution. Negotiating better shipping rates. Optimizing store layouts. Reducing late fee complaints. Making the existing system 3% more efficient each quarter. Proud of the polish.

The Netflix Founder (Builder):

Same year. Streaming is buggy. Selection is limited. Quality is inconsistent. But asking: What if movies came to you? What if there were no late fees? What if AI recommended what you'd love? Building the future badly.

We know who inherited the future.

The Corporate Manager (Maintainer):

Today. Perfecting the department AI will eliminate in 18 months. Creating detailed processes for tasks machines will do. Protecting headcount that won't exist. Managing decline with excellence.

The Forward Employee (Builder):

Same company. Learning to prompt AI. Building AI-assisted workflows. Creating value AI can't. Becoming the person who guides the machines. Building a bridge to relevance.

We know who'll thrive tomorrow.
The Universal Pattern

When change accelerates, Maintainers work harder at what's failing.

When change accelerates, Builders work different toward what's emerging.

The monastery scribes (Maintainers) made the most beautiful manuscripts just as the printing press (Builders) made them obsolete.

The telegraph operators (Maintainers) achieved peak efficiency just as the telephone (Builders) made them irrelevant.

The film photographers (Maintainers) perfected chemical processing just as digital (Builders) eliminated chemicals entirely.

Both paths are necessary.

We need those who preserve AND those who progress. We need those who perfect AND those who pioneer. We need those who protect AND those who provide.

But-and this is the crucial but-in times of change, Builders inherit the future.

And friend, look around. Is anything NOT changing?

The Choice You're Already Making

Every morning, you choose a path without knowing it.

When you perfect your budgeting system → Maintaining
When you learn a new skill → Building
When you optimize existing processes → Maintaining

When you create new solutions → Building
When you protect what you have → Maintaining
When you expand what's possible → Building

Neither is wrong. Both require effort. Both have honor.

But only one creates a future when the present is dissolving.

Both paths require effort.

Only one creates a future.

Which are you walking?

Not which do you admire. Not which sounds nice. But which are you actually walking today? This week? This year?

Your calendar knows. Your bank statement knows. Your browser history knows.

Most importantly, your future knows.

The Maintainer's path leads to a perfectly preserved position that won't exist.

The Builder's path leads to a messy creation that wouldn't exist without you.

One ends. One begins.

The choice is ancient. The consequences are immediate.

Which will you choose before the sun sets today?

The Farmer's Wisdom (A Story That Transcends Borders)

The drought came without warning. One season the rains failed. Then another. Then a third.

The sun baked the earth into concrete. Streams became memories. The soil cracked like broken promises. Every farmer in the region faced the same scorched fields, the same withering crops, the same terrible choice.

Four farmers. Same drought. Four different decisions. Four different futures.

The First Farmer

He looked at his seed corn-saved from better harvests, meant for planting. His children were hungry today. Tomorrow felt theoretical. The arithmetic was simple: eat now, worry later.

Each meal, he opened another seed bag. "Temporary," he told himself. "Just until the rains return." The seeds filled stomachs but emptied futures. He survived the drought one meal at a time.

When the rains finally came, he stood in his doorway watching neighbors plant. His fields remained empty. He'd eaten every tomorrow to survive today. Survived, yes. But with nothing to grow.

The Second Farmer

She planted during the worst of the drought. Neighbors thought her mad. "Wasting seeds in dead soil!" they cried. "Save them for when conditions improve!"

But she knew: Seeds stored too long lose vitality. Skills unused atrophy. Muscles resting weaken. So she planted. Most seeds died. But some, against all odds, sent roots deep, searching for hidden water.

When the rains returned, her fields already had roots. Deep roots. Drought-tested roots. While others were just planting, she was harvesting. The "wasted" seeds had become early advantage.

The Third Farmer

Fear ruled his decisions. He hoarded everything. Triple-wrapped his seeds. Buried them deep. Built locks upon locks. The drought would end someday, and he'd have the largest seed reserve. He'd be rich when others had nothing.

But seeds need air. Time is cruel to the inactive. His perfectly preserved cache slowly rotted in storage. Fungus spread through his fear-wrapped bundles. When the drought ended, he opened his vaults to find expensive compost.

He'd preserved his seeds to death.

He did something radical. During the worst of the drought, he shared seeds. Taught water conservation. Showed desert farming techniques his grandfather knew. Created a seed library where farmers could borrow and return.

"Foolish!" critics said. "Keep your advantages secret!"

But shared knowledge multiplies. Every farmer he helped succeeded. They shared back improved techniques. New drought-resistant varieties. Better methods. The network became resilience.

When rains returned, the entire region flourished. His generosity hadn't diminished him-it had created an ecosystem of abundance. He didn't just survive the drought. He transformed it into connection.

The Modern Drought

Your drought is here. Maybe it's economic. Maybe technological. Maybe personal. The ground feels hard. The future uncertain. Resources seem scarce.

You hold seeds. Not corn-time. Not grain-energy. Not harvest-potential.

What will you do?

Eating Seed Corn (Modern Version):

Spending	*learning*	*time*	*on*	*Netflix*
Using	*energy*	*for*		*complaining*
Trading	*future*	*skills*	*for*	*present*	*comfort*

Consuming your potential in small, daily surrenders

"Just until things improve," you say. But when improvement comes, you'll have nothing planted.

Planting in Drought (Builder's Way):

Learning	*during*	*unemployment*
Building	*skills*	*during*	*recession*
Creating	*during*	*criticism*

Investing when others retreat

"Waste of time!" they cry. But roots grow deep in difficult soil.

Hoarding in Fear (Scarcity Mindset):

Clinging   *to*   *outdated*   *methods*
Protecting   *obsolete*   *advantages*
Hiding   *knowledge*   *from*   *others*
Preserving what's already dying

Perfect preservation of dying things still equals death.

Sharing Seeds (Multiplier Method):

Teaching   *what*   *you*   *learn*
Building   *learning*   *communities*
Creating   *mutual*   *support*
Growing together

Shared growth creates exponential returns.

The Universal Truth

Builders plant during famine.

Maintainers ration during feast.

Builders see drought as planting season-hard soil makes deep roots.

Maintainers see drought as survival season-save everything, grow nothing.

When the economy crashes, Builders learn new skills.

When industries die, Builders birth new ones.

When paths close, Builders forge new trails.

When everyone retreats, Builders advance differently.

Your Drought Is Your Opportunity

That job loss? Planting season for new skills.

That industry disruption? Planting season for transformation.

That economic uncertainty? Planting season for innovation.

That personal crisis? Planting season for growth.

The drought isn't your enemy. It's your empty field. Your chance to plant while others eat their seeds. Your opportunity to grow deep roots while others wait for perfect conditions.

Four farmers. Same drought. Four choices:

One ate his future.

One planted through pain.

One preserved to death.

One multiplied through sharing.

The rains always return. They always have. They always will.

The only question: What will be growing in your field when they do?

Your seeds are in your hands. The drought is here. The choice is now.

Plant or eat?

Build or preserve?

Share or hoard?

The farmers who prospered didn't wait for rain. They planted for it.

Your drought isn't your curse. It's your planting season.

What will you plant today?

What Building Really Means

Forget everything you think "building" means.

It's not about launching startups. Not about becoming an entrepreneur. Not about side hustles or passive income or any of the usual suspects.

Building is simpler. And bigger.

Building is about expansion in any form.

Expanding   your   capabilities   (skills)
From knowing one thing to knowing ten things. From solving simple problems to solving complex ones. From following instructions to writing them. Every new ability multiplies your options.

Expanding   your   impact   (influence)
From helping yourself to helping one person. From helping one to helping ten. From helping ten to helping thousands. Same effort, amplified results. Impact compounds.

Expanding   your   value   (contribution)
From doing what's asked to anticipating what's needed. From completing tasks to improving systems. From solving problems to preventing them. Value isn't what you do-it's what happens because you did it.

Expanding   your   options   (opportunities)
From one path to multiple paths. From local to global reach. From single income to diverse sources. From dependent to autonomous. Options are oxygen for your future.

The Fundamental Questions

Listen to the questions people ask. They reveal everything.

Budgeters ask:

"How can I use less?"

"What can I cut?"

"How do I make it last?"

"What's the minimum I need?"

Every question shrinks life smaller. Even perfect answers lead to perfect reduction.

Builders ask:

"How can I create more?"

"What can I add?"

"How do I make it grow?"

"What's the maximum I can contribute?"

Every question expands possibility. Even imperfect answers lead to growth.

Same life. Same challenges. Different questions. Different futures.

The Physical Metaphor

Budgeting is making your box smaller so you fit inside. Cutting corners. Reducing dimensions. Shrinking until you fit the container life gave you.

Building is making yourself bigger so you need a larger box. Growing capabilities. Expanding impact. Becoming too valuable for your current container.

One accepts the box. One outgrows it.

Building in the Real World

The Nurse Who Builds

Maria started as a floor nurse. Good job. Steady pay. But she noticed the ICU always struggled with difficult IV placements. She practiced. Studied ultrasound-guided techniques. Became the go-to expert.

Now she trains entire departments. Speaks at conferences. Consults for medical device companies. Same license. Same hospital. Triple the income. Exponential impact.

She didn't start a business. She built expertise that the world desperately needed.

The Teacher Who Builds

James taught high school math. Decent reviews. Standard results. But he noticed students learned better with visualizations. Started creating animated lessons. Shared them freely.

Other teachers began using his materials. Test scores improved district-wide. Now he designs curriculum for the state. Trains educators globally. His methods reach 100,000 students annually.

He didn't become an entrepreneur. He built solutions that multiplied his teaching beyond his classroom.

The Accountant Who Builds

Priya processed invoices. Repetitive work. Limited growth. But she saw patterns in the inefficiencies. Learned basic automation. Created simple scripts that saved hours.

Showed her manager. Saved the company $50,000 annually. Then $500,000. Now she leads process improvement for the entire corporation. Her systems save millions. Her team prevents problems before they exist.

She didn't launch a startup. She built value that made her indispensable.

The Parent Who Builds

David struggled finding affordable childcare. So did every parent he knew. Instead of just complaining, he organized. Created a parent co-op. Shared pickup duties. Coordinated schedules.

What started with five families now includes 500. They share resources, support, knowledge. Negotiate group discounts. Provide emergency backup. His kids benefit, but so do hundreds of others.

He didn't start a business. He built a community that transforms lives.

The Common Thread

None of them became entrepreneurs. All of them became builders.

They expanded instead of contracted.

They created instead of consumed.

They multiplied instead of divided.

They grew instead of shrank.

They asked "How can I add value?" not "How can I reduce costs?"

They made themselves bigger, so life had to provide bigger boxes.

Building isn't about becoming an entrepreneur.
It's about becoming irreplaceable.

Irreplaceable to your patients because you solve problems others can't.

Irreplaceable to your students because you create outcomes others don't.

Irreplaceable to your company because you save money others miss.

Irreplaceable to your community because you build what others need.

Entrepreneurs are one type of builder. But every builder creates value that didn't exist. Every builder expands what's possible. Every builder makes tomorrow bigger than today.

The nurse builds health. The teacher builds minds. The accountant builds efficiency. The parent builds community.

What will you build?

Not what business will you start-what will you expand? What value will you create? What problems will you solve? What impact will you multiply?

Your job title doesn't matter. Your building does.

Your employer might be temporary. Your value is permanent.

Your position might be eliminated. Your capabilities can't be.

Build capabilities. Build impact. Build value. Build options.

Build yourself bigger than any box they try to put you in.

That's what building really means.

The Four Types of Builders (Global Gallery)

Every builder you admire falls into one of these categories. Sometimes multiple. Always powerful.

The Skill Builder

Definition: Continuously adds capabilities that multiply their value. Like a Swiss Army knife adding tools-each new blade makes previous ones more useful.

Real-World Example:

Sarah started as an emergency room nurse in Minneapolis. Good job, standard pay, typical progression. Then she noticed patterns.

Diabetic patients kept returning. She added diabetes management certification. Suddenly she wasn't just treating emergencies-she was preventing them. The hospital noticed. First raise.

Then wound care certification. Now she could handle the complex cases others avoided. The specialties started talking to each other. Diabetes knowledge improved wound healing. Wound expertise helped diabetic complications. Second raise.

The hospital asked her to train new nurses. She formalized her methods. Created protocols. Built systems. Now she's Director of Nursing Education. Same license she started with. Triple the salary. Ten times the impact.

The Stacking Secret: Every skill multiplies previous skills. Excel + presentation = powerful reports. Coding + marketing = unstoppable products. Writing + any expertise = thought leadership.

Skills don't add. They multiply.

Your Skill Builder Question: What skill could you add in the next 90 days that would double your value? Not a degree. Not a certification necessarily. What skill would make everything else you know more powerful?

The Problem Solver

Definition: Sees obstacles as opportunities to create solutions. Where others see walls, they see doors waiting to be built.

Real-World Example:

Marcus lived in a Brooklyn apartment complex. Packages got stolen constantly. Everyone complained. Marcus acted.

First, he organized residents to receive each other's packages. Simple WhatsApp group. Problem reduced. Building management noticed. Asked him to formalize it.

He researched smart lockers. Negotiated bulk pricing. Convinced management to invest. Theft dropped 90%. Other buildings heard about it. Asked for help.

Now Marcus runs CitySecure, providing package solutions for 20 buildings. Never intended to start a business. Just solved a problem he faced. Turns out thousands faced it too.

The Universal Truth: Every problem you solve for yourself, millions of others also face. Your solution is their salvation. Your fix is their freedom.

Your Problem Solver Question: What problem did you solve this week that others struggle with? What workaround did you create? What system did you build? That's your building opportunity hiding in plain sight.

The Connector

Definition: Creates value by linking people, ideas, or resources. The human router who makes the network work.

Real-World Example:

Maria worked in a Phoenix office park. Noticed two problems: coworkers complained about lunch options, food trucks sat empty across town.

She didn't cook. Didn't own a truck. But she could connect.

Created a simple schedule. Coordinated with building management. Invited food trucks to rotate through office parks. Set up pre-ordering system. Took 10% for coordination.

Now she manages lunch programs for 30 buildings. Food trucks get reliable customers. Office workers get variety. Maria gets paid for connecting dots. Never made a single meal. Feeds thousands daily.

The Network Effect: In the connection economy, the connector often creates more value than the connected. Uber connects drivers and riders. Airbnb connects homes and travelers. You can connect anything.

Your Connector Question: Who do you know who needs to know each other? What resource sits idle here that's desperately needed there? What obvious connection is everyone missing? You're probably sitting on a connection goldmine.

The Teacher

Definition: Multiplies impact by enabling others to succeed. Makes their knowledge immortal by embedding it in others.

Real-World Example:

David was "the Excel guy" in his Chicago accounting firm. Every complex spreadsheet landed on his desk. Bottleneck? Or opportunity?

Instead of hoarding knowledge, he taught. Created "Excel Fridays"-15-minute tips after lunch. Built template library. Recorded quick tutorials. Made everyone powerful.

His team's productivity soared. Other departments wanted training. He formalized the program. The company saved millions in efficiency. David? Promoted three times in two years. Now Chief Process Officer.

He multiplied himself. His methods work even when he's on vacation. His impact compounds daily. Teaching became his superpower.

The Multiplication Math: Do it yourself = 1X impact. Teach 10 people = 10X impact. Teach those 10 to teach = 100X impact. Teaching is the only legal cloning technology.

Your Teacher Question: What do people constantly ask you to help with? What seems obvious to you but amazes others? What knowledge do you have that could transform someone else's outcomes? That's your teaching opportunity.

The Builder's Truth

You won't be just one type. You'll be all four at different times.

Monday: Skill Builder (learning Python)

Tuesday: Problem Solver (automating a report)

Wednesday: Connector (introducing two colleagues)

Thursday: Teacher (showing someone your method)

Friday: All four combined in ways you didn't plan

The Progression Pattern:

Most builders evolve like this:

1. Build skills (foundation)
2. Solve problems with those skills (application)

3. Connect with others doing similar work (network)
4. Teach what you've learned (multiplication)

But you can start anywhere. Enter at any point. Switch between types as opportunities arise.

Master one, experiment with all.

Pick the type that feels most natural. That excites you most. That matches your current situation. Go deep. Become known for it.

But stay open to the others. The nurse who only builds skills hits a ceiling. Add teaching? Exponential growth. The problem solver who never connects stays small. Add networking? Global impact.

Your Building Starts With One Question:

Which type will you try first this week?

Will you add a skill that multiplies your value?

Will you solve a problem others share?

Will you connect resources that need each other?

Will you teach what you know to someone who needs it?

One type. One week. One start.

That's how every builder began. Including the ones whose stories you'll tell someday.

A Gallery of Builders (Beyond Money, Beyond Borders)

Building transcends bank accounts. The same physics that multiply income can multiply health, relationships, community, creativity. The same choice between managing decline and building growth exists everywhere.

The Health Builder

Tom stared at the blood test results. Pre-diabetic. Just like his father. His grandfather. His uncles. The family curse arriving on schedule.

The doctor's prescription was predictable: medication to manage the condition. Regular monitoring. Slow decline. Accept the inevitable.

Tom rejected the script.

Instead of managing disease, he decided to build health. Obsessively researched. Continuous glucose monitor to track real-time impact. Documented every meal, every walk, every weight session. His body became a laboratory.

Six months: Lost 40 pounds. Blood sugar normalized. Twelve months: Lost 70 pounds. Off all medications. Eighteen months: Better health at 48 than at 28.

But Tom didn't stop at personal transformation. He built beyond himself.

Started a blog: "The Reversal Diaries." Posted daily data. Shared failures alongside successes. Created meal plans. Exercise progressions. Mindset shifts. Raw truth about the journey.

Now thousands follow his protocols. Reversing their own diagnoses. Building their own vitality. His inbox fills with transformation photos. Lives saved. Futures reclaimed.

"I stopped managing disease and started building vitality. Turns out, the body wants to heal. We just need to stop preventing it."

The Relationship Builder

Jennifer's divorce was nuclear. Fifteen-year marriage ended in court battles. Kids caught in crossfire. Her ex-husband's new wife made everything harder. The standard playbook said: manage the damage, minimize contact, protect yourself.

Jennifer built instead.

Started with herself. Therapy. Books on attachment theory. Communication workshops. Not to fix the past but to build a better future. Learned about triggers. Patterns. Her own contribution to the chaos.

Then the brave part: applied it with her ex. Set boundaries with compassion. Communicated without attacking. Modeled the behavior she wanted to see. It was messy. Imperfect. Revolutionary.

The kids noticed first. Tension decreased. Transitions smoothed. Even the new wife softened. They started coordinating instead of competing. Built something nobody expected: a functional blended family.

Jennifer documented the journey. Started with a support group of five divorced parents. Now runs workshops across the country. Teaches what divorce lawyers don't: how to build new relationships from old ruins.

"I stopped managing damage and started building connection. Turns out, everyone wants peace. Someone just has to build the bridge."

The Community Builder

Mark's company transferred him to Denver. Knew nobody. Worked from home. The city might as well have been Mars. Weekends were Netflix and solitude. The standard solution: dating apps, meetup groups, manage the loneliness.

Mark built differently.

Bought a basketball. Went to the local park. Shot around alone that first Saturday. Posted in the neighborhood Facebook group: "Anyone want to play pickup basketball? Saturdays 10 AM, Jefferson Park. All skill levels welcome."

Week 1: Three people showed.
Week 4: Twelve people playing.
Week 12: Had to organize teams.
Year 1: Over 200 people in the WhatsApp group.

But basketball was just the beginning. Players became friends. Friends brought families. Barbecues after games. Kids' birthday parties. Job referrals. Three marriages so far. A entire community built from one basketball and consistent Saturdays.

Now there's a league. Sponsors. Youth programs. Mark accidentally built the social infrastructure for an entire neighborhood. Still plays every Saturday.

"I stopped managing loneliness and started building belonging. Turns out, everyone's looking for connection. Someone just has to create the first game."

The Creative Builder

Ashley's accounting job was slowly killing her soul. Good salary. Stable company. Logical career. But she felt like a ghost inhabiting someone else's life. The advice was standard: be grateful, hobbies on weekends, manage the emptiness.

Ashley built a different life inside her existing one.

5:30 AM alarm. Coffee. Canvas. Thirty minutes of painting before the spreadsheets. Bad paintings. Weird paintings. Her paintings. Posted them on Instagram. No strategy. Just proof of aliveness.

Month 1: Family likes and polite comments. Month 6: Strangers asking about purchasing. Month 12: First commission. Month 18: Consistent side income.

But the money wasn't the victory. The victory was feeling alive at 6 AM. Having something that was hers. Bringing creativity to accounting (her spreadsheets became art). Whole person instead of work robot.

Now she teaches other "practical professionals" to build creative lives. Her workshop: "Spreadsheets and Soul." Packed every time. Turns out, lots of ghosts want to become human again.

"I stopped managing emptiness and started building expression. The job pays my bills. The art pays my soul. Both are necessary. Neither is sufficient alone."

The Universal Pattern

Every builder story follows the same arc:

1. Face decline (health, relationship, community, creativity)
2. Reject management, choose building
3. Start small, stay consistent
4. Document and share the journey
5. Multiply impact by enabling others

Tom built health, then helped thousands build theirs.

Jennifer built peace, then taught others to build theirs.

Mark built community, then it built itself.

Ashley built expression, then freed other souls.

None of them meant to become leaders. They just wanted to stop shrinking and start growing. But when you build in public, you become a bridge for others.

Building isn't just about money.
It's about constructing the life you want to inhabit.

Money is one room in that life. But what good is a mansion with one beautiful room and the rest in ruins?

Build your health while building wealth.
Build relationships while building skills.
Build community while building career.
Build creativity while building security.

The same laws apply. The same physics work. The same choice exists:

Will you manage what's declining or build what could flourish?

Your bank account is just one building project.

Your life is the masterpiece.

What will you build today?

Your Chapter 3 Challenge (Build + Share = Momentum)

The Builder's Inventory

You have more to build with than you think. This inventory will prove it.

Right now, you're sitting on goldmines of value you've labeled "nothing special." Time to dig them up. Grab paper or open your phone. This takes 10 minutes and changes everything.

Step 1: List 10 Things You're Good At

Everything counts. Work skills. Life skills. Random talents. The weird stuff especially.

Don't filter. Don't judge. Just list.

Examples to break your brain open:

- Excel formulas that save hours
- Listening without interrupting
- Organizing chaotic spaces
- Cooking with whatever's in the fridge
- Explaining complex things simply
- Fixing things without calling repair people
- Calming anxious people
- Finding deals online
- Making strangers feel comfortable
- Remembering names and details

The Prompt That Unlocks Truth: *"What would friends say you're naturally good at?" They see what you've gone blind to.*

My 10 things:

1. _____
2. _____
3. _____
4. _____
5. _____
6. _____
7. _____
8. _____
9. _____
10. _____

Step 2: List 5 Problems You've Solved

Personal. Professional. Creative. Practical. All count.

You've overcome things. Fixed things. Figured things out. Those victories are building blocks.

Examples to trigger memory:

- Fixed a broken process everyone complained about
- Helped friend through divorce/crisis/career change
- Figured out cheap meal prep that actually tastes good
- Found way to exercise with bad knees/no time/small space

- Negotiated bill that seemed non-negotiable
- Organized system for chaotic situation
- Learned skill everyone said was too hard
- Recovered from setback others don't recover from

The Prompt That Reveals Gold: *"What obstacles have you overcome that others still face?"*

My 5 solved problems:

1. _____
2. _____
3. _____
4. _____
5. _____

Step 3: List 3 Things People Ask Your Help With

The recurring requests reveal your value. What people seek from you repeatedly is what you should build around.

Examples of hidden value:

- "Can you look at my resume?"
- "How do you make that dish?"
- "Can you help me understand this?"
- "What would you do in my situation?"
- "How did you fix that?"
- "Can you recommend a good...?"
- "You're so good at X, can you show me?"

The Prompt That Shows Your Worth: *"What do people assume you know about?"*

My 3 recurring requests:

1. _____
2. _____
3. _____

The Instant Action

Stop. Look at your lists. You just documented 18 pieces of evidence that you have value to offer.

Right now, do this:

1. Pick ONE item from any list.
2. Find ONE person who needs help with it.
3. Help them THIS WEEK.

Not next month. Not when you feel ready. Not after more preparation. This week.

Examples of instant action:

- Your Excel skills → Help coworker automate tedious report
- Your meal prep system → Share with overwhelmed parent
- Your career pivot experience → Guide someone considering change
- Your organizing skills → Tackle friend's closet chaos
- Your tech knowledge → Set up grandmother's new phone

One skill. One person. One week. One build.

The Multiplier Effect

After you help someone, share the story:

Post: #MyFirstBuild

"Just helped [who] with [what]. They were struggling with [problem], and I knew how to [solution]. Took me [time], saved them [result]. Felt amazing to build instead of just budget. Who else is building today?"

Include:

- What you helped with (skill/knowledge used)
- Who you helped (role, not name if private)
- What happened (specific result)
- What you learned (insight gained)

Real examples to inspire yours:

"Helped coworker automate report. 3 hours → 10 minutes. She almost cried. I almost cried. Building beats budgeting. #MyFirstBuild"

"Taught neighbor meal prep basics. Saved her $200/month on takeout. Trading recipes now. We both win. #MyFirstBuild"

"Showed friend LinkedIn optimization. Got three interviews next week. My knowledge = her opportunity. #MyFirstBuild"

Why This Matters

Your small win gives someone else permission to start.

Their win inspires another.

That person motivates five more.

This is how movements begin-one build at a time.

You're not just helping one person. You're proving to yourself that you have value to offer. You're shifting from consumer to creator. You're joining thousands of builders worldwide who chose expansion over contraction.

The Hidden Truth

Those 18 items you listed? That's your builder's toolkit. Most people go their entire lives without realizing they're walking around with treasure.

You just found yours.

Now use it.

One person. One problem. One solution. This week.

Then tell us about it. Your story becomes someone else's permission slip. Your build becomes their beginning.

The builders are waiting for your #MyFirstBuild post.

Don't make us wait long.

Your inventory is complete. Your value is documented. Your first build awaits.

The Builder's Choice Is Made

The Transformation Summary

You started this chapter seeing two options: spend less or earn more.

Now you see the real choice: manage decline or build growth. Maintainer or Builder. Consumer or Creator.

It's not about money. It's about identity. It's about choosing expansion over contraction in every area of life. It's about asking "What can I create?" instead of "What can I cut?"

The maintainer polishes what exists. The builder creates what's missing.

The maintainer perfects the map. The builder forges new paths.

The maintainer manages scarcity. The builder manufactures abundance.

You can't be both. Physics won't let you. Energy spent managing decline is energy not spent building growth.

Choose.

The Identity Bridge

Look at your Builder's Inventory again. Those 18 items you listed.

That's not a list of skills. That's a blueprint for transformation.

Every item is a seed that can grow into something that serves thousands. Your Excel knowledge could free a hundred small business owners from spreadsheet hell. Your meal prep system could help a thousand families eat better for less. Your listening skills could heal relationships, save marriages, transform lives.

You're not looking at what you have. You're looking at what you could build.

The distance between your current life and your desired life isn't measured in dollars. It's measured in builds. Each person you help. Each problem you solve. Each connection you make. Each lesson you teach.

You're not a consumer with skills. You're a creator with gifts.

The Momentum Check

Stop. Right now. Answer honestly:

Have you helped one person yet?

Have you taken ONE item from your inventory and used it to create value for ONE human being?

If not, put the book down. I'm serious. Open your phone. Scroll your contacts. Find someone who needs what you know. Send this:

"Hey, I've been learning about [skill/knowledge you have]. I know you've been dealing with [their problem]. Want me to show you what I've figured out?"

Start building. Now. Not tomorrow. Not after you finish the book. Now.

Books don't change lives. Builds do.

Reading about building while not building is just educated consumption. You're still a consumer, just a well-informed one.

One text. One offer. One build. That's the bridge from theory to transformation.

The Community Call

While you're on your phone, check #MyFirstBuild.

Watch the feed. See Sarah in Singapore helping her colleague automate reports. Watch Marcus in Miami teaching his neighbor smartphone photography. See Jennifer in Dublin organizing meal prep for her mother's friends.

Some builds are small-helped someone book a flight online.

Some are life-changing-taught someone interview skills that landed their dream job.

All are moving from consumer to creator.

You're not alone in this. Thousands are waking up to their builder potential. Taking inventory. Making offers. Creating value. Changing lives.

Your story belongs in that feed. Someone needs to see that a person just like them took action. Your small build is someone else's permission to start.

You now see the Builder's Path.

The four types are clear: Skill Builder, Problem Solver, Connector, Teacher. You know which one calls to you first. You have your inventory. You see others building.

But how do you walk this path consistently? What separates builders who thrive from those who try for a week and quit? What makes building inevitable rather than optional?

There are laws. Ancient laws. Universal laws. Laws that work in any economy, any situation, any life.

Chapter 4 reveals the first law-the one that changes everything else.

The Law of Active Growth: why standing still equals falling behind, and what to do about it. You'll discover why your skills are like ice cubes in the desert and what that means for your future.

But first, your build awaits.

One person needs what you know. Today. Right now. While you're reading about building, you could be building.

Which will you choose?

Tonight you sleep as someone with an inventory.

Tomorrow you wake as a builder.

Your first build awaits.

The sunrise doesn't wait for you to feel ready. Neither do the people who need what you can offer. Neither does your future.

Close the book. Open your phone. Make the offer. Start the build.

See you in Chapter 4-as a builder, not a reader.

Your transformation begins with your next action.

What will it be?

PART TWO: THE FOUR LAWS

CHAPTER 4: The Law of Active Growth.

All Value Decays Without Investment

"In a world of constant change, standing still is moving backward. You're either growing or dying. There is no maintaining."
The Universal Truth

Place an ice cube on a table.

In Miami, it melts in minutes. In Moscow, it takes longer. In the Sahara, it vanishes while you watch. In Stockholm, it lingers.

But it always melts.

Always.

The speed varies. The outcome doesn't. Without active cooling, ice becomes water becomes vapor becomes nothing.

Your economic value is that ice cube. The global economy is the heat.

And the temperature is rising everywhere.

Without active cooling-growth-you melt. Decay. Disappear.

This isn't motivation. It's physics. As real as gravity. As certain as sunrise. As universal as entropy.

Watch it happen in real time:

The Expert Programmer (2010): Master of PHP and Flash. Six-figure salary. Agencies fighting for his skills. "I'll just maintain my expertise," he said. Today? His resume is a museum of dead languages. Junior developers with React knowledge earn more than he ever did. He maintained perfectly. The world moved on.

The Successful Travel Agent (2000): Twenty years building client relationships. Knew every hotel, every route, every trick. "People will always need personal service," she said. Maintained her Rolodex religiously. Today? Her profession doesn't exist. Expedia and AI plan better trips in seconds than she could in hours. She maintained her expertise in a vanished world.

The Factory Supervisor (2015): Thirty years of experience. Could run the floor blindfolded. "These hands-on skills never go out of style," he believed. Maintained his methods. Perfected his systems. Today? One engineer with automation software does what his entire team did. He maintained. The factory evolved without him.

The Illusion of Maintaining

"But I'm not falling behind," you think. "My salary is the same. My skills still work. I'm maintaining."

Let's do the brutal math:

Your Salary "Maintains":

2019:	$60,000
2024:	$60,000

Looks stable, right?

Your Purchasing Power Melts:

2019:	$60,000	buys	$60,000	of	life
2024:	$60,000	buys	$48,000	of	life

20% of your ice cube melted while you weren't looking

Your Skills "Maintain":

2019:	Your	expertise	ranks	90th	percentile
2024:	Same	expertise	ranks	50th	percentile

Half your ice cube evaporated while you "maintained"

Your Industry "Maintains":

2019:	Your	company		employs		1,000
2024:	AI	and	automation	reduced	it	to	400

Your ice cube sits in a rapidly heating room

You're not maintaining. You're melting in slow motion.

The Acceleration of Heat

Your grandparents' ice cube melted over decades. Careers lasted lifetimes. Skills remained relevant for generations. The heat was gentle.

Your parents' ice cube melted over years. Careers needed refreshing. Skills required updating. The heat was warming.

Your ice cube? It's melting in months. Entire industries vanish between breakfast and lunch. Skills expire before you master them. The heat is scorching.

And it's accelerating:

- AI learns faster than you can
- Automation works while you sleep
- Global competition never rests
- Technology evolves exponentially

Standing still used to mean staying in place. Now it means being left behind at exponential speed.

There's no pause button on decay.

No timeout you can call. No safe plateau where you can rest. No maintenance mode that actually maintains.

You're either actively cooling your ice cube-growing, learning, building-or you're watching it disappear. Drop by drop. Day by day. Paycheck by shrinking paycheck.

The travel agent thought she was maintaining relationships. She was actually maintaining obsolescence.

The programmer thought he was maintaining expertise. He was actually maintaining irrelevance.

The supervisor thought he was maintaining standards. He was actually maintaining the past.

They all confused stillness with stability. Fatal error in a world where the ground itself is moving.

You can't stop the heat.

The economy will keep changing. Technology will keep advancing. Competition will keep intensifying. The temperature will keep rising.

Fighting it is like fighting weather. Denying it is like denying physics. Waiting for it to reverse is like waiting for time to flow backward.

The heat is here. The heat is real. The heat is rising.

But you can become something that thrives in it.

What if instead of protecting ice, you became fire?

What if instead of cooling desperately, you learned to generate your own heat?

What if instead of melting, you transformed?

That's what the Law of Active Growth teaches. Not how to preserve your ice cube longer-how to become something that feeds on change instead of being destroyed by it.

The choice is binary: Grow or decay. Build or melt. Transform or disappear.

Your ice cube is melting as you read this.

What are you going to do about it?

The Merchant's Wisdom (Lessons from the Silk Road)

The merchants of antiquity understood physics we've forgotten. Walk the ruins of any ancient marketplace-from Damascus to Venice, from Timbuktu to Xi'an-and you'll find the same wisdom carved in stone and whispered in legend.

Ancient merchants knew:

Silk   stored   too   long   rots   in   warehouses
The finest silk, hoarded in perfect conditions, still deteriorates. Moisture finds a way. Moths discover paradise. Time itself becomes the enemy. Merchants who stockpiled, thinking to wait for better prices, opened their warehouses to find expensive dust.

Spices   lose   their   potency   and   value
Black pepper from India. Cinnamon from Ceylon. Saffron from Persia. All commanding fortunes-when fresh. But hoard them? Their fire fades. Their aroma whispers, then silences. Yesterday's treasure becomes tomorrow's sawdust.

Gold   sitting   still   gets   stolen   eventually
Every merchant learned: stationary wealth attracts predators. Thieves. Officials. Wars. Taxes. Time. Gold that moves is hard to catch. Gold that sits is already caught.

Trade   routes   abandoned   become   overgrown
The path from Constantinople to Beijing. Used daily? A highway of wealth. Neglected for a season? Bandits move in. Two seasons? Nature reclaims. Three? It might as well have never existed.

Ships   in   harbor   rot   faster   than   ships   at   sea
Salt air eats at idle hulls. Barnacles claim still surfaces. Ropes deteriorate. Sails mildew. The ship preserved in harbor becomes unseaworthy. The ship battling storms stays strong.

Modern merchants know:

Skills   unused   become   rusty,   then   useless
That programming language you mastered five years ago? Try using it now. That design software you were expert in? Three versions obsolete. Skills are like muscles-use them or lose them. And in the digital age, losing happens at digital speed.

Knowledge   unshared   becomes   outdated
Hold your expertise close. Tell no one your secrets. Guard your methods. Then watch as the world develops better methods while you perfect yesterday's. Knowledge kept is knowledge killed.

Networks   unnurtured   wither   and   die
That contact list from your last job? How many numbers still work? Those LinkedIn connections you never message? Already strangers. Relationships are living things. Ignore them and they ghost you first.

Reputation   unstoked   fades   from   memory
"Remember when everyone called for Sarah's expertise?" Past tense. Reputation has the half-life of morning dew. Stop demonstrating value and the world forgets you had any.

Innovation   stopped   becomes   irrelevance
The company that perfected the pager. The expert in fax machine repair. The

master of yesterday's innovation. Innovation isn't a destination. It's a velocity. Stop moving and you're already irrelevant.

The Timeless Law

From Silk Road to Silicon Valley, the law remains unchanged:

> *Value requires movement.*
> *What doesn't flow, decays.*
> *What doesn't grow, dies.*

The medium changes-silk to skills, spices to software, gold to knowledge. The physics don't.

A Tale of Two Merchants

Isfahan, ancient Persia. Two brothers inherited equal wealth from their merchant father. Same gold. Same goods. Same opportunity. Different philosophies.

The First Brother-The Hoarder:

"Preserve wealth by protecting it," he declared. Built the finest warehouse. Hired guards. Counted inventory daily. Reduced risk to zero. No dangerous journeys. No uncertain trades. No trusting strangers.

He watched market prices obsessively. Waited for perfect moments. Analyzed endlessly. Acted rarely. His silk remained pristine. His spices perfectly preserved. His gold meticulously counted.

The Second Brother-The Trader:

"Create wealth by moving it," he believed. Loaded camels monthly. Traded silk for spices, spices for silver, silver for silk again. Each journey brought risk. Storms. Bandits. Bad trades. Lost shipments.

But also: new routes discovered. Relationships built. Reputation spread. Knowledge accumulated. Each trade taught lessons. Each journey revealed opportunities. Each risk brought either profit or education.

Ten Years Later:

The Hoarder's warehouse stood magnificent. Inside: silk turned to threads, spices to dust, gold depleted by guards and maintenance. Perfect preservation of declining value. He'd protected his inheritance to death.

His greatest achievement? Slowing the decay. His reward? Watching wealth evaporate slowly instead of quickly. He'd managed decline with excellence.

The Trader's warehouse was often empty-goods flowing in and out like tides. But his network spanned continents. His reputation opened doors. His knowledge commanded premiums. Young merchants sought his mentorship.

He'd lost individual shipments but built an empire. Failed at preservation but succeeded at multiplication. His wealth wasn't in any warehouse-it was in the movement itself.

The merchant's greatest asset wasn't his goods.
It was his movement.
Your greatest asset isn't your current skills.
It's your growth velocity.

The Hoarder asked: "How can I protect what I have?"

The Trader asked: "How can I create what I don't?"

The Hoarder feared loss above all.

The Trader feared stagnation above all.

The Hoarder optimized storage.

The Trader optimized flow.

One preserved. One prospered.

The same choice faces you. Your skills are silk-use them or watch them rot. Your knowledge is spice-share it or feel it fade. Your network is gold-activate it or lose it to time.

You can build the finest warehouse. Install the best security. Create perfect conditions.

But you can't stop the decay. You can only outrun it through growth.

The ancient merchants knew. The modern builders know.

Now you know.

Will you hoard or trade? Preserve or prosper? Manage decline or create growth?

The caravan is forming. The ships are sailing. The trades are happening.

With or without you.

Global Decay, Global Growth

Two forces shape every life, every economy, every future. One is automatic. One requires intention. Understanding both changes everything.

What Decays (The Melting Ice)

Money: Inflation as Termites Eating Cash

Picture termites. You can't see them, but they're always feeding. Silent. Relentless. Structural.

Your money has termites. They're called inflation, and they never sleep.

The Feeding Frenzy:

- $10,000 saved in 2020 = $8,200 in purchasing power today
- That "safe" savings account paying 0.5% while inflation eats 3-6%
- The retirement fund that will buy half what you planned
- The emergency fund emergently shrinking

You're not losing dollars. You're losing life. The vacation gets smaller. The retirement gets delayed. The dreams get downsized. All while the number stays the same.

The termites don't care about your discipline. They eat savers and spenders equally. The only difference? Savers document their decay better.

Skills: Technology as the Great Obsolescence Machine

Travel agents once commanded respect and income. They knew every route, every deal, every insider secret. Today? Expedia knows more in milliseconds.

Photo developers were chemists and artists. Dark room wizards creating memories. Today? Instagram filters do it better, faster, free.

Video store managers curated culture. They knew every film, every actor, every recommendation. Today? Netflix's algorithm never sleeps.

All experts. All obsolete. All replaced by technology they didn't see coming.

Today's Version:

- That cutting-edge React framework? Next year's legacy code
- Your Excel mastery? ChatGPT does it in seconds
- Your industry expertise? AI is training on it right now
- Your specialized knowledge? Being digitized and democratized

The obsolescence machine runs 24/7. No holidays. No mercy. No exceptions.

Relationships: Distance and Time as Universal Eroders

Remember your college crew? "Friends forever!" you swore. Now it's birthday texts and awkward reunions.

That mentor who changed your life? When did you last connect? They've probably forgotten your name.

Your professional network from your last job? Those business cards are archaeological artifacts. Those LinkedIn connections are digital strangers.

The Erosion Pattern:

Daily contact → Weekly → Monthly → Yearly → "Whatever happened to...?"

Deep conversations → Surface updates → Emoji reactions → Silence

Would do anything for each other → Would maybe respond to emergency → Would need reminder of who you are

Relationships are like muscles. Use them or lose them. And most people are losing them to the scroll.

Health: Time's Non-Negotiable Tax

At	20:	Bounce	back	from	anything	overnight
At	30:	Need	a	day	to	recover
At	40:	Need	a	week	and	supplements

At 50: Need medical intervention

The Decay Curve:

- Muscle mass: Losing 3-8% per decade after 30
- Flexibility: Decreasing unless actively maintained
- Energy: Depleting with each passing season
- Recovery: Slowing to a crawl
- Vitality: Dimming like a battery with no charger

Gravity always wins. Time always collects. Without active intervention, you don't maintain-you manage decline.

Relevance: Change as the Great Eliminator

Blockbuster had 9,000 stores. Perfect inventory systems. Optimal locations. Customer loyalty. All irrelevant when streaming arrived.

Kodak invented digital photography. Then buried it to protect film sales. Protected themselves into bankruptcy. Perfected irrelevance.

Nokia made indestructible phones. "Connecting people" was their motto. Then smartphones connected everything, and Nokia became a museum piece.

Current Casualties:

- Traditional media (papers closing daily)
- Retail stores (malls becoming ghost towns)
- Banks (fintech eating their lunch)
- Universities (online learning disrupting everything)
- Your industry (probably next)

Relevance has an expiration date. And it's getting shorter.

What Grows (The Compound Effect)

But while ice melts, other things multiply. While value decays, other forces compound. The builders know this secret.

Learn   Excel.   Useful.
Learn   Excel   +   Python.   Powerful.
Learn Excel + Python + Data Visualization. Unstoppable.

Each skill doesn't add. It multiplies.

The Multiplication Magic:

- Writing + Any expertise = Thought leadership
- Coding + Any industry = Digital transformation
- Design + Any skill = Premium positioning
- Teaching + Any knowledge = Scalable impact
- Sales + Any passion = Profitable purpose

Watch builders stack:

- Morning: Learn new skill
- Afternoon: Apply to current work
- Evening: Combine with existing skills
- Result: Exponential value creation

One skill makes you useful. Two make you valuable. Three make you irreplaceable. Four make you a category of one.

You help one person. They remember. They mention you to someone. Opportunity appears. That someone knows someone. Doors open. Suddenly you're "the person who..."

The Network Effect:

- Each relationship opens 10+ potential connections
- Weak ties (acquaintances) often more valuable than strong
- Digital amplifies everything (local help, global reach)
- Reputation compounds faster than money
- Trust transfers across networks

Real example: Designer helps local bakery. Bakery owner's sister runs marketing agency. Agency needs design help. Designer now has steady client. Client refers to others. Six months later: full practice from one free logo.

Knowledge is the only asset that multiplies when divided.

Teach one person coding. Your knowledge remains, theirs begins. They teach someone. Now three people code. Create a tutorial. Thousands learn. Your knowledge didn't shrink. It exploded.

The Teaching Multiplier:

- Explaining deepens your understanding
- Questions reveal new perspectives
- Students become collaborators
- Documentation becomes products
- Reputation attracts opportunities

The teacher learns twice. The documented lesson teaches forever. The shared skill creates allies everywhere.

Create a solution for yourself. Impact: 1
Share with your team. Impact: 10
Package for your company. Impact: 100
Release to your industry. Impact: 1,000
Open source to world. Impact: 1,000,000

The System Scale:

Personal solution → Team system
Team system → Company standard
Company standard → Industry practice
Industry practice → Global methodology

Every builder's path: Solve once, scale forever.

Real examples:

- A spreadsheet template that saves millions of hours
- A communication method that transforms organizations
- A teaching approach that revolutionizes education
- A simple habit that changes lives globally

Your solution to a personal problem is someone else's salvation. Your system for efficiency is another's path to excellence. Your method for success is a movement waiting to happen.

Decay is automatic.

Ice melts without intervention.
Skills expire without updating.
Relationships die without nurturing.
Relevance fades without evolution.

Growth is intentional.

Capabilities must be built.
Connections must be cultivated.
Knowledge must be shared.
Impact must be designed.

One happens to you. One happens through you.

One is gravity. One is flight.

One is default. One is decision.

Which are you choosing with today's 24 hours?

Right now, as you read this, both forces are at work. Your money is decaying. Your skills are aging. Your relationships are eroding. Your relevance is fading.

But also right now, you could be learning. Connecting. Teaching. Building.

The ice cube melts regardless.

Will you just watch it disappear? Or will you become something that grows instead?

The next 24 hours will pass either way.

How will you spend them-documenting decay or creating growth?

The choice is binary. The results are exponential.

Choose wisely. Choose now. Choose growth.

You can see this law anywhere. The same law applies to this book's reach. Either its impact is growing or decaying. One of the only ways this book grows is with you. If you find this book interesting, one way you can help it grow is by leaving a review or sharing the ideas with someone who could use this.

The Anti-Decay Protocol (Works in Any Time Zone)

Decay is aggressive. Your defense must be systematic. Here's your daily dose of anti-obsolescence-25 minutes that change your trajectory forever.

Think of this as vitamins for value preservation. Miss a day, feel fine. Miss a month, feel the decline. Make it daily, become unstoppable.

The 25-Minute Anti-Decay Protocol

Total time: Less than a sitcom episode. Total impact: Exponential.

15 Minutes: Learn One New Thing

Not random YouTube surfing. Intentional skill acquisition.

Options for different lives:

- Commuting? Podcast on negotiation skills
- At desk? YouTube tutorial on Excel formulas you don't know
- Exercising? Audiobook on your industry's future
- Waiting rooms? LinkedIn Learning on your phone
- Making breakfast? TED talk on communication

Real examples that compound:

- Monday: Learn VLOOKUP in Excel
- Tuesday: Learn keyboard shortcuts for your main software

- Wednesday: Learn one presentation technique
- Thursday: Learn basics of ChatGPT prompting
- Friday: Learn how to read financial statements

Key: Related to your growth area, not random. Building JavaScript skills? Stay in that lane. Growing leadership? Focus there. Scattered learning equals scattered results.

5 Minutes: Apply Immediately

Knowledge without application is entertainment. You're not here to be entertained. You're here to grow.

The 60-Minute Rule: Apply within one hour or it dies in your head.

Instant applications:

- Learned VLOOKUP? Fix that messy spreadsheet right now
- Learned negotiation technique? Use it in your next email
- Learned productivity hack? Implement before lunch
- Learned design principle? Redesign one slide
- Learned communication method? Try it in next meeting

Make it ridiculously small:

- Can't rebuild entire spreadsheet? Fix one formula
- Can't negotiate salary? Negotiate deadline
- Can't redesign presentation? Fix one slide
- Can't transform communication? Change one email

Small application beats perfect procrastination every time.

2 Minutes: Share With One Person

Teaching is the multiplier. Share to solidify. Explain to expand.

Zero-friction sharing:

- Text coworker: "Just learned this Excel trick that saves 10 min..."

- Slack message: "Found productivity hack: [link]. Game changer"
- Dinner conversation: "Discovered interesting thing about our industry..."
- WhatsApp group: "This negotiation tip actually worked today..."
- LinkedIn post: "Today I learned... [insight]"

The selfish reason to share: You remember 90% of what you teach, 10% of what you read. Sharing isn't nice. It's strategic.

The multiplier effect: Your share helps someone. They share back. Knowledge network activated. Value compounds in all directions.

3 Minutes: Document the Insight

Your brain is for creating, not storing. Document to compound.

Pick one method, use it forever:

- Notes app: Date + category + insight + application
- Voice memos: "October 5th learning: VLOOKUP saved 20 minutes on report"
- Journal: Three sentences before bed
- Social media: Tweet the lesson (public documentation)
- Email yourself: Subject: [LEARNING] Today's growth

Format that works:

Date:		Oct			5
Learned:		VLOOKUP			formula
Applied:	Fixed		sales		report
Result:	20	min	→	2	min

Note: Use for all cross-sheet data

Six months later, you have 180 documented growths. That's a personal curriculum nobody else has.

The Compound Math

Let's get mathematical about your transformation:

Daily:		25			minutes
Weekly:	175	minutes	(nearly	3	hours)

Monthly: 750 minutes (12.5 hours)
Yearly: 9,125 minutes (152 hours)

152 hours = 19 full workdays = Nearly a month of growth

While colleagues decay, you're investing a full month in compound growth. They're managing decline. You're manufacturing ascent.

But the real math is exponential:

Day 1: Learn one thing

Day 30: Know 30 things that interconnect

Day 90: Skills start combining multiplicatively

Day 180: Recognized as "the person who knows..."

Day 365: Different human being entirely
Make It Inevitable

Motivation is unreliable. Systems are unstoppable.

The Setup (do this now):

Phone alarm: Set for tomorrow. Label: "🚀 Anti-Decay Protocol"

Stack it: Attach to existing habit

- Morning coffee + learning
- Commute + podcast
- Lunch + application
- Evening shower + documentation

Track simply:

- √ Learned
- √ Applied
- √ Shared
- √ Documented

Phone notes or paper. Complexity kills consistency.

Recovery protocol:

- Missed today? Tomorrow is 30 minutes
- Missed a week? Start fresh, no guilt
- Perfection isn't the goal. Persistence is.

The Accountability Hack:

Find one person. Text them now: "Doing daily 25-min growth protocol. Join me?"

When two people commit, success rate triples. When you have to report to someone, excuses evaporate.

Common Excuses Destroyed:

"No time" → You spent 25 minutes scrolling today

"Too tired" → Decay doesn't care about your energy

"Won't matter" → 152 hours of growth always matters

"I'll start Monday" → Decay started years ago
Decay happens in the margins. So does growth.

The 25 minutes you waste on social media. The 25 minutes you spend on news that changes nothing. The 25 minutes you use complaining about your situation.

That's where your future is hiding.

Not in grand gestures. Not in perfect plans. Not in ideal circumstances.

In the margins. In the minutes. In the daily decision to grow instead of decay.

25 minutes daily tips the scale forever.

Ice cubes don't melt in 25-minute chunks. They melt drop by drop, minute by minute, in the margins of inattention.

Growth happens the same way. Small. Daily. Compounding. Inevitable for those who show up.

Your alarm is set. Your protocol is clear. Your decay has an enemy.

Tomorrow morning, you join thousands worldwide who chose growth over gravity.

25 minutes. Every day. Forever changed.

The ice cube melts regardless.

But you? You're becoming fire.

One protocol at a time.

Universal Applications (Proof from Every Continent)

The Law of Active Growth doesn't care about categories. It works on money, muscle, minds, and marriages equally. Same physics. Different applications. Universal transformation.

Money Growth: From Obsolete to Essential

Jennifer had been a bookkeeper in Seattle for fifteen years. Steady work. Decent income. Then she watched AI do her job in seconds. QuickBooks automation. Receipt scanning apps. Her expertise evaporating in real-time.

The typical response? Panic. Protect. Pretend it's not happening.

Jennifer's response? Grow.

Her 15-Minute Protocol:

- Morning learning: YouTube tutorials on data visualization
- Coffee break application: Added one chart to a client report
- Lunch sharing: Showed colleague what she discovered
- Evening documentation: Noted which visualizations clients loved

The Evolution:

- Month 1: Basic charts replacing boring numbers

- Month 3: Interactive dashboards clients couldn't stop sharing
- Month 6: Charging 3X for "financial insight consulting"
- Year 1: Teaching other bookkeepers to transform

She doesn't do bookkeeping anymore. She translates numbers into stories. AI can crunch data. Jennifer creates understanding.

"I stopped protecting old skills and started building new ones. Turns out clients never wanted bookkeeping. They wanted clarity."

Health Growth: From Managing Pain to Mastering Movement

Mark's back pain story was boringly common. Desk job. Long hours. Annual deterioration. By 40, he needed help putting on socks. The typical prescription: painkillers, careful movement, accept the decline.

"Just part of aging," his doctor shrugged.

Mark disagreed.

His 15-Minute Protocol:

- 6 AM learning: Mobility videos, movement science, pain research
- 6:15 AM application: One new stretch or movement pattern
- Evening sharing: Posted progress in back pain support group
- Bedtime documentation: Pain levels and what helped

The Transformation:

- Week 1: Discovered hip flexors were the real issue
- Month 1: Could touch toes for first time in decade
- Month 6: Deadlifting more than in his twenties
- Year 1: Teaching "Rebuild Your Back" workshops

His MRI still shows disc degeneration. But Mark moves like a dancer. The structure aged. The function improved.

"I stopped managing decline and started building resilience. My spine didn't get younger. I got smarter about using it."

119

Relationship Growth: From Roommates to Lovers

David's marriage wasn't bad. That was the problem. No fights. No passion. Just two polite strangers sharing a mortgage. Date nights were restaurant interviews. Conversations were logistics. Love had quietly flatlined.

Counseling felt dramatic. Divorce felt premature. Decay felt inevitable.

Until David decided to grow.

His 15-Minute Protocol:

- Morning learning: Gottman Institute videos on connection
- Lunch application: Sent one appreciative text to wife
- Dinner sharing: Practiced one new communication technique
- Bedtime documentation: What sparked connection today?

The Renaissance:

- Week 1: Wife noticed him actually listening
- Month 1: Laughing together again
- Month 6: Planning adventures, not just errands
- Year 1: Mentoring other couples

Same house. Same jobs. Same kids. Completely different marriage.

"I stopped assuming love maintains itself and started building it daily. Turns out my wife was starving for connection too. We just forgot how to create it."

Creativity Growth: From Corporate Drone to Published Author

Sarah's creative obituary was already written. Marketing manager. Good salary. Soul-crushing PowerPoints. The artist in her had died somewhere between college and mortgage payments.

"Maybe when I retire," she told herself at 35.

Then she did the math. Thirty more years of death-by-deck. The ice cube of her creativity wouldn't last that long.

Her 15-Minute Protocol:

- 5:30 AM learning: Writing craft videos while coffee brewed
- 5:45 AM application: Wrote one scene, one page, one paragraph
- Lunch sharing: Posted snippets in online writing group
- Evening documentation: Word count and what worked

The Creation:

- Day 1: 150 terrible words
- Month 1: 10,000 words and a habit
- Month 6: First draft complete
- Month 18: Published novel, kept day job, found joy

She still makes PowerPoints. But now she also makes worlds.

"I stopped waiting for inspiration and started building creative discipline. My job pays the bills. My writing pays my soul."

Leadership Growth: From Boss to Builder

Tom inherited a team in trouble. Turnover at 40%. Engagement scores in the basement. Everyone doing minimum required. The usual fixes-pizza parties, motivational posters, performance reviews-changed nothing.

His manager suggested "stronger accountability." Tom tried stronger growth.

His 15-Minute Protocol:

- Lunch learning: Simon Sinek, Brené Brown, leadership podcasts
- Afternoon application: One new leadership behavior
- Team meeting sharing: "Here's what I'm trying..."
- Evening documentation: Team response and energy

The Revolution:

- Week 1: Started with genuine "How are you?" conversations
- Month 1: Team members staying late voluntarily

- Month 6: Engagement scores up 40%
- Year 1: Zero turnover, three promotions

Same team. Same work. Same challenges. Completely different culture.

"I stopped managing people and started growing leaders. Turns out everyone wants to matter. I just had to learn how to show them they did."

Same protocol. Different domains. Universal results.

Jennifer	grew	financial	value.
Mark	grew	physical	capability.
David	grew	emotional	connection.
Sarah	grew	creative	expression.
Tom grew human potential.			

None of them had more time. All of them had the same 24 hours. They just spent 25 minutes of those hours differently.

The Pattern is Clear:

1. Identify area of decay (skills, health, relationships, creativity, leadership)
2. Commit 15 minutes daily to learning
3. Apply immediately, however small
4. Share to solidify and multiply
5. Document to compound
6. Transform decay into growth

Where will you apply it?

Your money might be stable, but your health is decaying.

Your relationship might be strong, but your creativity is dying.

Your leadership might be growing, but your skills are obsolescing.

Everyone has ice cubes melting somewhere. The question isn't whether you're experiencing decay. The question is whether you'll do something about it.

Pick one area. Start tomorrow. Set the alarm.

Because here's the truth no one mentions:

Growing in one area creates energy for others. Jennifer's financial growth gave her confidence to improve health. Mark's physical transformation sparked creativity. David's relationship growth made him a better leader.

Growth is contagious. Even to yourself.

So pick one domain. Any domain. Start the protocol. Watch it spread.

The ice melts everywhere. But fire spreads too.

Which will you choose?

Your alarm is waiting. Your growth domain is calling.

Answer tomorrow morning. 25 minutes. Life changed.

Same protocol. Your domain. Universal transformation.

Where will you apply it?

Your Chapter 4 Challenge (With Accountability Loop)

The 7-Day Growth Sprint

Theory is interesting. Experience is transformative. Here's your proof that decay is a choice-and so is growth.

Not next month. Not "when things calm down." Starting tomorrow morning. Seven days that prove the Law of Active Growth in your actual life.

Step 1: Pick ONE Area (The One Screaming Loudest)

Don't overthink. Don't optimize. Pick the one where decay is most obvious:

Money (skills that multiply income)

- That skill gap making you nervous
- The AI threat to your position
- The income that's not keeping pace

- The expertise becoming irrelevant

Health (energy that compounds)

- The vitality that's fading
- The pain that's increasing
- The stamina that's vanishing
- The flexibility that's gone

Relationships (connections that matter)

- The marriage on autopilot
- The friendships fading
- The network withering
- The family drifting

Creativity (expression that fulfills)

- The spark that's dying
- The dreams gathering dust
- The art you "used to do"
- The voice going silent

Which one just made your stomach tighten? That's your answer. Circle it. Commit. No backsies.

Step 2: Commit to 15 Minutes Daily

The Non-Negotiables:

- Same time each day (morning momentum preferred)
- Same growth area all week (no scatter-shot learning)
- Phone on airplane mode (YouTube rabbit holes don't count)
- Timer set for exactly 15 minutes (not 14, not 20)

Lock it in right now:

My growth time: _____ AM/PM
My growth area: _____
My learning source: _____

Set the alarm. Label it "Growth Sprint Day 1." Do it now before your brain talks you out of it.

Step 3: Apply Immediately (The 60-Minute Rule)

Learning without application is entertainment. You're not here for entertainment.

Within 60 minutes of learning, apply:

- Learned negotiation tactic? Use it in next email
- Learned mobility exercise? Do it before shower
- Learned connection technique? Try at dinner
- Learned writing method? Write one paragraph

Even microscopic application counts:

- Can't rebuild full spreadsheet? Fix one formula
- Can't overhaul diet? Add one vegetable
- Can't have deep conversation? Send appreciation text
- Can't write chapter? Write one true sentence

Small application beats perfect procrastination. Always.

Step 4: Post Daily Progress (Public Accountability)

Shame is a terrible motivator. But public commitment? That's rocket fuel.

Daily post template:

"#GrowthSprint Day [X]
Area: [Money/Health/Relationships/Creativity]
Learned: [Specific thing]
Applied: [Specific action]
Result: [What happened]
Tomorrow: [What's next]"

Real examples to model:

"#GrowthSprint   Day   3
Area: Money
Learned: Python   automation   basics
Applied: Automated   daily   sales   report
Result: Saved   30   min,   boss   impressed
Tomorrow: Automate inventory tracking"

"#GrowthSprint   Day   5
Area: Relationships
Learned: 'Bids   for   connection'   concept
Applied: Noticed wife's 3 bids, responded to all
Result: Best   conversation   in   months
Tomorrow: Make my own bids"

Specificity matters. Vague posts = vague results.

Step 5: Tag One Friend (Growth Becomes Contagious)

Alone, you might quit on Day 3. Together, quitting becomes impossible.

Send this text right now:

"I'm doing a 7-Day Growth Sprint in [area]. Every day: 15 min learning, immediate application, public accountability. Join me? We can keep each other going. Starts tomorrow. You in?"

Why this works:

- They don't want to let you down
- You don't want to let them down
- Competition makes it fun
- Success becomes shareable
- Growth becomes normal

When they say yes (they will), create a mini accountability chat. Two people. Seven days. Lives changed.

The Predictable Journey

Day 1-2: Feels Forced
"This is awkward. Is 15 minutes enough? What should I even learn? Maybe

this   is   stupid."
Normal. Push through. Everyone feels this.

Day   3-4:   Becomes   Easier
"Oh, I actually look forward to this. Found good resources. Starting to see patterns."
The habit is forming. The resistance is weakening.

Day   5-6:   Connections   Appear
"Wait, this connects to what I learned Tuesday. I can combine these. This is actually   working."
Knowledge compounds. Skills cross-pollinate. Magic begins.

Day   7:   Don't   Want   to   Stop
"Can't believe the week's over. Already planned next week's learning. This is who   I   am   now."
Identity shifted. Builder born. Decay defeated.

The Multiplier Effect

When you tag someone and they succeed, you've done more than accountability. You've:

- Broken their decay cycle
- Proven growth is possible
- Created a growth partner
- Started a ripple effect

When they tag someone else, you've started a growth epidemic.

The Hidden Magic:

This isn't just about your seven days. When you post progress, someone watching thinks: "If they can do it..."

Your Day 3 struggle gives someone permission to start.
Your Day 5 breakthrough shows it's possible.
Your Day 7 transformation proves it's worth it.

You're not just growing. You're giving others permission to grow.

Seven days from now, you'll have proof:

- Growth is a choice
- Decay is a choice
- 15 minutes matters
- Applied knowledge compounds
- Public commitment works
- You're capable of transformation

But only if you start.

Not Monday. Tomorrow. Set the alarm now.

Not alone. Text a friend now.

Not perfect. Just committed.

The clock's ticking. Ice cubes are melting. Skills are expiring. Relationships are fading.

But you? You're about to spend seven days proving that growth is always possible. Always available. Always a choice.

Your friend is waiting for that text. Your alarm is waiting to be set. Your growth area is waiting for attention. Your future is waiting for you to choose.

Seven days from now, you'll have proof that growth is a choice.

So is decay.

Choose now.

#GrowthSprint starts in the morning. With or without you.

But why would you choose without?

Set the alarm. Text the friend. Pick the area.

See you at sunrise, builder.

The Growth Imperative
The Decay/Growth Scorecard

Let's be brutally honest. No sugar-coating. No excuses. Look at your life one year ago versus today:

Skills: More   or   less   valuable? That expertise you were proud of-does it command more respect or feel more obsolete?

Income: Buying   more   or   less? Same salary might look stable. But what about purchasing power? That $1000 goes how far now?

Health: Stronger   or   weaker? Energy levels. Flexibility. Pain. Recovery time. Trending up or down?

Relationships: Deeper   or   shallower? Those important connections-are they strengthening or becoming Facebook birthday posts?

Joy: Increasing   or   decreasing? Sunday night feeling. Morning alarm response. Overall life satisfaction. Growing or shrinking?

Count your answers. How many "growing"? How many "decaying"?

Most people score 1 out of 5. Maybe 2. Rarely more. Because most people aren't actively growing. They're passively decaying. And passive always loses to physics.

The Truth Bomb

Here's what this chapter proved beyond doubt:

If you're not intentionally growing, you're automatically decaying.

There is no neutral. No pause button. No maintenance mode that actually maintains.

The ice cube is always melting. Always. In every area. At different speeds but same direction. The only question is: Are you actively cooling it or passively watching it disappear?

- Your skills are either expanding or expiring

- Your health is either building or breaking

- Your relationships are either deepening or dying

- Your relevance is either rising or retreating
- Your joy is either multiplying or melting

Physics doesn't check your intentions. Decay doesn't care about your busy schedule. Time doesn't pause for your perfect moment.

The Identity Shift

You started this chapter thinking growth was optional-something for ambitious people. For entrepreneurs. For the young and hungry. For people with time and energy you don't have.

Now you see it's mandatory-something for people who want to avoid decay. For humans who want to remain relevant. For anyone who refuses to document their decline in perfect spreadsheets.

That's not motivation. That's mathematics.

Growth isn't about becoming exceptional. It's about avoiding extinction. It's not about thriving. It's about surviving in a world where standing still means falling behind.

You don't need to become Elon Musk. You need to become tomorrow's version of yourself instead of yesterday's.

The Challenge Check

Stop. Answer these questions:

- Have you picked your growth area?
- Have you set your alarm for tomorrow?
- Have you tagged your accountability partner?
- Have you committed to the 7-Day Growth Sprint?

If not, stop reading. Put the book down. Open your phone. Take the actions. Decay is happening while you hesitate. Every minute you spend thinking about growing instead of growing is a minute donated to decay.

Books don't stop decay. Actions do. And your first action is setting that alarm.

Still reading without acting? Then you're still choosing decay, just with more information about it.

The Movement Moment

While you're on your phone, check #GrowthSprint.

Watch the feed fill with people choosing growth over decay. Sarah in Sydney starting health protocols. Marcus in Miami beginning financial learning. Jennifer in Jakarta tackling relationship growth. Different areas. Same choice. Same physics. Same rebellion against decay.

You're not alone in this choice. Thousands are setting alarms, picking areas, tagging partners. All deciding that today decay stops and growth begins.

Your post belongs in that feed. Someone needs to see that a person exactly like them chose growth today. Your Day 1 gives someone else permission to start.

Now you understand the First Law: All value decays without investment.

The ice cube melts. Skills expire. Relevance fades. Joy diminishes. Unless you actively intervene.

But knowing decay exists isn't enough. Where should you invest first? What deserves your initial growth energy? How do you ensure your effort creates abundance instead of just busy-ness?

Because here's what nobody mentions: You can grow in the wrong direction. You can invest energy in areas that don't matter. You can be busy decaying-active but still declining.

Chapter 5 reveals the Second Law-the one that determines whether your growth creates abundance or just activity.

The Law of Priority Investment: What you fund first flourishes. What you fund last famishes.

You'll discover why most people grow but still struggle. Why they're learning constantly but earning sporadically. Why they're busy building but still slowly sinking.

The answer will transform how you allocate your most precious resources: time, energy, and attention.

But first, you have an alarm to set. A partner to tag. A sprint to start.

Tonight, decay stops.

Tomorrow, growth begins.

Your alarm is set.

Your future is calling.

Will you answer? Or will you read about growth while decay continues its patient work?

The ice cube doesn't care about your decision. But your future self desperately does.

Choose growth. Choose now. Choose daily.

See you at sunrise, builder. The #GrowthSprint is waiting for your Day 1 post.

Don't make us wait long.

CHAPTER 5. The Law of Priority Investment

"What You Fund First Flourishes"

"Show me your bank statement and calendar, and I'll show you your future. What you fund first flourishes. What you fund last famishes."

The Timeless Sequence (A Lesson from Ancient Traders)

The Phoenician merchants gathered at dawn, their camels groaning under possibility. Before them: the Sinai Desert. Forty days of scorching passage. Behind them: the markets of Memphis, bursting with buyers.

Every merchant faced the same mathematics. Each camel could carry 300 pounds. The choice was binary and brutal:

Load the valuable trade goods first-silks, spices, precious metals-then squeeze in whatever water remains?

Or secure water first-life itself-then pack whatever goods the remaining space allows?

The profit-minded did their calculations. "Silk brings fifty times its weight in gold. Water brings nothing. Load the goods! We'll ration carefully."

The survival-minded did different calculations. "Gold can't purchase water where none exists. Load the water! We'll trade whatever fits."

The caravan departed. Forty days of sun. Thirty days of heat. Twenty days of hell.

The Sequence Revealed Its Truth

By day fifteen, the first group was rationing sips. Mouths like sand. Goods pristine.

By day twenty-five, they were drinking camel blood. Surrounded by fortune. Dying by degrees.

By day thirty-five, the desert claimed them. Perfectly preserved silk wrapping perfectly dead merchants. They died wealthy. They died anyway.

The second group? They arrived with less merchandise. Some had only copper where others planned gold. But they arrived. Traded. Profited. Returned. Lived to trade for decades.

The sequence mattered more than the amount.
Still does.

The Modern Caravan

Your bank account is your camel. Your monthly income, its carrying capacity. Every payment is a choice: survival resource or trade good?

Watch the modern merchant's loading sequence:

First funded (the "valuable goods"):

- Netflix, Spotify, Disney+ - $45
- Dining out - $400
- New clothes - $200
- Latest phone - $100/month
- Car payment for image - $500

Last funded (if anything remains):

- Skills courses - "maybe next month"
- Health investment - "when I have extra"
- Books/learning - "if there's anything left"
- Career development - "after the holidays"
- Future self - "when things calm down"

Loading entertainment before education. Comfort before growth. Status before skills. Image before improvement.

Loading trade goods before water. Every. Single. Month.

The Brutal Modern Math

She pays for eight streaming services but "can't afford" the Excel course that would double her income.

He finances a $40,000 car but "doesn't have money" for the $40 book that would change his mindset.

They fund restaurants religiously but claim they're "too broke" for the gym membership that would add ten years to their lives.

Everyone's camel is loaded. The question is: with what?

Today's Version of Dying Rich in the Desert

Perfect credit score. Empty skill set.

Impressive Instagram. Depressing bank balance.

Premium subscriptions. Poverty mindset.

Comfortable today. Obsolete tomorrow.

They're dying with full entertainment packages and empty growth accounts. Perishing with perfect comfort and zero capability. Fading with every luxury except the ones that matter.

The Payment Autopsy

Pull up your bank statement. Right now. Look at the autopay sequence. The order reveals everything:

1. 1st: Landlord (survival)
2. 2nd: Utilities (necessity)
3. 3rd: Car (transportation)
4. 4th: Insurance (protection)
5. 5th-15th: Comfort and entertainment
6. ...
7. Last: You (if anything remains)

You're the last person you pay. The last priority in your own life. The water at the bottom of the camel after all the silk is loaded.

Your ancestors knew: Survival resources first, profit second.

They understood that water in the desert is worth more than gold. That food for the journey matters more than goods at the destination. That arriving alive beats dying wealthy.

Have you forgotten this wisdom in monthly autopay?

The Phoenicians would watch you fund Netflix before knowledge and weep. They'd see you prioritize DoorDash over development and know your fate. They'd observe you loading entertainment before education and start preparing your desert grave.

Because they knew what you've forgotten:

What you fund first flourishes.
What you fund last famishes.

And right now, you're funding everyone else's future first and yours last.

The merchants who survived the desert didn't have more resources. They just loaded them in the right order. Water first. Life first. Future first. Then whatever else fit.

Your modern camel stands ready. Your monthly load awaits. The autopay sequence is set.

But sequences can be changed. Priorities can be reversed. Futures can be rewritten.

The question is: Will you keep loading silk before water? Or will you finally understand why the sequence matters more than the amount?

The desert doesn't care about your entertainment subscriptions. But your future self is dying of thirst while you stream another show.

Time to reload the camel.

Time to change the sequence.

Time to fund your future first.

The merchants who survived would approve.

The Default Sequence (Worldwide)

Every month, resources flow through your hands. London or Lagos, Delhi or Detroit-the order determines everything.

Pull up your banking app. Watch the sequence. It's the same tragedy playing out in every currency:

1. Landlord/Bank (Shelter) - 30-50% Gone

First withdrawal. Biggest bite. Before you've even had coffee on the 1st, your largest payment vanishes. Your landlord's mortgage gets paid with your labor. The bank builds wealth with your work.

You wake up on payday already broke.

2. Utilities (Survival) - Another 10%

Electricity to see. Heat to survive. Water to drink. Internet to work. The basics of existence in the modern world. Non-negotiable. Auto-drafted. Gone before you notice.

3. Transport (Movement) - 15% Disappears

Car payment to the bank (building their assets). Insurance to the company (funding their profits). Gas to get to work (to make money for everyone else). The machine that enables you to generate income for others.

4. Food (Sustenance) - 15% Consumed

Groceries inflating faster than wages. Restaurants because you're too exhausted from funding everyone else to cook. The fuel to keep you productive for your creditors.

5. Everyone Else (Obligations) - 20% Scattered

Netflix gets funded before your knowledge. Spotify gets paid before your skills. Amazon Prime before your progress. Credit card minimums maintaining your past mistakes. Phone bills, subscriptions, the thousand tiny vampires drinking your future dry.

6. You (Growth) - If Anything Remains

Usually 0-10%. Often negative. The course that could double your income? "Can't afford it." The book that could change your mindset? "Maybe next month." The gym membership for your health? "When things stabilize."
The Brutal Truth in Your Payment Order:

Your landlord gets paid before you do. They're building equity. You're building their equity.

Netflix gets funded before your knowledge. They're growing their empire. You're growing their user base.

Your past (debt) gets paid before your future (growth). Yesterday's mistakes funded before tomorrow's possibilities.

Everyone eats first at your financial table. You get scraps. If there are any. Usually, you go hungry while everyone else gets fat on your labor.

The Mathematical Mugging

Let's expose this with real numbers:

Average Income: $5,000/month

After fixed costs (rent, utilities, transport): Started with: $5,000
Remaining: $1,500 (70% gone to necessities)

After food and basics: Started with: $1,500
Remaining: $500 (another 20% gone)

After everyone else (subscriptions, obligations, minimums): Started with: $500
Remaining: $50-100 (if lucky)

For building your future: Whatever crumbs remain.

That's $50 to transform your life. $50 to learn new skills. $50 to invest in growth. $50 to escape the sequence that's strangling you.

No wonder you're stuck. You're trying to build a future with pocket change while funding everyone else's empire with paper bills.

The Sequence Psychology

This isn't accidental. The system is designed for you to pay everyone else first:

- **Rent due on the 1st?** Ensures they get first dibs
- **Auto-pay everything?** Removes your choice
- **Late fees on their stuff?** Punishes different priorities
- **No late fees on your growth?** Because nobody profits from your improvement

You've been programmed to fund others before yourself. Trained to see their obligations as necessities and your growth as luxury. Conditioned to believe everyone else's claims on your income matter more than your own future.

Here's the life-changing reframe:

You're not poor. You're last.

Big difference. Massive difference. Life-altering difference.

Poor is about amount. Last is about order.

Poor is about income. Last is about sequence.

Poor is about math. Last is about priorities.

You don't have an income problem. You have a sequence problem. You don't need more money. You need a different order.

The Revolutionary Question

What if you flipped this sequence?

What if you went first instead of last?

What if, before anyone else got paid, you invested in your growth? Before Netflix got their $15, you got your knowledge? Before your landlord got their thousands, you got your future?

What if you treated your growth like you treat your rent-non-negotiable, first funded, automatic?

The Phoenician merchants would tell you: Load water before silk. Fund life before luxury. Invest in tomorrow before you pay for today.

Everyone else can wait. Your future can't.

Your landlord won't evict you for paying on the 3rd instead of the 1st. Netflix won't cancel you for pausing a month. The restaurants won't close because you cooked at home.

But your opportunity window? It's closing every day you fund last. Your skills gap? It's widening every month you pay yourself scraps. Your future? It's fading every time everyone else goes first.

The sequence is killing you.

Not the amount. The order.

You have enough. It's just going to everyone else first.

Time to change the sequence. Time to go first. Time to fund your future before their profits.

The merchants who died in the desert had the same resources as those who survived.

They just loaded them in the wrong order.

How are you loading yours?

Why Priority Works (The Psychology is Universal)

When you pay yourself first, your brain shifts operating systems. Not gradually. Instantly. Like switching from black-and-white to color television.

The Brain's Two Programs

Your mind runs one of two programs. Only one. Never both. The sequence of your spending determines which one boots up each month.

Program 1 (Default): Scarcity Management

Triggered when you pay everyone else first, then manage what remains.

- **Question:** "How do I cover everything?"
- **Focus:** Stretching what exists
- **Energy:** Conservation and fear
- **Creativity:** Finding ways to need less
- **Result:** Creative ways to stay poor

This is your brain on leftovers. Calculating how to divide crumbs. Optimizing decline. Your creativity channels into coupon combinations, sale stacking, need reduction. Brilliant solutions to the wrong problem.

You become a genius at poverty management. A master of making less work. An artist of decline documentation.

Program 2 (Priority): Abundance Creation

Triggered when you pay yourself first, then solve for the gap.

- **Question:** "How do I cover everything AND invest in growth?"
- **Focus:** Expanding what's possible
- **Energy:** Innovation and possibility
- **Creativity:** Finding ways to create more
- **Result:** Creative ways to grow rich

This is your brain on priority. Calculating how to generate solutions. Optimizing growth. Your creativity channels into value creation, opportunity recognition, resource multiplication. Brilliant solutions to the right problem.

You become a genius at value creation. A master of making more exist. An artist of abundance manufacturing.

Same brain. Different question. Opposite life.

The Constraint Creates Creativity

Here's what nobody understands: Your brain is lazy until threatened. Comfortable until constrained. Passive until pressured.

Before Priority Investment: "I can't afford that $200 course. Maybe when I have extra money. Maybe next month. Maybe never."

Brain status: Sleeping. No problem to solve. No urgency to create. No pressure to perform.

After Priority Investment: "I bought the $200 course. Rent is due in 10 days. Now what?"

Brain status: DEFCON 1. Problem immediate. Solutions needed. Innovation required.

The Sarah Experiment

Sarah was a graphic designer, living paycheck to paycheck for five years. Same salary. Same expenses. Same "I can't afford to learn new skills" story.

Then she flipped the sequence.

Moved her $200 monthly learning budget to the TOP of her priorities. Before rent. Before food. Before Netflix. First. Automatic. Non-negotiable.

"I was terrified," she admits. "Rent was due in two weeks, and I'd just spent $200 on a UX design course."

Her brain went into hyperdrive. Not panic-purpose. Not fear-focus.

- **Day 3:** Posted in freelance groups: "Quick design work available"
- **Day 5:** Found logo project: $300
- **Day 7:** Delivered early, got bonus: $400 total
- **Day 10:** Client referred her to friend: Another $500 project
- **Day 14:** Rent paid, course funded, $200 extra

Would she have looked for freelance work without the pressure? "Never. I was comfortable enough to complain but not uncomfortable enough to create."

The Neuroscience Is Clear

Your brain has two modes:

Default Mode: Energy conservation. Routine maintenance. Autopilot operation. Active when comfortable.

Survival Mode: Solution generation. Pattern recognition. Resource multiplication. Active when constrained.

Paying yourself last keeps you in default mode. Why innovate when bills are paid? Why hustle when Netflix is funded? Why create when comfortable?

Paying yourself first triggers survival mode-but for growth instead of decline. Your brain treats your development as survival necessity. Solutions appear. Opportunities emerge. Resources materialize.

Constraint + Priority = Innovation

It's not motivation. It's mathematics. It's not willpower. It's brain wiring.

The Uncomfortable Truth

When you have "enough" for bills, your brain sleeps.

When you prioritize growth first, your brain works.

When rent is secured, innovation hibernates.

When growth is funded, solutions activate.

When comfort is guaranteed, creativity atrophies.

When priority creates pressure, genius emerges.

Real Examples of Priority-Driven Innovation:

Marcus: Paid for coding bootcamp before securing rent. Brain found weekend warehouse work he'd never considered. Now senior developer.

Jennifer: Invested in certification before groceries. Brain noticed consulting opportunity in company newsletter. Now runs her own firm.

David: Funded home gym before car payment. Brain created online fitness coaching to cover gap. Now full-time trainer.

All had the same resources before. All found new resources after. The only difference? Priority sequence creating productive pressure.

Your brain is wired to solve immediate problems.
Make your growth the immediate problem.

Not someday growth. Today growth. Not eventual development. Urgent development. Not comfortable learning. Necessary learning.

When growth is optional, it never happens.

When growth is first, solutions always appear.

The Priority Paradox

The more comfortable your sequence, the less creative your solutions.

The more priority your growth, the more innovative your income.

Comfort whispers: "Manage what you have."

Priority demands: "Create what you need."

Comfort kills creativity.

Priority creates it.

Your brain has genius-level problem-solving ability. But it only activates under constraint. Pay everyone else first, and your genius sleeps. Pay yourself first, and your genius works.

The Phoenician merchants understood: When water is optional, you die calculating. When water is priority, you find a way.

Your growth is water in the modern desert.

Fund it first, or perish calculating how to manage the decline.

The choice-and the sequence-is yours.

Real Stories from Real Places

Three people. Three moments of terror. Three decisions that changed everything. None of them had "extra" money. All of them found it anyway.

Michael's Reversal (The Engineer's Awakening)

Michael had been a mechanical engineer in Detroit for eight years. Same desk. Same CAD software. Same salary with 2% annual raises. Same financial sequence: bills first, whatever remained for "someday improvement."

That whatever? Usually $50. Sometimes nothing.

"I kept waiting for a month when I'd have extra to invest in learning," he recalls. "Five years of waiting. The 'extra' never appeared."

Then he watched a junior engineer get promoted past him. The difference? AI and automation skills.

That month, Michael did something insane. Before paying a single bill, he enrolled in a $300 AI course. First purchase of the month. Non-negotiable. Automatic.

"My stomach dropped the second I hit 'buy.' Utilities were due in two weeks. I had no idea how I'd cover them."

But something shifted. His brain switched from "manage what exists" to "create what's needed."

144

The Innovation: Within 48 hours, Michael approached his manager. "I'm learning AI automation. Let me automate our reporting system. If I save the department 20 hours a week, how about a one-time bonus?"

Manager agreed. Michael delivered in three weeks. Bonus: $2,000.

Six months later: Leading the automation initiative. Salary increased 40%. Now invests $1,000/month in continuous learning-still first, before any bills.

"I was budgeting for survival. Now I'm investing for transformation. Turns out I never had an income problem. I had a sequence problem."

Jennifer's Choice (The Teacher's Leap)

Fourth-grade teacher. Single mom. Cleveland. Two kids. Every month the same story: bills, kids' needs, groceries, nothing left. The American dream in reverse.

"I made spreadsheets proving I couldn't afford to learn new skills," Jennifer laughs now. "Really detailed ones. I was excellent at documenting why I was stuck."

The breaking point: Watching her own students use technology she didn't understand. Teaching becoming obsolete in real-time.

Jennifer made the choice that made her family think she'd lost her mind. $150/month for coding bootcamp. Before groceries. Before utilities. Before her kids' wants.

"My mother called me selfish. My sister said I was irresponsible. 'Your kids need food, not your dreams.'"

The pressure was immediate. Groceries were needed in days. Her teacher brain-used to finding resources from nothing-kicked into overdrive.

The Innovation: Posted on local parent Facebook groups: "Teacher offering online evening tutoring." Five responses in two days. Rate: $40/hour. Covered groceries in one week.

Twelve months later: Remote curriculum development role for ed-tech company. Salary: $95,000 (double her teaching salary). Still tutors because she loves it. Kids in better schools. Mother apologizes weekly.

"Everybody said feed your kids first. But building my skills feeds them for life. I wasn't taking food from their mouths. I was building their future."

Robert's Gambit (The Accountant's Calculation)

CPA for fifteen years. Houston. Everything by the book. Bills automated in "responsible" order. Pride in never missing a payment. Credit score: 798. Growth investment: whatever crumbs remained.

Those crumbs averaged $0-75 monthly. Fifteen years of crumbs don't make a meal.

"I calculated everyone else's wealth while documenting my own decline," Robert reflects. "Perfect records of standing still."

Then a client half his age hired him. An entrepreneur who'd built three companies. During tax prep, she asked Robert: "Why are you still doing individual returns?"

That stung. That night, Robert did something his CPA brain screamed against. Enrolled in a $500/month business coaching program. Before his car payment. Before his mortgage. First.

"I'd never been late on anything. The thought made me nauseous. But I'd also never been early to my own future."

Car payment due in ten days. No savings to tap. His analytical brain faced a new equation: create or be late.

The Innovation: Reached out to five small business owners he'd met through tax work. "I'm adding CFO consulting services. First month discounted for early adopters." Three said yes. Monthly retainer: $1,500 each.

One year later: Robert's firm has twelve fractional CFO clients. Revenue: $350,000. He buys cars with cash now. Credit score: Still 798, but who cares?

"One late payment, lifetime of different payments. I spent fifteen years optimizing the wrong sequence."

None of them had "extra" money.

Michael had the same salary when he bought the course.

Jennifer had the same teaching check when she started bootcamp.

Robert had the same income when he joined coaching.

They had priority clarity.

They stopped waiting for margin and created it through sequence. Stopped hoping for extra and manufactured it through pressure. Stopped managing what existed and built what they needed.

The Pattern is Universal:

1. Flip the sequence (growth first)
2. Feel the pressure (bills still due)
3. Find innovation (brain activates)
4. Create value (solutions appear)
5. Transform life (new normal)

Your story is waiting.

You don't need more money. You need Michael's courage to buy first. You don't need perfect timing. You need Jennifer's clarity on what matters. You don't need permission. You need Robert's willingness to be uncomfortable.

Every transformation started with terror. Every success began with "How will I cover this?" Every new life was born from priority pressure.

They flipped the sequence. They felt the fear. They found the way.

Your turn.

What will you fund first tomorrow?

Breaking Global Barriers

Every culture has sacred financial sequences. Every family has money myths. Every brain has barriers. Let's shatter them with truth.

"But I Have Responsibilities!"

The most common prison. The most noble chain. The most destructive excuse.

Question back: "Is your growth not a responsibility?"

To your family who depends on your income? To your children who inherit your limitations? To your future self who pays for today's choices? To the people you could help if you had resources?

The Comfortable Lie: "I sacrifice for others."

The Uncomfortable Truth: "I use others as an excuse to stay small."

Staying poor doesn't help anyone you're responsible for. It just makes you all poor together. Misery might love company, but poverty destroys families.

The Tale of Two Fathers:

Father One: "I can't invest in myself. Kids come first." Twenty years of noble poverty. Kids grow up stressed about money. Learn scarcity. Inherit fear. College? "Too expensive." Wedding? "Keep it small." Help with house? "Sorry, wish I could."

Father Two: "I must invest in myself. Kids deserve better." One year of uncomfortable growth. Twenty years of expanding resources. Kids grow up seeing possibility. Learn abundance. Inherit confidence. College? "Which one?" Wedding? "Dream big." House? "Here's your down payment."

Both loved their kids. One loved them into limitation. One loved them into opportunity.

Growing wealth helps everyone you care about.
Staying broke helps no one, including you.
Your growth isn't selfish. Your stagnation is.

"But I'll Get Evicted/Divorced/Disowned!"

The fear feels real. The math isn't.

Reality check from every continent:

Most bills have 15-30 day grace periods. Your landlord won't evict you for paying on the 5th instead of the 1st. Your spouse won't leave over one strategic choice. Your family won't disown you for investing in your future.

The Communication Solution:

"Hi [Landlord/Creditor], I'll be one week late this month due to an investment in professional development. Payment will arrive by [date]. This is a one-time situation."

99% say: "Thanks for letting us know."

1% complain: Still won't evict you.

The Mathematical Truth:

One week late on rent: $50 late fee (maybe)
Lifetime of skills gained: $500,000+ income increase
ROI: 10,000X

One month of side-eyes: Temporary discomfort
One year of transformation: Permanent elevation
Trade-off: Obviously worth it

This isn't about being irresponsible.

It's about being strategic.

The Phoenician merchants didn't skip water. They prioritized it. You're not skipping bills. You're reordering them. Once. To change your life forever.
"But I Literally Have Zero Extra!"

Everyone says this. From Manhattan to Mumbai. Let's expose the lie.

Start with time (the universal currency):

You have zero extra money? Fine. Do you have zero extra time?

- 30 minutes of growth before 30 minutes of Netflix
- 15 minutes of learning before 15 minutes of Instagram
- 5 minutes of reading before 5 minutes of complaining

Time invested in growth becomes money. Time invested in entertainment becomes nothing.

Start tiny (the crumb strategy):

- $10 for a used book before $10 for takeout

- $5 for an app course before $5 for a latte
- $1 for paid newsletter before $1 for lottery ticket

The amount matters less than the sequence. Tiny prioritized beats large leftover every time.

Start creative (the builder's way):

No money? Barter. Trade. Create.

- Fix someone's computer for course access
- Babysit in exchange for textbooks
- Clean offices for conference tickets
- Write reviews for learning subscriptions

Builders find ways. Budgeters find excuses.

Real Examples of Starting from Zero:

Lagos: Adaeze had literally zero. Walked to library daily. Used free computers. Learned graphic design. First client paid for internet café access. Now runs design agency.

Mumbai: Raj sold his lunch daily to buy data. Hungry but learning. YouTube University graduate. Now teaches what he learned. Hunger was temporary. Skills are permanent.

Detroit: Maria collected cans for course money. $0.10 at a time. Neighbors thought she was crazy. Learned social media marketing. Now manages accounts worth millions.

Zero money doesn't mean zero options. It means creative priorities.

"But What About Emergencies?"

The ultimate objection. The fear of all fears. The reasonable-sounding excuse that keeps millions poor.

Counter: "What about the emergency of staying poor forever?"

Your car might break down someday. You ARE broken down today.

Your health might fail eventually. Your wealth IS failing currently.

Your job might disappear tomorrow. Your skills ARE disappearing now.

Which emergency deserves priority? The hypothetical one or the happening one?

Truth: Your current sequence creates perpetual emergency.

Living paycheck to paycheck IS an emergency. Having no savings IS an emergency. Skills becoming obsolete IS an emergency. Being one crisis from catastrophe IS an emergency.

You're not preventing emergencies. You're living in one. Permanently.

New frame: Investment in growth prevents future emergencies.

Skills can't be repossessed. Knowledge can't be stolen. Capabilities can't be fired. Networks can't be foreclosed.

Every dollar invested in growth creates emergency-proof income. Every skill learned creates crisis-resistant value. Every connection made creates catastrophe insurance.

The best emergency fund? Ability to create value anywhere, anytime, for anyone.

Every objection assumes the current sequence is sacred.

It's not. It's just familiar.

Familiar feels safe. But familiar is what got you here. Reading a book about building because you can't afford to build. Dreaming of transformation while funding stagnation.

Your objections aren't protections. They're prison bars. And prison bars only feel like safety until you realize you're inside them.

The Phoenician merchants faced the same objections:

- "But we need trade goods!" (But I have responsibilities!)
- "But we'll anger the buyers!" (But I'll upset people!)
- "But we have no extra space!" (But I have no extra money!)
- "But what if bandits come?" (But what about emergencies!)

151

The ones who listened to objections died rich in the desert.

The ones who prioritized water lived to tell the tale.

Your water is your growth. Everything else is silk in the sand.

Your Chapter 5 Challenge (The 30-Day Reversal)

Time to stop theory and start practice. For 30 days, you're going to do what terrifies you: pay yourself FIRST.

Not "when convenient." Not "if there's extra." FIRST. Before anyone or anything else gets a penny.

Step 1: Choose Your Investment

Pick ONE. Based on your next growth edge, not your comfort zone:

Skill Course ($50-500)

- That Excel mastery you keep postponing
- The coding basics you "can't afford"
- The marketing skills you need
- The AI tools everyone else knows

Coaching Program ($100-1000)

- Business strategy you're missing
- Career transition you're dreaming of
- Leadership skills you need
- Life design you're craving

Tools/Software for Building ($20-200)

- Design software to create
- Automation tools to scale
- Learning platforms to grow
- Building blocks for your future

Books/Resources ($50-100)

- The knowledge you're lacking
- The strategies you need
- The mindset requiring upgrade
- The blueprint for transformation

Don't overthink. Your gut knows what you need. The thing you keep saying "someday" about? That's your pick.

Step 2: Pay It FIRST

The moment money hits your account:

1. Open laptop/phone
2. Buy the investment
3. Close laptop/phone
4. Feel the terror

Before rent. Before utilities. Before groceries. Before your morning coffee. Before your brain can object.

First means first. Not second. Not "after I calculate." FIRST.

Step 3: Figure Out the Rest

Now the magic happens. Watch your brain shift from "I can't" to "I must."

What to expect:

- **Hour 1-24:** Panic ("What have I done?")
- **Day 2-5:** Innovation ("Maybe I could...")
- **Day 6-10:** Action ("Let me try this...")
- **Day 11-30:** Transformation ("Why didn't I always do this?")

Document everything:

- Solutions you find
- Opportunities that appear
- Money that materializes

- Mindset that shifts

Your brain on priority is genius-level. You're about to meet it.

Step 4: Post Daily Proof

Accountability + Community = Unstoppable Force

Day **1** **Post:**
"Just did something crazy. Invested in [specific thing] BEFORE paying bills. Terrified and excited. Figuring out the rest. #FirstFunded #30DayReversal"

Daily **Posts:**
"#FirstFunded Day [X]
Challenge: [What you faced]
Solution: [What you found]
Lesson: [What you learned]
Tomorrow: [What's next]"

Be specific:

"Needed $200 for groceries. Posted in neighborhood group about organizing services. Booked 3 closets. Made $300."

"Electric bill due. Offered to build spreadsheet for colleague. Took 2 hours. Paid week's expenses."

"Rent short by $100. Listed old textbooks online. Sold for $150. Profit from priority."

Specificity inspires. Vagueness dies. Share real numbers, real solutions, real transformation.

Step 5: Create the Chain

You're not just changing your life. You're starting a revolution.

Daily chain-building:

- Tag one new person: "You talked about wanting [change]. Join me? #FirstFunded"
- Share their wins when they start

- Connect chains to each other
- Watch network effects multiply

The Multiplier Math:

Week 1: You + 7 others = 8 builders
Week 2: Those 7 bring 7 each = 56 builders
Week 3: Exponential growth = 400+ builders
Week 4: Movement in motion = Thousands changing sequences

Your reversal becomes their permission. Their success becomes someone else's catalyst. The chain reaction builds new futures.

Real Examples to Model:

Singapore Sarah: "Invested in Python course first. Rent due in 5 days. Brain found freelance data entry. Made course cost in 2 days. Mind = blown. #FirstFunded"

Detroit David: "Coaching program before car payment. Scariest click ever. Used coach's advice to negotiate raise same week. Covered everything plus extra. #FirstFunded"

Mumbai Monica: "Bought design software before groceries. Family freaked. Created logos for local shops. Groceries covered, software paid, confidence soaring. #FirstFunded"

Why This Works:

Pressure creates diamonds. Comfort creates complacency. When growth is optional, it never happens. When growth is first, solutions always appear.

Your brain is waiting. It has genius-level problem-solving ability that only activates under productive pressure. Give it a problem worth solving.

Community compounds courage. Alone, you might quit day 3. Together, quitting becomes impossible. Your win becomes their fuel. Their fuel becomes movement.

Start NOW or Stay Last Forever

Right now, while you're feeling it:

1. Choose your investment
2. Set calendar reminder for payday
3. Post commitment: "Starting #FirstFunded on [date]. Who's with me?"
4. Screenshot this challenge
5. Share with one person who needs it

The clock is ticking:

Every day you delay is another day paying everyone else first. Another day as last priority in your own life. Another day choosing familiar poverty over uncomfortable growth.

30 days from now, you'll be one of two people:

Person A: Still reading about priority investment. Still paying everyone else first. Still finding reasons it won't work. Still last.

Person B: Living priority investment. Brain rewired for solutions. Network built on growth. Life transformed by sequence. Finally first.

30 days. One reversal. Lifetime of different results.

The Phoenician merchants would be proud. You're about to load water before silk. Fund life before lifestyle. Choose growth before groceries.

Your current sequence has you exactly where you are. A different sequence creates a different life.

Which life do you want?

The movement starts with your first purchase. The chain begins with your first tag. The transformation launches with your first reversal.

#FirstFunded is waiting for your Day 1 post.

Don't make us wait long.

Your reversal starts with your next paycheck.

Or your excuses continue forever.

Choose.
The Future You're Funding

Pull out your last three bank statements. Go ahead. Open your banking app. Look at the sequence of payments. That pattern you see? That's not just your spending.

That's the future you're funding.

The Two Futures

Future A (Your Current Sequence):

Landlord   first   =   Building   their   wealth
Every month, their mortgage gets paid with your labor. Their equity grows. Their retirement funds. Their kids' inheritance builds. With your life energy.

Subscriptions   second   =   Funding   their   growth
Netflix adds to their billion-dollar valuation. Spotify multiplies their market cap. Amazon grows their empire. Every automatic payment is a vote for their expansion over yours.

You   last   =   Ensuring   you   stay   there
The crumbs that remain-if any-go to your growth. Usually nothing. Sometimes debt. Always insufficient. You're not just last in line. You're ensuring you remain there.

This sequence isn't neutral. It's a wealth transfer system. From you to everyone else. Every. Single. Month.

Future B (The Reversed Sequence):

You   first   =   Building   your   capabilities
Skills that compound. Knowledge that multiplies. Networks that expand. Health that energizes. Every investment in yourself pays dividends forever.

Growth   second   =   Creating   abundance
From scarcity management to value creation. From budget juggling to income multiplication. From surviving to thriving.

Others   after   =   From   your   overflow
Pay bills from abundance, not anxiety. Fund others from surplus, not sacrifice. Give from growth, not guilt.

Same money. Different order. Opposite futures.

The Choice Point

Every month, you vote with your sequence.

For five years, ten years, maybe twenty-you've been voting for everyone else's future while yours starves. Funding their dreams while yours die. Building their empires while yours crumbles.

Time to vote differently.

This isn't about having more money. It's about directing the money you have toward the future you want instead of the poverty you fear.

The Identity Declaration

Say this out loud. Right now. Even if it feels uncomfortable:

"From this moment: I am not the leftover person. I am the priority person."

"I don't get what remains. I take what I need to grow. Then figure out the rest."

"I am not last in my own life. I am first."

"My growth is not optional. It's essential."

"Everyone else can wait. My future can't."

Feel different? Good. Identity shifts before behavior. Behavior creates results. Results build the new life.

The Challenge Check

Stop. Answer honestly:

- Have you chosen what to invest in?
- Have you committed to the 30-day reversal?
- Have you set the date for your first priority payment?

If not, stop reading. This book won't change your life. Your next action will.

Open your banking app. Right now. Set up the automatic transfer for when your next payment arrives. Not to savings. To growth. To that course. That program. That investment in your future.

Make it automatic so fear can't stop you.

Make it first so nothing comes before it.

Make it real so theory becomes transformation.

Still reading without acting? Then you're choosing Future A. Choosing to stay last. Choosing everyone else's wealth over your own.

The Movement Moment

Open another tab. Check #FirstFunded.

Watch the feed fill with reversals. Sarah investing $75 in design skills before groceries. Marcus putting $200 toward certification before rent. Jennifer funding coaching before car payment.

Some investing $50. Some $500. All going first instead of last.

They're not special. They're not fearless. They're just tired of funding everyone else's future while theirs withers.

Your reversal gives others permission to reverse. Your courage creates theirs. Your first-funded post might be the exact push someone needs to flip their own sequence.

You now understand the Second Law: What you fund first flourishes.

The Phoenician water traders proved it. Modern builders live it. Your future depends on it.

But here's what's coming: Investment without multiplication is just spending with better timing.

Chapter 6 reveals the Third Law-how to make every investment multiply beyond your imagination.

The Law of Value Multiplication: why 1+1 equals 11 in the builder's world. How small investments create exponential returns. Why your unique combination of skills, problems, and connections is worth more than you imagine.

You'll discover:

- Why intersection points create fortunes
- How to stack skills for exponential value
- The multiplication method that turns hundreds into thousands
- Real examples of ordinary people creating extraordinary returns

But none of that matters if you stay last.

Tonight you decide: Stay last or go first.

Not eventually. Tonight. Before you sleep. Before another day passes funding everyone else's dreams.

Set up the automatic payment. Choose your investment. Commit to the reversal.

Or close this book and keep your comfortable, familiar sequence that's slowly killing your future.

Tomorrow your bank account reveals your choice.

Will it show the same sequence-everyone else first, you last?

Or will it show the reversal-you first, finally?

Your landlord doesn't need your priority. Netflix doesn't need your loyalty. The old sequence doesn't need your obedience.

But your future? Your skills? Your growth? Your family's transformation? They desperately need you to go first.

Just once. Just tomorrow. Just to see what happens when you flip the sequence that's been flipping you.

Your future is watching.

And it's hoping-praying-you finally choose it first.

The alarm is set. The investment is chosen. The reversal awaits.

Will you?

The next transaction tells all.

Chapter 6: The Law of Value Multiplication.

"Value Multiplies at Intersections"

"Don't get better at one thing. Connect two things. That's where fortunes hide—in the intersections nobody else sees."

The Silk Road Secret

The year: 200 BCE. The place: Chang'an, ancient China's capital. The discovery: A multiplication principle that would create more wealth than all the gold in the empire.

Chinese merchants had silk. Beautiful, valuable, desired. A luxury that commanded high prices in local markets. Good business. Profitable trade. Linear growth.

Then someone noticed something that changed everything.

Romans, thousands of miles away, had never seen silk. Would pay anything for it. Had gold, silver, spices to trade. But geography was brutal. Deserts. Mountains. Bandits. Distance.

Silk was valuable. Maybe 10 taels of silver per bolt locally.

Silk + Western demand? Same silk now worth 100 taels of silver. Not because the silk improved. Because the intersection was discovered.

But merchants who tried the journey often died. Bandits. Weather. Starvation. The multiplication was theoretical until someone added the third element.

The breakthrough: Safe routes.

Not just any path—mapped routes with water sources. Protected passages with way stations. Reliable guides who knew the terrain. Suddenly, the impossible became inevitable.

Silk = 10 taels (valuable)
Silk + Western demand = 100 taels (10X multiplication)
Silk + Western demand + Safe route = 1,000 taels (100X multiplication)

The silk didn't get better. The merchants didn't work harder. They just connected three elements that multiplied each other.

162

Modern Multiplication (Same Physics, Different Century)

Watch it happen today:

Basic web design

You learn HTML, CSS, JavaScript. Charge $50/hour. Compete with millions globally. Race to the bottom on freelance platforms. Good skill. Linear income. Slowly drowning.

Web design + Conversion optimization

You notice clients don't just want pretty sites. They want sites that sell. Add conversion rate optimization knowledge. Study psychology. Learn A/B testing. Same design work, but now you guarantee results. $150/hour. 3X multiplication. Not from working three times harder. From connecting two valuable things.

Web design + Conversion optimization + Subscription model

The final multiplication. Instead of one-time projects, you offer ongoing optimization. Monthly retainer. Continuous improvement. Predictable revenue. Ten clients at $1,500/month = $15,000 monthly. Same skills. Different intersection. 300X multiplication from where you started.

The Pattern Reveals Itself

Single elements add value. Combinations multiply it.

Ancient		**version:**
Silk	=	Valuable
Transportation	=	Valuable
Security	=	Valuable
Combined = Fortune		

Modern		**version:**
Coding	=	Valuable
Marketing	=	Valuable
Psychology	=	Valuable
Combined = Fortune		

Your		**version:**
[Your skill]	=	Valuable
[Market need]	=	Valuable
[Delivery method]	=	Valuable
Combined = Your fortune		

The Breakthrough Insight

The Silk Road traders didn't get rich from having the best silk. Chinese silk was always excellent. They got rich from connecting silk to distant buyers through safe routes.

The multiplication happened at the intersection.

Modern fortunes hide in the same place:

- Not in being the world's best programmer. In connecting programming to business problems through automation.
- Not in being the perfect writer. In connecting writing to marketing through conversion copy.
- Not in being an amazing teacher. In connecting teaching to global students through digital platforms.
- Not in mastering one thing. In connecting multiple things.

Fortune isn't in perfecting one thing.
It's in connecting multiple things.

The ancient traders knew: Don't just improve your silk. Connect it to those who've never seen it. Create the path between.

Today's builders know: Don't just improve your skill. Connect it to urgent problems. Bridge the gap others can't see.

The Multiplication Question

Every Silk Road fortune started with someone asking: "What if we connected...?"

- What if we connected Eastern silk to Western gold?
- What if we connected scattered routes into a safe path?
- What if we connected individual traders into caravans?

Every modern fortune starts the same way:

- What if we connected riders needing rides to drivers with cars? (Uber)
- What if we connected empty rooms to traveling strangers? (Airbnb)
- What if we connected local restaurants to hungry homes? (DoorDash)

Simple connections. Exponential value. Multiplied fortunes.

What are you connecting?

- What skill do you have that could multiply with market need?
- What problem do you see that could connect to a solution?
- What separated elements could you bridge?

You don't need the best silk. You don't need to perfect one thing. You need to see the intersection others miss.

The Silk Road created more millionaires than gold mines. Not from extraction. From connection.

Your fortune isn't hiding in perfection. It's waiting at an intersection.

What will you connect today?

The Four Multipliers (With Global Proof)

Value multiplication isn't magic. It's math. Four specific types of fusion that turn ordinary resources into extraordinary results. Master one, and you thrive. Master all four, and you become unstoppable.

Skill Fusion (1+1=10)

Definition: Combining complementary skills that create exponential value. Not learning more of the same thing—connecting different things that amplify each other.

The Multiplication Pathway:

Watch Sarah's progression from commodity to premium:

Year 1: Accounting degree = $45,000 salary
Basic bookkeeping. Competing with software. Replaceable.
Year 2: Accounting + Advanced Excel = $65,000
Now she automates reports. Saves companies time. More valuable.
Year 3: Accounting + Excel + Data Visualization = $95,000
Turns numbers into insights. Creates dashboards executives love. Irreplaceable.
Year 4: Accounting + Excel + Data Visualization + AI Tools = $300/hour consulting

Predicts trends. Prevents problems. Transforms decisions. Exponential value.

Each skill didn't add 20% more value. Each multiplied everything before it.

Real Story: The Accidental Multiplier

Jake in Portland. Decent photographer—thousands like him. Decent writer—millions more. Separately, both skills were commodity. $50 for photos. $0.10/word for writing.

Then a startup asked: "Can you tell our story visually?"

Jake combined both skills. Visual storytelling for brands. Photos that narrate. Words that paint. Stories that sell.

Now? $10,000 per project. Same skills. Different intersection. 100X multiplication.

"I spent years trying to be the best photographer. Then years trying to be the best writer. Turns out I needed to be the only visual storyteller in my niche."

Your second skill multiplies your first. Your third multiplies both.

- Coding + Design = Full-stack value
- Marketing + Psychology = Conversion expertise
- Teaching + Technology = Scalable education
- Sales + Empathy = Relationship millions

Stop perfecting one thing. Start connecting multiple things.

Network Fusion (Bridging Worlds)

Definition: Creating value by connecting disconnected groups. You don't produce anything. You bridge everything.

The Connection Economy:

Sarah discovered this accidentally. College friends were launching startups—brilliant ideas, no experience. Church community had retired executives—decades of wisdom, empty calendars.

Two groups. Same city. Never intersecting. Until Sarah built the bridge.

100 connections in Group A (founders)
× 100 connections in Group B (executives)
= 10,000 potential valuable interactions

Sarah facilitates introductions. Takes 5% equity for successful connections. Zero production. Zero expertise needed. Pure multiplication through connection.

Year 1: 10 introductions, 2 succeed = $50K in equity value
Year 2: 50 introductions, 10 succeed = $500K in equity value
Year 3: System automated, reputation established = $2M portfolio

Real Examples Everywhere:

- **Mumbai Raj:** Connected Indian developers with US startups. Never wrote code. $30K/month in placement fees.
- **London Emma:** Linked British antique dealers with Chinese collectors. Never touched an antique. 7-figure business.
- **São Paulo Carlos:** Introduced Brazilian musicians to gaming companies needing soundtracks. Can't play an instrument. Revolutionized an industry.

Every group you belong to is a multiplication opportunity with every other group.

Your gym × Your office = Corporate wellness programs
Your neighborhood × Your profession = Local expert status
Your hobby group × Your industry = Unique consulting angle
Stop trying to be the expert. Start being the bridge.

Time Fusion (Double Dipping)

Definition: Stacking activities to multiply output from same time investment. Not time management—time multiplication.

The Stacking Revolution:

Unsuccessful people see time as single-use:

- Commute = Dead time
- Exercise = Just fitness
- Cooking = Just food
- Walking = Just movement

Successful people stack value:

- Commute + Podcast = Mobile university
- Exercise + Audiobooks = Body and mind training
- Cooking + YouTube = Audience building
- Walking + Client calls = Relationship deepening

Real Story: The Commute That Paid

Lisa from Boston. 45-minute commute each way. 90 minutes daily. 450 minutes weekly. Most people scroll Instagram. Lisa enrolled in Python bootcamp.

The Stack:

Commute = Getting to work
+ Audio lessons = Learning to code
+ Practice problems = Skill application
+ Community forum = Network building

Six months later: Remote Python developer. No commute. Those same 90 minutes now earning $150/hour instead of costing gas money.

450 weekly minutes × 26 weeks = 11,700 minutes = 195 hours = Full bootcamp completed in "dead" time.

Normal use: 1 hour = 1 outcome
Double stack: 1 hour = 2 outcomes
Triple stack: 1 hour = 3 outcomes
Master stack: 1 hour = Exponential outcomes

Examples to implement tonight:

- Dishes + Phone calls to neglected connections
- Dog walking + Voice memo brainstorming
- Meal prep + Skill tutorial videos
- Cleaning + Educational podcasts

Unsuccessful people have spare time. Successful people have leveraged time.

Every moment can be single-use or multiplied. Same 24 hours. Exponentially different results.

Problem Fusion (One Solution, Million Applications)

Definition: Solving your personal problem in a way that helps countless others. Your struggle becomes their salvation.

Personal problem → Systematic solution → Scalable product → Global impact

Real Story: The Budget Tracker That Built an Empire

Marcus was broke. Really broke. Negative bank balance broke. Built an Excel budget tracker out of desperation. Color-coded. Automated. Foolproof. Finally got finances under control.

Shared with roommate. Roommate shared with sister. Sister shared with coworkers. Requests poured in.

Version 1: Personal use (saved his finances)
Version 2: Friends and family (20 users)
Version 3: Added tutorials ($47 price point)
Version 4: Full course + community ($497)
Version 5: Enterprise version for companies ($4,997)

Now: 50,000 customers. $2M revenue. Same spreadsheet. Just multiplied.

Examples Everywhere:

- Your back pain solution? Millions of office workers need it
- Your meal prep system? Every busy parent wants it
- Your anxiety management? The whole world seeks it
- Your productivity method? Everyone craves more hours

The Multiplication Truth:

You're not unique in your struggles. You're unique in your solutions.

Every problem you face, millions face. But most people:

- Complain about problems
- Accept problems
- Work around problems

Builders:

- Solve problems systematically
- Document the solution
- Share with others facing same problem
- Scale the solution

Every problem you solve for yourself, millions of others also face.

Your divorce recovery becomes their healing guide. Your debt elimination becomes their financial freedom. Your fitness transformation becomes their health revolution.

Not because you're special. Because you solved it and shared it.

The Master Multiplier Formula:

- Fuse skills that amplify each other
- Bridge networks that need connection
- Stack time for exponential output
- Scale solutions to universal problems

**Do   one?   You   succeed.
Do all four? You explode.**

The Silk Road traders understood: Don't just have silk. Connect it to buyers through safe routes. Modern builders understand: Don't just have skills. Multiply them through fusion.

Your current value = X
Your multiplied value = X^{2n}
Same person. Same resources. Exponential results.

Real Multiplication Stories

Three people. Three intersections. Three fortunes hidden in plain sight. None of them special. All of them multiplied.

The Accidental Empire (Skills Multiply)

Emma taught third grade in Phoenix for seven years. $45,000 salary. Summer breaks. Standard story. Except Emma had a secret weapon she didn't know was loaded.

She made her worksheets pretty.

Not revolutionary. Just basic Canva skills learned from YouTube. Borders here. Fonts there. Colors that made kids smile. Other teachers noticed. "Can I have that worksheet?" became the daily request.

Year 1-3: The Teacher Phase

Teaching skill: Strong
Income: $45,000
Future: 2% raises until retirement

Year 4: The Design Addition

Started sharing designed worksheets with her grade team. Then her school. Then a Facebook group. Teachers went crazy. "These actually make kids want to learn!"

Emma saw the intersection: Teachers desperate for engaging materials + Design skills = Opportunity.

Year 5: The Store Launch

Teachers Pay Teachers account. First product: $3 math worksheet pack. First month: $180. "Beer money," she laughed. Kept uploading.

Year 6: The Marketing Multiplication

Emma noticed: Great products sat invisible. Learned Pinterest. Studied SEO. Created email list. Same worksheets, now with audience.

Teaching alone: $45K (linear)
Teaching + Design: $60K (helpful)
Teaching + Design + Marketing: $300K (explosive)

Today: The Empire

- 100,000 teachers on email list
- 500+ products in store
- $300K annual revenue
- Still teaches (because she loves it)
- Works 2 hours daily on business

"I didn't become a better teacher. I connected teaching with design and marketing. The intersection was worth more than the sum of parts."

The Stack Evolution:

- Teacher who designs (common)
- Designer who understands teachers (uncommon)
- Marketer of teaching designs (rare)
- All three in one person (category of one)

Emma didn't invent teaching. Didn't invent design. Didn't invent marketing. Just connected them in a way nobody else saw.

The Translator (Bridges Multiply)

Marcus had a weird childhood. Dad coded since the 80s. Mom ran a medical practice. Dinner conversations jumped between debugging and diagnoses. He absorbed both languages without realizing their value.

Became a nurse. Good job. Decent pay. Frustrating reality: Hospitals buying million-dollar tech that nobody could use. Vendors speaking tech. Doctors speaking medicine. Nobody translating.

The Lightning Moment

Hospital board meeting. Tech vendor pitching new system. Doctors glazing over. Millions about to be wasted. Marcus raised his hand.

"What they're saying is the API will integrate with your EMR to reduce documentation time by 40%. What you're hearing is tech gibberish. Let me translate..."

Fifteen minutes later, both sides understood each other for the first time. Deal restructured. Hospital saved $2 million. CEO pulled Marcus aside: "Can you do this regularly?"

The Bridge Business

Marcus didn't learn anything new. Just realized his intersection was worth a fortune.

Healthcare knowledge (from work) + Tech fluency (from childhood) = Translation superpower

Started consulting part-time:

Year 1: $50K side income
Year 2: Quit nursing, $150K
Year 3: Team of 3, $350K
Year 4: $500K practice
Year 5: Tech companies on retainer

The Multiplication Magic:

Average	tech	consultant:	$150/hour
Average	healthcare	consultant:	$200/hour
Marcus (both languages): $500/hour			

"I'm not the smartest tech person or healthcare expert. I'm the bridge.
Turns out bridges are worth more than either shore."

His Client Base:

- Hospitals hiring tech (need translation)
- Tech companies selling to healthcare (need translation)
- Doctors evaluating systems (need translation)
- Investors in health tech (need translation)

Every meeting between tech and healthcare becomes his opportunity. He doesn't create. He connects. The multiplication happens in the middle.

The Stack Master (Problems Multiply)

Ashley was a burned-out marketing manager in Chicago. Stress eating. No time for health. Rock bottom moment: Couldn't fit into her sister's wedding dress. Six months to fix it.

Problem 1: Needed to Meal Prep

Created a system out of desperation. Sunday prep. Container system. Recipe rotation. Labeled everything. Lost 30 pounds. Felt amazing. Posted transformation photos.

Problem 2: Friends Wanted the System

"How did you do it?" flooded her inbox. Created a simple PDF guide. Shared with 20 friends. They wanted more. Facebook group born. 100 members in a month.

Problem 3: People Wanted It Done for Them

"I love your system but hate cooking. Can you just make my meals?" Lightbulb. Started weekend meal prep service. Five clients. Then ten. Then waitlist.

Commercial kitchen rental. Delivery routes. Hired help. Business exploding. New problem: Couldn't scale beyond Chicago.

Problem 4: Service Hard to Scale Geographically

Revelation: Don't scale the service. Scale the system. Created certification program for meal prep coaches. Teach others to run local services using her system.

Today: The Multiplication Machine

- 200+ certified coaches in 35 states
- Each pays $2,000 for certification
- Plus monthly licensing fees
- Plus approved supplier commissions
- Total: Seven-figure business

"Each solution created a new problem with 10X the opportunity. I thought I was solving my weight problem. Turns out I was building an empire, one problem at a time."

The Problem Evolution:

Personal problem (weight) → Personal solution (meal prep)
Friends' problem (want system) → Shared solution (guide)
Market problem (want service) → Business solution (local prep)
Scale problem (geographic limits) → Certification solution (teach others)
Next problem brewing → Next multiplication waiting

Each problem wasn't an obstacle. It was an opportunity in disguise. Each solution created value. Each value created new problems. Each new problem meant bigger opportunity.

None of them invented anything new.

- Emma didn't invent teaching, design, or marketing. She connected them.
- Marcus didn't invent healthcare or technology. He bridged them.
- Ashley didn't invent meal prep or certification. She systematized then scaled them.

174

They just connected things that already existed.

Your fortune isn't hiding in innovation. It's waiting at an intersection. Between skills you already have. Between worlds you already know. Between problems you've already solved.

The Silk Road traders would recognize these stories. Same principles. Different century. Identical multiplication.

They connected silk to buyers through routes. Emma connected teaching to design through marketing. Marcus connected tech to healthcare through translation. Ashley connected problems to solutions through systems.

All multiplication. All available to you. All waiting at your intersections.

The Multiplication Mindset

Most people see skills like items on a grocery list. Learn this. Add that. Improve here. Linear progress in a world that rewards exponential results.

Builders see skills like chemical elements. Hydrogen is useful. Oxygen is useful. Together they create water—entirely new properties, exponentially more valuable.

Time to rewire your brain for multiplication.

From Linear to Multiplicative Thinking

Linear Thinking (Addition)—How 99% Think:

"I'll get better at Excel"

Today:	Basic	user
Year 1:	Advanced	user
Year 2:	Expert	user
Year 3:	Master	user

Progress: 1→2→3→4 (adding competence)

"I'll expand my network"

Month 1:	100	connections
Month 2:	200	connections
Month 3:	300	connections

Progress: Adding people to same pool

"I'll learn marketing"

Week 1:		Basics
Week 4:		Intermediate

175

Progress: Deeper into single subject
Linear thinking asks: "How can I get better at this?"

Multiplicative Thinking (Intersection)—How Builders Think:

"I'll	**use**	**Excel**	**to**	**solve**	**marketing**	**problems"**
Analytics		dashboards			for	campaigns
ROI		calculators			for	clients
Automated			reporting			systems

Progress: 1→2→6→24 (multiplying value)

"I'll	**connect**	**my**	**gym**	**network**	**to**	**my**	**work**	**network"**
Corporate			wellness			programs		born
Executive			fitness		accountability			groups
Health-focused				business				mastermind

Progress: Two separate groups become exponential opportunities

"I'll	**teach**	**marketing**	**to**	**Excel**	**users"**
They	need		to	track	campaigns
You		bridge		both	worlds
Course:		"Excel		for	Marketers"

Progress: Intersection creates new category
Multiplicative thinking asks: "What could this connect with?"

Same effort. Exponential results. Different question.

The Daily Practice

Every evening, before the day's lessons fade, ask four questions:

1. **What did I learn today?**
   Maybe you discovered a new Excel function. Learned about customer psychology. Understood a market trend. Picked up a productivity hack. Anything counts.

2. **What do I already know?**
   Your existing skills. Your background. Your network. Your experiences. Your unique combination of knowledge that nobody else has exactly.

3. **How could they connect?**
   This is where magic happens. Force connections. Play with combinations. What if your Excel skills helped photographers track bookings? What if your psychology knowledge improved your coding? What if your network needed your new insight?

4. **Who would pay for that connection?**
   Every intersection solves someone's problem.
   Photographers hate business tracking. Coders struggle with
   user psychology. Your network seeks specific solutions.
   Who desperately needs what you just connected?

Real Example from Last Tuesday:

Sarah's Evening Review:

- **Learned:** TikTok algorithm basics (from YouTube video)
- **Already knew:** Local restaurant operations (previous job)
- **Connection:** Restaurants failing at TikTok because they
  think like restaurants, not creators
- **Who pays:** Local restaurants desperate for young
  customers

Result: Now consulting for five restaurants on TikTok strategy.
$2,000/month each. Intersection discovered on a Tuesday. Implemented by
Friday. Income multiplied by month end.

Spotting Intersections Everywhere

Once your brain switches to multiplication mode, you see intersections
everywhere:

Restaurant Server + Social Media = Food Influencer
Not just serving tables. Documenting culinary experiences. Behind-scenes
stories. Chef interviews. Suddenly making more from sponsorships than tips.

Nurse + YouTube = Health Educator
Not just treating patients. Teaching prevention. Explaining conditions.
Demystifying treatments. Reaches millions instead of dozens. Impact
multiplied infinitely.

Mechanic + Teaching = DIY Course Creator
Not just fixing cars. Empowering owners. Saving families thousands.
Building trust through education. Course income exceeds shop income within
year.

Parent + Organization = Productivity Consultant
Not just managing chaos. Systematizing it. Teaching other overwhelmed
parents. Corporate clients want same skills. Parenting hacks become business
systems.

Every profession has multiplication opportunities:

- Accountant + Storytelling = CFO consultant who explains numbers
- Teacher + Technology = EdTech curriculum designer
- Lawyer + Writing = Legal content creator
- Therapist + Group dynamics = Corporate team builder

The intersections are infinite. Your combination is unique.

The Multiplication Filter

Before learning anything new, run it through this filter:

"What could this multiply with?"

Learning   **Spanish?**
$\times$ Your profession = Bilingual premium (2X rates)
$\times$ Your location = Cultural bridge business
$\times$ Your network = International opportunities

Learning   **Video**   **Editing?**
$\times$ Your expertise = Course creation ability
$\times$ Your hobby = YouTube channel monetization
$\times$ Your job = Become the company's media person

Learning   **Sales?**
$\times$ Your passion = Monetized hobby business
$\times$ Your knowledge = Consulting practice
$\times$ Your connections = Affiliate income streams

Learning   **Coding?**
$\times$ Your industry = Automation consultant
$\times$ Your problems = Scalable solutions
$\times$ Your creativity = Technical artist

Never learn in isolation. Always seek multiplication.

The Compound Question

Every time you consider learning something, ask:

"Will this add to what I know or multiply it?"

- **Adding:** Learn accounting after finance (similar, linear)
- **Multiplying:** Learn psychology after finance (different, exponential)
- **Adding:** Learn another programming language (depth)

- **Multiplying:** Learn design with programming (breadth)

- **Adding:** Get another certification in your field
- **Multiplying:** Learn complementary skill from different field

Real Builder Examples:

Tom: Learned five programming languages (adding). Still competing on freelance sites. $50/hour.

Amy: Learned programming + music theory. Creates algorithmic music tools. $500/hour consulting for music software companies.

Both learned. One added. One multiplied.
Stop collecting skills like baseball cards.

Baseball cards sit in albums. Isolated. Pretty but static. Each worth only its individual value. Linear collection.

Start connecting skills like Lego blocks.

Lego blocks click together. Create structures. Build systems. Each block multiplies the possibilities of others. Exponential creation.

Your skills aren't collectibles. They're building blocks. Stop asking "What else can I learn?" Start asking "What can I build with what I'm learning?"

The Silk Road traders understood: Don't just improve your goods. Connect them to new markets. Create new routes. Build new possibilities.

Modern builders understand: Don't just improve your skills. Connect them to pressing problems. Create new categories. Build multiplied value.

Your multiplication moment is waiting.

In the intersection between what you know and what you're learning. Between your background and your future. Between your network and your knowledge. Between today's discovery and tomorrow's application.
Stop adding. Start multiplying.

The intersections are everywhere, waiting for eyes trained to see them.

Train your eyes. Tonight. With those four questions.

Watch your value multiply.

The Hidden Multiplication Opportunities

Everyone looks for multiplication in the obvious places. Skills. Networks. Problems. But the biggest multipliers hide where nobody thinks to look. In gaps. In differences. In what you take for granted.

Let's expose the invisible goldmines you walk past daily.

Geographic Arbitrage Multiplication

The world is flat for income. The world is steep for costs. The gap between them? Pure multiplication.

Live in low-cost area + Work for high-cost market = Lifestyle multiplication

Real Example:

Jake, developer in Wichita, Kansas. Previous job: Local bank, $65,000. Comfortable but limited. Then he discovered remote work for coastal companies.

The Multiplication:

San Francisco junior developer salary: $120,000
Kansas living costs: 60% less than SF
Effective purchasing power: $300,000 SF equivalent
Multiplication factor: 3X lifestyle upgrade
Same skills. Same hours. Same Jake. Triple the life.

Modern Examples Everywhere:

- Filipino VA earning US wages: 10X local salaries
- European designer charging US rates: 2X purchasing power
- Indian developer working for London: 5X lifestyle multiplication
- Mexican marketer serving Canadian clients: 4X income arbitrage

The Hidden Truth: Your location is negotiable. Your income doesn't have to be.

Companies pay for value, not your zip code. They care about output, not your overhead. The developer in Silicon Valley costs them more but doesn't deliver more. You're not cheaper labor. You're smarter economics.

Experience Stack Multiplication

Your biggest failure is someone else's expensive prevention.

Past failure + Current success = Paid wisdom

Nobody pays for theory. Everyone pays to avoid pain they see coming.

Real Example:

Sandra built a restaurant. Invested everything. Failed spectacularly. Lost $200,000. Devastating. "Career over," she thought.

Two years later, she noticed other restaurants making her exact mistakes. Started consulting: "Restaurant Rescue Services."

The Multiplication:

Failed restaurant:		-$200,000
Lessons learned:		Priceless
Consulting rate:	$5,000/month per	client
Current clients:		20

Monthly income: $100,000

Her failure was tuition. Her success is the multiplication.

Universal Pattern:

- Failed startup founder → Startup advisor
- Divorced person → Relationship coach
- Bankruptcy survivor → Financial recovery consultant
- Addiction overcomer → Recovery specialist
- Disease survivor → Health advocate

Your worst experience × lessons learned = valuable expertise

People pay premium to avoid premium pain. Your scars are their roadmap. Your mistakes are their shortcuts. Your recovery is their hope.

Stop hiding failures. Start multiplying them.

Access Multiplication

What's boringly normal to you is impossibly valuable to others.

Your normal × Others' impossible = Premium value

You have access to things others can't reach. Not because you're special. Because of where you are, who you know, or what you routinely encounter.

Real Example:

David in New York. Had Netflix, HBO, Disney+. Normal for him. Created detailed watching guides for best content. Seemed pointless—everyone has streaming, right?

Wrong. Millions globally have VPNs but no idea what to watch. Different catalogs. Language barriers. Cultural confusion.

Started blog: "What to Actually Watch" for international audiences.

The Multiplication:

Streaming subscriptions: $50/month (his cost)
Blog monetization: $8,000/month (ads + affiliates)
Multiplication: 160X return on "normal" access

Access You Take for Granted:

- English fluency → Premium tutoring for global learners
- US Amazon account → Personal shopping for restricted countries
- Local farmer's market → Exotic goods for urban dwellers
- University library → Research service for entrepreneurs
- Industry conferences → Insider reports for outsiders

What's ordinary to you × scarce elsewhere = multiplication opportunity

Your everyday access is someone's impossible dream. Stop overlooking it. Start multiplying it.

Timing Multiplication

The sun never sets on opportunity. Your breakfast is someone's bedtime. The gap? Money.

Your timezone × Their need = Premium service

Time zones aren't barriers. They're multiplication machines.

Real Example:

Lisa, East Coast developer. Noticed West Coast companies always needed "emergency" fixes at 6 PM their time—9 PM her time. Started advertising: "Overnight Development Solutions."

The Multiplication:

Regular	hourly	rate:		$100
"Overnight"	delivery	premium:		$200
Same	work,	different	timing: 2X	rates

Bonus: Done while competitors sleep

Global Timing Arbitrage:

- Australian accountant doing "same-day" US tax work
- Indian designer delivering "overnight" to Europe
- Brazilian writer providing "morning content" to Asia
- UK consultant offering "end-of-day" analysis to US

Work while they sleep × urgent delivery = premium pricing

Your 9 AM is someone's emergency hour. Your evening is someone's crucial morning. Your weekend is someone's workweek.

Time zones multiply value for those who see opportunity instead of obstacle.

Platform Multiplication

Why whisper once when you can echo everywhere?

One creation × Multiple platforms = Exponential reach

Most people create content like it's 1995. One thing, one place, one time. Builders create once and multiply everywhere.

Real Example:

Maria, nutritionist in Miami. Spent week creating comprehensive guide: "Healing Your Gut Naturally." Previously would have been single blog post. Maybe 500 readers.

Instead, she multiplied:

The Distribution:

- Blog post: 2,000 readers
- YouTube video: 15,000 views
- Podcast episode: 8,000 downloads
- Instagram carousel: 25,000 reaches

- LinkedIn article: 5,000 professionals
- Email course: 3,000 subscribers
- Paid guide: 500 customers × $47

Total reach: 58,500 people. **Revenue:** $23,500. From one week's creation.

Platform Multiplication Stack:

1. Core content (the meat)
2. Video version (visual learners)
3. Audio version (commute learners)
4. Social snippets (micro-learners)
5. Email sequence (deep learners)
6. Paid product (serious learners)

Create once × Distribute everywhere = Maximum leverage
Same effort. 50X results. Pure multiplication.

The Hidden Multiplication Menu:

- Your Location × High-cost markets = Geographic arbitrage
- Your Failures × Lessons learned = Experience arbitrage
- Your Access × Others' restrictions = Access arbitrage
- Your Timezone × Their urgency = Timing arbitrage
- Your Content × All platforms = Platform arbitrage

Multiplication opportunities hide in plain sight.

In the gap between your costs and their budgets.
In the space between your failures and their fears.
In the bridge between your access and their absence.
In the hours between your morning and their night.
In the reach between one platform and all platforms.

You walk past them daily.

Dismissing geographic differences as inconvenience instead of income. Hiding failures as shame instead of sharing them as wisdom. Taking access for granted instead of taking it to market. Cursing time zones instead of cashing in on them. Creating for one platform instead of conquering them all.

The Silk Road traders saw deserts where others saw death. Modern builders see multiplication where others see mundane.

Your mundane is someone's miracle. Your normal is someone's necessity. Your everyday is someone's extraordinary.

Stop walking past multiplication. Start working it.

The opportunities aren't hiding. You just haven't trained your eyes to see them.

Train them. Today. Look around with multiplication vision.

What	gaps	can	you	bridge?
What	differences	can	you	leverage?
What	access	can	you	share?
What	timing	can	you	exploit?

What creation can you multiply?

The hidden opportunities are hiding in plain sight.

Time to expose them.

Your Chapter 6 Challenge (The Intersection Map)

The Intersection Mapping Process

Time to discover your hidden multiplication opportunities. This exercise has created more breakthroughs than any other. Fortunes hide at intersections. Yours are about to be revealed.

Grab paper. Draw three overlapping circles. Your future lives where they meet.

Step 1: Draw Three Circles (Venn Diagram)

Make them big. Overlapping. Like the Olympic rings had a profitable baby.

Circle 1: What You Know

Brain dump everything. Skills, knowledge, expertise. The impressive and the mundane.

Professional: Excel, customer service, project management, industry specific knowledge, software you use, processes you've mastered

Personal: Cooking, organizing, parenting, gaming, fitness, languages (even broken ones), hobbies, random YouTube rabbit holes

Hidden assets: What comes "too easy" to count, what people always ask you about, what you do without thinking, skills from old jobs, knowledge from failed ventures

Don't filter. Your "obvious" is someone's impossible.

Circle 2: Who You Know

Every network is a multiplication opportunity.

Professional networks: Current colleagues, former coworkers, industry contacts, LinkedIn connections, conference contacts, clients/customers

Personal networks: Gym buddies, parent groups, hobby communities, neighbors, church/temple/mosque, school connections

Online networks: Facebook groups, Discord servers, Reddit communities, Instagram followers, WhatsApp groups, gaming clans

Weak connections count: That person you met once at a party, your dentist's receptionist, your kid's teacher, the barista who knows your order

Networks multiply value. Include everyone.

Circle 3: Problems You've Solved

Your struggles are someone's salvation.

Personal challenges: Weight loss, debt escape, divorce recovery, illness management, addiction overcome, anxiety conquered, move to new city

Work problems: Inefficient process fixed, difficult boss managed, career transition navigated, skill gap closed, team conflict resolved

Life situations: Elderly parent care, special needs child support, long-distance relationship success, immigration process, scholarship applications

Every solution you've found, someone desperately needs.

Step 2: Find the Intersections

This is where magic lives. Where circles overlap, fortunes hide.

Two-Circle Overlaps (10X Opportunities):

- **Know + Know:** Excel skills + Parent network = Budget training for families
- **Know + Solved:** Marketing knowledge + Weight loss = Fitness marketing consultant
- **Network + Solved:** Gamer friends + Overcame anxiety = Mental health gaming community

Three-Circle Overlap (100X Opportunity):

This is your goldmine. Where all three meet, category-defining businesses are born.

Example: Know project management + Know exhausted parents + Solved household chaos = Household CEO training program

Look for non-obvious connections. The weirder, the better. Weird means untapped.

Step 3: The Multiplication Question

For each intersection, ask: **"Who would pay for this combination?"**

Be specific. Not "businesses" but "Dental offices in suburbs." Not "parents" but "Dual-income parents with special needs kids." Not "people who need help" but "Female executives managing aging parents."

The more specific your who, the more valuable your what.

Test each intersection:

- Who desperately needs this?
- What would they pay to solve it?
- How many of them exist?
- Can I reach them?

One intersection with clear answers beats ten fuzzy maybes.

Step 4: Share Your Map

Knowledge shared multiplies. Hiding your map helps nobody.

Post with #MyIntersections:

"Just mapped my multiplication opportunities. Mind = blown 🤯

Found: Excel skills + Teacher network + Solved classroom chaos = Automated grading systems for overworked teachers

Never saw this intersection until I mapped it. What intersections am I still missing?"

Include:

- Photo of your actual map (messy is fine)
- One surprising intersection you discovered
- The multiplication opportunity it represents
- Question asking what else others see

Vulnerability creates value. Your shares inspire others to map.

Step 5: Help Others See

Your fresh eyes see their hidden gold.

When you see others' maps:

- Comment with intersections they missed
- Share how their combinations could multiply
- Connect dots they can't see
- Tag people who need their intersection

Example comments:

"Your nursing + gaming + parent stress could be gaming therapy for special needs families!"

"Wait, you know corporate executives AND organize closets AND solved work-life balance? That's a premium executive home organization service!"

"Your accounting + DJ skills + helped friends budget for weddings = Financial planning for creative professionals!"

Your comment could unlock someone's fortune. Their breakthrough could inspire yours.

Real-Life Intersection Victories:

Sarah's Map:

Knows: Excel, basic teaching
Network: Teacher friends, online educator groups
Solved: Lesson planning chaos eating weekends
Intersection: Excel templates specifically for elementary teachers
Result: Started with one free template. Teachers begged for more. Now sells template packs. $5K/month from intersection she never noticed.

Marcus's Map:

Knows: Car maintenance, YouTube editing
Network: Car enthusiasts, young drivers
Solved: Expensive repair bills through DIY
Intersection: YouTube channel teaching car maintenance to broke college students
Result: 100K subscribers. $8K/month ads and affiliates. Mechanic shops pay him to refer complex jobs.

Jennifer's Map:

Knows: Organization, social media
Network: ADHD support groups, overwhelmed professionals
Solved: ADHD chaos through systems
Intersection: ADHD-friendly organization systems shared on Instagram
Result: Course launch sold out. $50K in first month. Intersection she thought was "too niche."

Your map contains at least three income streams you've never noticed.

They're hiding where your "normal" meets others' "need it now." Where your "easy" meets their "impossible." Where your "obvious" meets their "revolutionary."

What you know × Who you know × Problems you've solved = Hidden fortune

But only if you map it. Only if you share it. Only if you let others help you see it.

Right now, do this:

1. Draw three circles
2. Fill them honestly (include the "stupid" stuff)
3. Find five intersections minimum
4. Share your map: #MyIntersections
5. Help someone else see their gold

The Multiplier Effect:

You map and find three opportunities. You share and inspire ten others to map. They find thirty opportunities collectively. Everyone helps everyone see more. Hundreds of hidden fortunes revealed.

Your intersection map isn't just personal discovery. It's community multiplication.

Stop wondering where opportunity hides. Start mapping where it lives.

Your three circles are waiting. Your intersections are calling. Your multiplied future is hidden in plain sight.

Draw the map. Share the discovery. Find the fortune.

The builders are waiting to see your intersections. Don't make us wait long.

Your hidden multiplication opportunities expire every day you don't see them.

Map them. Today. Now. Before another intersection passes unnoticed.

#MyIntersections awaits your breakthrough.

What will you discover?

The Multiplication Revolution

The Single vs Multiple Paradigm

You've been taught to specialize. Get better at one thing. Go deeper. Be the expert. Master your craft. Stay in your lane.

That's addition thinking in a multiplication world.

It's buying better silk when you should be building trade routes. It's perfecting your horse carriage while others connect engines to wheels. It's organizing deck chairs on the Titanic of single-skill careers.

The advice made sense when careers lasted forty years. When industries moved slowly. When local was enough. When depth beat breadth.

That world died. You're living in its ruins, following its ghost rules.

The New Wealth Equation

Look at every fortune created in the last twenty years. None came from being best at one thing. All came from connecting multiple things.

Wealth isn't in the depth of one skill but the connection between multiple elements:

Google: **Search** + **Advertising**
Not the best search engine. Not the best ad platform. But the intersection? Worth a trillion.

Uber: GPS   +   Spare   time   +   Cars
Didn't invent GPS. Didn't create cars. Didn't discover spare time. Connected them. Revolutionized transport.

Airbnb: Empty space + Travel need + Trust system
No hotels. No construction. No staff. Just connected existing elements. Hospitality reimagined.

Amazon: Books   +   Internet   +   Logistics
Started with simple intersection. Kept adding connections. Now intersects everything.

All billion-dollar intersections. All obvious in hindsight. All available to someone else first.

But they were busy going deeper into single skills. Perfecting one thing. Missing the multiplication.

Your Intersection Inventory

Stop. Look at your life right now. Not with addition eyes. With multiplication vision.

Skills collecting dust separately:

- Excel expertise sitting alone
- Writing ability in isolation
- Organization skills unused
- Teaching gift unmonetized

Each powerful. Together, exponential.

Networks never introduced:

- Work contacts who don't know your gym friends
- Hobby group unaware of professional network
- Online community separate from local circles
- Family connections untapped for business

Living in silos when they could be synergizing.

Problems solved in isolation:

- Helped yourself get fit (personal win)
- Fixed process at work (local impact)

- Organized your finances (private victory)
- Navigated life challenge (solo triumph)

Each solution worth sharing. Together, worth fortune.

Time used for single purposes:

- Commute = just traveling
- Exercise = just fitness
- Cooking = just food
- Walking = just movement

Single-use time in a multiplication economy.
These aren't separate assets. They're multiplication opportunities.

- Your Excel + Teaching + Parent network = Course empire
- Your fitness journey + Writing + Work stress = Corporate wellness program
- Your organization + Technology + Busy professionals = Productivity consulting
- Your commute + Learning + Content creation = Mobile university

Stop seeing ingredients. Start seeing combinations. Stop counting assets. Start multiplying value.

The Identity Shift

Close your addition eyes. Open your multiplication mind.

You're no longer a single-skill person.

Not just an accountant. An accountant who connects numbers to stories. Not just a teacher. A teacher who bridges knowledge to need. Not just a parent. A parent who multiplies solutions to problems. Not just an employee. An employee who sees intersections everywhere.

You're an intersection creator. A multiplier. A connector of unconnected value.

The world has enough specialists going deeper into smaller holes. It needs multipliers connecting across chasms. Builders bridging islands of value.

That's you now. Not because you learned something new. Because you learned to connect what you already knew.

The Movement Moment

Open your phone. Check #MyIntersections.

Watch minds explode in real-time:

"Never realized nursing + gaming could = therapeutic gaming for patients 🎮"

"My accounting + DJ background = financial planning for creatives. WHAT."

"Teaching + Fitness + Anxiety = Movement therapy for stressed teachers. Starting tomorrow!"

See people finding fortunes in their overlaps. Discovering gold in their intersections. Building bridges they never knew existed.

Your map will inspire ten others to map. Their maps inspire hundreds. The multiplication multiplies.

You now see how value multiplies at intersections.

The Silk Road secret is yours. The multiplication method is clear. The intersections are mapped. The opportunities are obvious.

But here's what kills most multipliers: They see the intersection but never build the bridge. They map the opportunity but never create momentum. They understand multiplication but die in contemplation.

Chapter 7 reveals the Fourth Law—how to turn your intersections into unstoppable momentum.

The Law of Momentum: why small actions compound into transformation. How daily tiny bridges become superhighways. Why most fail at day 60 and how to breakthrough at day 90.

You'll discover:

- The momentum timeline that predicts success
- Why the Valley exists and how to survive it
- The compound effect that turns drops into oceans
- Real stories of intersection creators who pushed through

But none of that matters if you don't activate an intersection first.

Tonight   you   have   skills. Sitting separately. Adding slowly. Aging quickly.

Tomorrow   you   have   intersections. Mapped and visible. Ready for connection. Waiting for activation.

Next month you have multiplication. If you build the bridges. If you create the connections. If you activate the intersections.

The only question: Which intersection will you activate first?

Not eventually. Tomorrow. Which connection will you make? Which bridge will you build? Which multiplication will you manifest?

Your map shows ten possibilities. Your fear says try none. Your future says try one.

Just one. The smallest. The easiest. The most obvious.

Because activated intersections attract more intersections. Built bridges enable bigger bridges. Small multiplications compound into transformations.

The Silk Road started with one merchant connecting one load of silk to one distant buyer through one safe route. The multiplication built empires.

Your empire starts with one intersection. Activated tomorrow. Built into bridge. Multiplied into fortune.

Which one will it be?

The builders are watching. The intersections are waiting. The multiplication is inevitable.

For those who act.

Your skills remain addition until connected. Your value stays linear until multiplied. Your future stays single until intersected.

Connect something. Multiply anything. Start tomorrow.

The revolution isn't in having more. It's in connecting what you have.

Welcome to the multiplication revolution.

Which intersection launches it for you?

Chapter 7: _The Law of Momentum._

"Small Actions Compound Into Transformation"

"Everyone wants the breakthrough. Nobody wants the thousand invisible actions that create it. But that's exactly how breakthroughs work—worldwide."

The Great Wall Principle

Stand at the base of the Great Wall of China. Look up. 13,000 miles of impossibility made real. Winding over mountains. Spanning deserts. Visible from space. A monument to human determination that makes you feel small.

Now bend down. Pick up a single brick.

This brick? Insignificant. Laughable. Who cares about one brick? What difference could it possibly make? Throw it in the valley—wall remains. Add it to the wall—still invisible progress.

Yet 3.8 billion bricks later: a wonder of the world.

Each brick seemed pointless. Each worker's daily contribution felt meaningless. "What's my dozen bricks against infinity?" Years passed laying stones into void. No visible progress. No glory. No recognition.

But compound math doesn't care about feelings. It only cares about consistency.

Brick one: Nothing.
Brick thousand: Still nothing visible.
Brick million: Wait, is that a wall?
Brick billion: History made visible.
    Your transformation works the same way.

Today's Brick: That 15-minute learning session that feels pointless

You watch the Python tutorial. Struggle with basic syntax. Feel stupid. Close laptop discouraged. "What's the point? I'll never be a programmer."

That's brick one. Invisible. Insignificant. Essential.

Tomorrow's Wall: The expertise everyone sees and envies

Five years later, you're the technical co-founder of a startup. People say you're "naturally gifted with code." They never saw the thousand invisible tutorials. The daily syntax struggles. The debugging at midnight. The bricks laid in darkness.

They see your wall. They never counted your bricks.

The Masters Prove the Principle

Warren Buffett's Invisible Library

500 pages. Every. Single. Day. For 60 years. That's 10,950,000 pages. Nearly 11 million bricks of knowledge.

Young Buffett reading annual reports? Pointless. Middle-aged Buffett reading trade journals? Obsessive. Elderly Buffett still reading? "That's why he's the Oracle."

Nobody counts the pages. Everyone counts the billions.

Jerry Seinfeld's Chain of X's

One joke. Every. Single. Day. Calendar on the wall. Write joke, mark X. Don't break the chain.

Day 1: Terrible joke nobody would laugh at.
Day 100: Slightly better terrible jokes.
Day 1,000: Professional comedian.
Day 10,000: Comedy legend.
  "How did you become Seinfeld?"

"I didn't. I just didn't break the chain. The chain became Seinfeld."

Steph Curry's Invisible Gym

500 made shots. Every. Single. Practice. Before teammates arrive. After they leave.

Shot 1: Routine, boring, forgettable.
Shot 100: Still warming up.
Shot 500: Muscle memory building.
Shot 500,000: "Greatest shooter in history."
  Reporters see the impossible shots in games. They never see the invisible shots at dawn. The bricks laid in empty gyms. The wall built in solitude.

The Compound Timeline Nobody Mentions

Days 1-10: The Excitement Bricks

"This is it! I'm changing my life!" Energy high. Motivation fresh. Every brick feels meaningful.

Days 11-50: The Doubt Bricks

"Is this working? I don't see changes." Energy dropping. Results invisible. Bricks feel pointless.

Days 51-89: The Darkness Bricks

"This is stupid. I'm wasting time." No visible progress. Want to quit daily. Every brick is agony.

Day 90: The First Glimpse

"Wait... is that... progress?" Squint and you might see it. The faintest outline of a wall. Others can't see it yet. But you know.

Days 91-365: The Momentum Bricks

Each brick adds to visible structure. Progress compounds. Others start noticing. "Have you been working out?" "Did you get promoted?" "You seem different."

Year 2+: The Wall Rises

Now everyone sees it. Wishes they had one. Asks your secret. You tell them: "Daily bricks." They want the wall without the bricks. Doesn't work that way.

Breakthroughs are just momentum finally becoming visible.
The novelist's overnight success? Ten years of daily pages. The startup's explosive growth? Thousand days of invisible building. The fitness transformation? 500 workouts nobody saw. The career breakthrough? Evening skill-building while others Netflix'd.

All walls. All built brick by brick. All invisible until suddenly undeniable.

The Brick-Layer's Secret

197

Great Wall workers had a saying: "不怕慢，只怕站" (Don't fear going slow, fear standing still).

One brick daily for a year: 365 progress points.
Zero bricks but perfect planning: 0 progress points.
Small actions beat grand intentions. Always.

Your Daily Bricks Are Waiting

That 15-minute morning routine you're considering? Brick. That evening skill practice you're debating? Brick. That weekend project you're postponing? Brick. That daily writing you're avoiding? Brick.

Each feels pointless in isolation. "What's 15 minutes against a lifetime?" But lifetimes are built in 15-minute increments. Walls are built one brick at a time. Transformations happen invisibly, then suddenly.

The Modern Wall-Builders

She wakes at 5 AM to write. Page by invisible page. Now published author.

He practices design after kids sleep. Project by invisible project. Now creative director.

They study investing during lunch. Lesson by invisible lesson. Now financially free.

You do... what? Daily. Invisibly. Until your wall becomes undeniable.

Everyone sees the wall. Nobody counts the bricks.

They see the entrepreneur's success. Not the thousand failed pitches. They see the athlete's medals. Not the predawn training. They see the artist's gallery. Not the daily practice. They see the transformation. Not the accumulation.

But the bricks are everything.
Without them, you're just another person wishing for walls. Another dreamer sketching blueprints. Another talker explaining future empires.

With them, you're inevitable. Mathematical. Unstoppable.

Not because you're special. Because momentum doesn't care about special. It only cares about consistent. Because compound effects don't require talent. They require time. Because walls don't ask your IQ. They count your bricks.

Tomorrow you'll lay a brick. It will feel pointless. Insignificant. Invisible.

Lay it anyway.

That's how Great Walls are built. That's how great lives are constructed. That's how greatness becomes inevitable.

One brick. One day. One compound effect at a time.

The breakthrough everyone wants is just momentum becoming visible. The thousand invisible actions nobody wants are just bricks becoming walls.

Which brick will you lay today?

The wall is waiting. The compound effect is mathematical. The momentum is available.

But only for brick-layers. Only for the daily builders. Only for those who understand:

Everyone sees the wall. Nobody counts the bricks.

But the bricks are everything.

Start counting.

Why Most Fail (The Universal Pattern)

The graveyard of abandoned dreams has visiting hours. Walk through. Read the headstones. Every single one has the same epitaph: "Quit Too Soon."

The Quitting Timeline (Death by Impatience)

Watch the massacre unfold. Same pattern. Every continent. Every pursuit. Every dreamer becoming a statistic.

Day 30: Sarah Stops Her Design Practice

"Not improving fast enough. Still making amateur mistakes. This is pointless."

Closes laptop. Cancels Adobe subscription. Returns to scrolling job boards. Tells friends "It wasn't meant to be."

Day 45: Marcus Abandons His Writing

"Nobody's reading anyway. Forty-five days, twelve articles, 97 total views. My mom accounts for 30 of those."

Deletes drafts. Lets domain expire. Goes back to consuming instead of creating. "At least I tried."

Day 60: Jennifer Quits Learning Code

"Still can't build anything real. Two months and all I have are broken tutorials and error messages."

Closes VS Code for last time. Sells barely-used MacBook. Returns to Excel sheets. "Coding isn't for people like me."

Day 75: David Gives Up on Investing

"No returns yet. Actually down 3%. YouTubers promised quick gains. This is just gambling with extra steps."

Withdraws remaining funds. Closes brokerage account. Back to savings account earning 0.01%. "At least it's safe."

Day 89: Lisa Stops Her Business

"Almost three months. Zero traction. Three inquiries, no sales. Everyone says 90 days to success—lies."

Takes down website. Dissolves LLC. Returns to job applications. "Entrepreneurship is for trust fund kids."

Each quit. Each returned to safety. Each chose familiar suffering over unfamiliar struggle.

Now let's pull back the cosmic curtain and see what they couldn't:

The Tragedy They'll Never Know

Sarah: First client inquiry would have arrived day 92. Local boutique needing rebrand. Would've led to five referrals. Year later: full design studio.

Marcus: His article about overcoming failure—written from pain on day 60—would've gone viral on day 62. Publisher would've reached out day 71. Book deal by day 180.

Jennifer: Day 90 was her breakthrough day. Suddenly code would click. Day 105: first working app. Day 200: recruited by startup. Day 365: senior developer.

David: Market correction on day 91 would've turned his positions green. Compound effect would've kicked in. His diversified portfolio set for 15% annual returns. Retirement secured.

Lisa: Day 94. That's it. Day 94 her SEO would've kicked in. First organic customer. Then word-of-mouth. Then momentum. Then empire. Missed by five days.

The Tragedy Pattern

They were passengers who got off the plane during taxi, missing the takeoff by minutes.

They were miners who stopped digging three feet from gold, selling their claims for nothing to someone who struck rich with one more swing.

They were marathon runners who quit at mile 25, never knowing the finish line was around the next corner.

They were farmers who abandoned fields in August, missing September's harvest.

They were sculptors who threw away the stone one chisel strike before revealing the masterpiece.

They were tea kettles removed from heat at 211 degrees, never knowing one more degree meant transformation.

The Statistical Slaughter

The numbers are brutal in their clarity:

90% quit in first 30 days

The excitement wears off. Reality sets in. First obstacle appears. Mass exodus. Dreams die in infancy.

9% quit in days 31-90

The warriors. They survived the first wave. But the messy middle claims them. Progress too slow. Doubts too loud. The sophisticated quitters.

1% push through to day 100

The unreasonable ones. The ones who trust the process over the progress. The brick-layers who count bricks, not walls.

That 1% gets 99% of the results.

Not because they're special. Because they're still there when momentum becomes visible. Because they're still laying bricks when walls become undeniable. Because they're still rowing when the current finally turns.

The Universe's Cruel Test

Here's what nobody tells you: The universe tests your commitment by making progress invisible until right before breakthrough.

Like it's checking: "Do you really want this? Or are you just another tourist?"

Days 1-89: "Let's see if you're serious."
Day 90+: "Okay, you passed. Here's everything."

It's not fair. It's not linear. It's not logical.

It's just true.

The Valley of Despair Geography

Every journey has the same topography:

- **Start:** Hope Mountain (Everyone's excited)
- **Days 10-30:** Reality Foothills (Harder than expected)
- **Days 31-89:** Valley of Despair (The killing fields)
- **Day 90+:** Momentum Mesa (Survivors celebrate)

The valley floor is littered with skeletons. Each one a dreamer who mistook the valley for the destination. Each one quit in the darkness before dawn.

The Morning They Never Saw

Sarah's teaching design thinking to Fortune 500s now. But not our Sarah. A different Sarah who didn't quit on day 30.

Marcus is a bestselling author. But not our Marcus. The Marcus who pushed through day 45.

Jennifer leads engineering at a unicorn. But not our Jennifer. The Jennifer who survived day 60.

David retired at 45. But not our David. The David who trusted the process past day 75.

Lisa's company just got acquired. But not our Lisa. The Lisa who lasted past day 89.

The cemetery of dreams is full of people who quit on day 89 of a 90-day journey.
Their headstones all read the same:

"Here lies potential. Murdered by impatience."

"Almost made it. Almost doesn't count."

"Quit at dawn. Never saw sunrise."

"Was three feet from gold. Settled for dirt."
Don't add your name to this graveyard. Don't become another statistic in the 99% who quit before compound effects kick in.

Your day 89 is coming. It will feel like failure. It will look like wasted time. It will seem like proof you should quit.

That's the test. That's the universe asking: "Tourist or builder?"

The breakthrough you want is scheduled. It has a date. It's probably around day 100. But it only keeps appointments with those who show up.

Will you?

Or will you join Sarah, Marcus, Jennifer, David, and Lisa in the graveyard of what could have been?

The compound effect doesn't care about your feelings. It only counts your days. Make sure you're still counting when it's ready to reward.

The cemetery has room for one more quitter. Or the world has room for one more winner.

Day 89 decides which you become.

Choose wisely. Choose daily. Choose to continue.

The dead don't get second chances. But you're still breathing. Still building. Still possible.

Don't stop now. Not when you're this close. Not when the universe is about to reward your unreasonable persistence.

Not when you're three feet from gold.

The Compound Timeline (Same Everywhere)

Every builder faces the same journey. Silicon Valley or rural village. Creative pursuits or corporate climbing. Health transformation or wealth creation. The curve never changes. Only your position on it.

Days 1-30: The Invisible Foundation

What's happening: Your brain is literally rewiring. New neural pathways forming like ant trails in virgin forest. Habits taking root in subconscious soil. Skills accumulating in invisible storage. Foundation being poured for future skyscraper.

What you feel: Excited but embarrassed. Energy but no evidence. "I'm doing the thing!" but nothing to show. Like being pregnant on day 20—you know something's happening, but nobody can see it.

What others see: Nothing. Worse than nothing—delusion. "There goes Michelle, waking at 5 AM to write. To write what? For whom?" Eye rolls. Concerned whispers. "Phase she's going through."

Michelle's Reality Check:

Day 1: Wrote 200 terrible words. Felt like a writer. Day 7: Wrote 500 mediocre words. Momentum building. Day 14: Missed morning. Guilt. Back at it. Day 21: Husband asks "How long is this experiment?" Day 30: 10,000 words written. Zero readers. Zero evidence this matters.

The Truth: You're building roots. Roots grow down before trees grow up.

Every master started here. In the dark. Underground. Invisible. Your foundation is setting like concrete—unseeable but essential. The skyscraper everyone will admire requires this basement work nobody witnesses.

Neural pathway formation takes 21-30 days. You're literally building brain architecture. Of course it's invisible. Of course it feels pointless. Construction sites look like destruction before they look like creation.

Days 31-90: THE VALLEY OF DESPAIR

What's happening: Skills solidifying but not yet useful. Like knowing alphabet but not words. Like having ingredients but not recipes. Competence building but not confidence. The messy middle where most dreams die.

What you feel: "This isn't working" becomes your morning mantra. "Why am I doing this?" your evening prayer. Every day a fresh argument with yourself about continuing. Motivation dead. Discipline tested. Faith evaporating.

What others see: "I told you so" in their eyes if not their words. Vindication for their own quit dreams. Relief that you're not making them look bad. "When are you going to focus on real things?"

Michelle's Valley Journey:

Day 35: Shared article. Six views (checked 47 times). Day 42: "Maybe I'm not a writer" journal entry. Day 50: Skipped three days. Nearly quit entirely. Day 63: Crying at keyboard. Words feel pointless. Day 71: Friend says "Still doing that writing thing?" Day 85: Googled "How to know when to quit"

The Psychology: Your brain is screaming for dopamine hits. Getting none. Used to instant feedback—likes, hearts, validation. Now getting silence. Dopamine-deprived brain creates suffering. "Make it stop!" it begs. "Go back to scrolling! At least that felt good!"

Valley Survivors Say:

"The Valley isn't your enemy. It's your filter. It's asking 'Tourist or resident?' Most are tourists."

"Day 73 wanted to die. Day 94 changed my life. Twenty-one days between death and birth."

"The Valley is where you discover if you're doing it for love or applause. Applause comes later. Love gets you through."

Key Insight: The Valley is where hobbies become habits and habits become careers. Where dabblers become practitioners. Where interest becomes identity. But only for those who traverse it.

The Valley kills 90% of dreams. Not because it's hard. Because it's boring. Because progress is invisible. Because dopamine is absent. Because easier paths call constantly.

Days 91-120: First Green Shoots

What's happening: Compound effect becoming visible. Skills reaching usable threshold. Networks noticing consistency. Algorithms rewarding persistence. The underground work breaking surface.

What you feel: "Wait, something's happening." Disbelief mixed with hope. Afraid to jinx it. Small wins feeling huge. Energy returning. Faith rebuilding. "Maybe I wasn't crazy."

What others see: "Lucky break." "Right place, right time." "Must be nice." Missing the 90 days of foundation. Seeing flower, not roots.

Michelle's Breakthrough:

Day 92: Article shared by influencer. 5,000 views overnight. Day 94: First email: "Your writing helped me." Day 98: First paid gig offered. $50. Felt like $5,000. Day 102: Three guest post invitations. Day 108: Husband: "Maybe this writing thing has potential." Day 115: Can't keep up with opportunities.
The Revelation: It was never about luck. It was about lasting.

The influencer shared because 90 days of consistency caught her eye. The paid gig came because portfolio existed. The opportunities multiplied because foundation was solid. Lucky break? No. Compound effect becoming visible.

Green shoots look like sudden growth. But the growth happened underground for 90 days. Now it's just showing. Now others can see what you've been building in darkness.

Days 121-365: The Exponential Explosion

What's happening: Momentum becomes unstoppable. Skills sharp enough to create real value. Network activated by consistent presence. Reputation building on itself. Success breeding success. Compound effect in full force.

What you feel: "I can't imagine NOT doing this." Identity shifted. From "trying to write" to "I'm a writer." From "learning to code" to "I'm a developer." From "getting healthy" to "I'm an athlete." Not discipline anymore—identity.

What others see: "Overnight success." "Natural talent." "So inspiring!" Memory of your Valley erased. Your struggle invisible. Your 5 AMs forgotten. Only seeing current success.

Michelle's New Reality:

Day 150: Quit job to write full-time. Day 200: First five-figure month. Day 250: Book deal discussion. Day 300: Speaking at conferences. Day 365: Teaching others the path.
The New Problem: Too many opportunities, not enough time. From starvation to feast. From "please someone notice" to "I need boundaries." From chasing to choosing.

The Reality: 120+ days of invisible work created this visible success.

Every "overnight success" has a hidden morning routine. Every "natural talent" has a Valley story. Every "lucky break" has compound math behind it.

Michelle's conference keynote? Built on 5 AM sentences nobody read. Book deal? Constructed from Valley tears. Success? Just momentum made visible.

Same curve. Same timeline. Same pattern.

From	Mumbai	to	Memphis:	Days	1-30	invisible
From	corporate	to	creative:	Days	31-90	Valley
From	health	to	wealth:	Days	91-120	breakthrough

From nobody to somebody: Days 121+ explosion

The only variable? Who quits and who continues.

Sarah	quit	day	30.	Never	saw	shoots.
Marcus	quit	day	45.	Missed	his	moment.
Jennifer	quit	day	60.	Abandoned	her	ascent.

Lisa quit day 89. Five days from fortune.

Michelle continued. Now teaching thousands.

You're reading this on day what?

The timeline is predictable. The pattern is proven. The compound effect is mathematical. The only uncertainty is you.

Will you be explaining your success on day 365? Or explaining why you quit on day 60?

The curve doesn't care. It rewards those who complete it. Punishes those who abandon it. Transforms those who trust it.

Where are you on the curve today? More importantly, where will you be tomorrow?

The compound timeline is waiting. Your day count is ticking. Your transformation is scheduled.

But only if you show up for it.

Day after day after day after day.

Until invisible becomes inevitable.

Valley Survivor Stories from Every Continent

The Valley has a 90% kill rate. These are the 10% who survived. Not because they were special. Because they were still there on day 91.

The Programmer's Persistence

Jake from Austin. Marketing degree. Decent agency job. Watched his cousin make $150K coding. Decided to learn. How hard could it be?

Days 1-30: The Honeymoon Code

YouTube University enrollment. FreeCodeCamp every evening. Built a calculator. Built a to-do list. Built confidence. "I'll be job-ready in three months!" Posted #100DaysOfCode tweets. The future looked binary—and bright.

Day 45: Reality.exe Has Crashed

"I can't even center a fucking div."

That's the text Jake sent his cousin. Three tutorials on CSS Grid. Four on Flexbox. Still can't make things line up. Wife peering over his shoulder: "How long will this take exactly? Wasn't it supposed to be three months?"

Day 67: The Reddit Confession

Posted to r/learnprogramming at 2 AM:

"67 days in. Feel stupider than when I started. Tutorial hell is real. Everything I build looks like garbage. Works like garbage. Is garbage. I want to quit. Someone tell me it gets better."

50 replies. 49 saying "me too." 1 saying "push through."

Day 75: The Almost Deletion

Cursor hovering over project folder. Select all. Delete. So close. So tired. So done with error messages. Done with imposter syndrome. Done with dreams that mock reality.

Wife found him at kitchen table, laptop closed, staring at nothing.

"I'm not cut out for this."

Day 89: The Breaking Point

One last project. Rock-paper-scissors game. Followed tutorial exactly. Still broken. Syntax error. Another syntax error. Undefined is not a function.

Tears. Actual tears. Grown man crying over semicolons.

"I'm done. I'm fucking done. Three months of my life wasted."

Day 94: The Shift

Fixed the semicolon. Game worked. Felt... different. Tried adding features without tutorial. They worked. Built another small app. It worked. Something had clicked while he wasn't looking.

Posted working app to Reddit. Someone commented: "Hey, could you make something similar for my small business?"

First client. $500. Might as well have been $5 million.

Day 180: New Reality

Full-stack developer at Austin startup. The same concepts that broke his brain now feel obvious. Mentoring others through their div-centering disasters. Valley survivor turned Valley guide.

Today: The Valley Prophet

Senior developer. Runs "Valley Survivors" Discord. 10,000 members. Daily encouragement for those on day 67, 75, 89. His pinned message:

"The Valley is where tutorials become skills. Where copying becomes creating. Where confusion becomes clarity. I almost quit three feet from gold. Your gold is scheduled for day 91+. Don't you dare delete those files."

Every month, someone messages: "Day 91. It clicked. Thank you for keeping me alive."

The Content Creator's Crucible

Amanda from Phoenix. CMO laid off at 44. "Too senior" for most roles. "Too expensive" for others. Started posting marketing insights on LinkedIn. Had knowledge. Had time. Had no idea what was coming.

Days 1-30: Publishing to the Void

209

Daily posts. Marketing strategies. Leadership insights. Twenty years of experience distilled into 1,300-character wisdom. Average views: 12. Mom accounted for 3.

"Building my personal brand," she told unemployed friends. They nodded politely.

Day 60: The Statistics of Sadness

60 posts. 420 total views. 7 views per post. 3 comments total. 2 from recruiters selling services. 1 from ex-colleague saying "keep going!"

Posted about innovative marketing campaign she'd run. 4 views. Her cat videos on Facebook got 400.

Day 88: The Existential Post

Wrote from the heart:

"Why am I doing this? 88 days of shouting into the void. Sharing 20 years of experience with no one. Maybe I'm just another unemployed executive pretending to be a thought leader. Maybe it's time to accept reality and take that call center job."

12 views. 0 comments. The void confirmed her fears.

Day 89: The Almost Deletion

LinkedIn profile open. Cursor on "Delete All Activity." Two decades of expertise reduced to ignored posts. The call center paid $18/hour. Benefits. Stability. Defeat.

Finger on mouse. Click away from erasure.

Phone rang. Call center HR. "Can you start Monday?"

"Let me call you back."

Day 91: The Tiny Spark

Posted about brand authenticity. Used call center temptation as example. How brands lose soul chasing short-term survival. How professionals do too.

50 views. Not viral. Not breakthrough. But 5X normal. Three meaningful comments. One DM: "This resonated. Can we talk?"

Day 105: The First Client

That DM became coffee. Coffee became contract. $5,000/month marketing consultation. Ex-CMO had her first client. Posted about it. 200 views. More DMs.

Day 365: The New Chapter

Six-figure consulting practice. Speaking at conferences she used to attend. Clients include former competitors. LinkedIn following: 45,000. Average post views: 5,000.

Call center? They filled her position. She built her future.

"The Valley taught me consistency beats talent. Algorithms reward persistence, not perfection. My worst Valley days—when nobody watched—built my best future days. Day 88 me would be shocked. Day 1,000 me is grateful she didn't click delete."

The Artist's Ascent

Yuki from Tokyo. Banker by day. Artist by soul. Started posting one sketch daily on Instagram.

90 days: Total likes: 847. Followers: 73. Comments: mostly friends being polite.

Day 93: Stranger from Germany DM'd. "Do you take commissions?" First paid art. €50. Cried at her desk. Boss thought it was work stress.

Day 95: Second commission. From Australia. Word spreading through art hashtags.

Year 2: Quit banking. Gallery showings in three countries. Teaching workshops. Living as artist, not banker who draws.

"The Valley was my art school. Those 90 days of posting to silence taught me to create for creation, not validation. Validation came anyway. After the Valley. Always after the Valley."

Every success story has a Valley.

Between "started" and "succeeded" lies 60 days of darkness. Between amateur and professional lies 90 days of doubt. Between dream and reality lies the Valley that kills most dreams.

Jake survived his code Valley. Amanda survived her content Valley. Yuki survived her art Valley.

They're not special. They're just Valley survivors. The 10% who discovered that day 91 exists. That compound effects are scheduled. That breakthroughs have addresses—always past the Valley.

The only question: Will you survive yours?

You're reading this from somewhere on the timeline. Day 1 full of hope? Day 45 questioning everything? Day 75 cursor hovering over delete?

Read these stories again. Screenshot them. Save them for your Valley days. Because your Valley is coming. Or you're in it. Or you just survived it.

But wherever you are, remember: Every master was once a disaster in the Valley. Every expert was once crying over basics. Every success story has 60 days of "this isn't working."

The only difference between Jake's deleted folders and his senior developer role? He didn't delete them.

The only difference between Amanda's call center application and her consulting empire? She posted on day 90.

The only difference between Yuki's private sketches and her gallery showings? She kept posting through silence.

Your Valley is not your grave. It's your graduation requirement.

Will you graduate? Or will you add your name to the 90% who quit before the compound curve turned upward?

Day 91 is coming. Make sure you're there to meet it.

The Psychology of Momentum

Your Valley isn't just difficult. It's neurologically engineered to make you quit. Understanding the brain science transforms the Valley from mysterious suffering to predictable psychology. From personal failure to universal pattern.

Your Brain in the Valley

Your brain runs on dopamine. Not happiness—dopamine. The anticipation chemical. The "this might be good" molecule. And the Valley is a dopamine desert by design.

Days 1-30: Dopamine from Novelty

New activity floods brain with excitement chemicals. "I'm learning to code!" Dopamine. "I'm finally writing!" Dopamine. "This is my transformation!" Dopamine waterfall.

Your brain loves novelty like addicts love fixes. Every new tutorial, new lesson, new attempt triggers reward chemicals. You're high on possibility. Drunk on potential. This is why everyone starts strong.

Days 31-90: Dopamine Withdrawal (The Valley)

Novelty wears off. Now it's just work. Brain expects dopamine hits that don't come. Same tutorials feel boring. Progress invisible. Effort unrewarded.

Your brain, like a spoiled child, throws tantrums:

"This isn't fun anymore!" *(No novelty dopamine)*
"We're not getting results!" *(No achievement dopamine)*
"Let's do something else!" (Seeking new dopamine source)
You're not weak. You're in withdrawal.

Like caffeine withdrawal. Like sugar withdrawal. But from the future-projection chemicals that made starting feel magical. Your brain is literally detoxing from hope hormones.

Days 91+: Dopamine from Progress

Suddenly, different dopamine. Not from novelty but mastery. Not from starting but improving. The first working code. The first shared article. The first pound lost that stays off.

Progress dopamine is sustainable. Novelty dopamine is cocaine—intense but fleeting. Progress dopamine is coffee—steady and renewable. But you must survive withdrawal to reach it.

Why You Want to Quit

It's not personal failure. It's predictable neurology. Every brain in the Valley screams "quit!" because every brain wants easy dopamine. Instagram. Netflix. Snacks. Anything but the hard work of building new neural pathways.

Your ancestors' brains quit picking berries when easy prey appeared. Quit hard when easy appeared. It kept them alive. It's keeping you average.

The Compound Math Nobody Sees

Progress isn't linear. It's exponential. But exponential curves look linear until they don't.

The Deceptive Curve:

Day 1: 1 unit of skill (1^1)
Excited! Making progress! This is easy!

Day 30: 30 units (looks linear)
One month, 30X improvement. Solid pace. Still motivated.

Day 60: 90 units (still feels linear)
Wait, only 3X improvement in second month? Slowing down? Valley doubts creeping in.

Day 90: 270 units (3X acceleration begins)
Multiplication starting but still invisible. Feels like grinding. Is like compounding.

Day 120: 810 units (9X from day 30)
Whoa. When did this happen? Same daily effort, exponential results. Compound effect visible.

Day 365: 133,225 units (exponential reality)
Incomprehensible from day 1. "Overnight success" to observers. Compound math to you.

The Perception Problem:

Days 1-60 feel like 1+1+1+1 (addition)
Days 61-90 feel like waste (Valley blindness)
Days 91+ reveal it was 1×1.1×1.1×1.1 (multiplication)

You were never adding. Always multiplying. But multiplication disguises itself as addition until the curve goes vertical. Most quit while curve still looks flat.

The Invisible Becomes Visible

Every skill follows the same emergence pattern:

Writing Progression:

Days 1-30: Bad (but you can't tell)
Days 31-60: Readable (but you hate it)
Days 61-90: Good (but you don't believe it)

Days 91-120: Very good (others notice)
Days 121+: Excellent → Viral → Voice of generation

Hemingway was terrible before good. King was rejected before acclaimed. Every writer sucked until they didn't. The Valley is where suck transforms to skill.

Coding Evolution:

Week 1: Syntax errors everywhere
Month 1: Working code (ugly but functional)
Month 2: Cleaner code (still amateur)
Month 3: Elegant solutions emerging
Month 6: "How did I not understand this?"
Year 1: Teaching others what broke your brain

Fitness Transformation:

Day 1: Everything hurts
Day 30: Still hurts but less
Day 60: Wait, is that muscle?
Day 90: Others asking "Have you been working out?"
Day 180: New human entirely
Day 365: Teaching transformation

Network Building:

Month 1: Nobody knows you exist
Month 2: Few recognize your name
Month 3: Many engage with your content
Month 6: Influential in your niche
Year 1: "How do I network like you?"

The progression is predictable. The timeline is consistent. The emergence is mathematical. But only visible to those who last.

The Identity Shift Timeline

This is the real transformation. Not the skill. The identity. Watch how self-perception evolves:

Days 1-30: "I'm trying to be a..."

"I'm trying to be a writer." Tentative. Apologetic. Experimenting with identity like trying on clothes. Imposter syndrome screaming. But trying.

Days 31-90: "Maybe I'm not cut out for..."

"Maybe I'm not cut out for coding." The Valley whispers lies. Evidence seems to confirm. Identity retreating. Safety beckoning. Old self calling.

Days 91-120: "I might actually be a..."

"I might actually be a developer." Surprise in voice. Disbelief at progress. Identity crystallizing. Old self fading. New self emerging.

Days 121+: "I am a..."

"I am a writer." No qualification. No apology. No explanation needed. Identity complete. Not doing writing—being writer. Not learning code—being coder. Not getting fit—being athlete.

The Neurology of Becoming

Your brain literally rewires. New default patterns. New automatic responses. New identity pathways. You're not the same person who started. Literally. Neurologically. Measurably.

Brain scans of day 1 you vs day 365 you = different humans. Same body. Rebuilt brain. This is why quitters can't imagine continuing. And continuers can't imagine quitting. Different wiring. Different beings.

Momentum isn't about the actions.

It's about who you become through the actions.

The daily writing isn't creating articles. It's creating a writer. The daily coding isn't building apps. It's building a developer. The daily workouts aren't shaping muscle. They're shaping identity. The daily practice isn't changing habits. It's changing humans.

Jake didn't become senior developer by learning JavaScript. He became senior developer by surviving the Valley where Jake-the-marketer died and Jake-the-developer was born.

Amanda didn't build a consulting practice by posting content. She built it by enduring withdrawal from external validation until internal identity emerged.

The Valley isn't punishment. It's metamorphosis.

Caterpillars don't become butterflies by adding wings. They dissolve completely. Become soup. Reorganize at cellular level. Emerge unrecognizable.

Your Valley is your cocoon. The dopamine withdrawal is dissolution. The compound math is reorganization. The identity shift is emergence.

But only if you stay in the cocoon. Only if you trust the process. Only if you understand:

You're not building skills. You're building a new you. You're not creating content. You're creating identity. You're not developing habits. You're developing into who you were meant to become.

The momentum isn't in what you do. It's in who you become by doing it. Day after day. Through novelty and withdrawal. Through invisible and exponential. Through trying and being.

Until one day you wake up and realize: You're not practicing anymore. You're living. You're not becoming. You've become.

That's momentum. That's transformation. That's what waits on the other side of your Valley.

If you survive it.

Your Chapter 7 Challenge (The 100-Day Chain)

The 100-Day Chain That Changes Everything

This is it. The challenge that separates builders from dreamers. Simple to understand. Hard to complete. Life-changing if you do.

Not another 30-day sprint you'll forget. Not a week-long experiment that changes nothing. 100 days. Through excitement. Through the Valley. Through to transformation.

The Rules

1. Pick ONE Daily Action

One. Not three. Not "whatever I feel like." ONE.

Requirements:

- 15 minutes minimum (more is fine, less is broken chain)
- Same action every day (consistency creates compound)
- Must be building, not consuming (creating, not watching)
- Must be specific and measurable

Examples that work:

- Write 300 words
- Code one function/feature
- Design one element
- Practice instrument 15 minutes
- Create one piece of content
- Learn one language lesson
- Build one business asset

Examples that don't:

- "Work on stuff" (too vague)
- "Watch tutorials" (consuming)
- "Think about business" (not building)
- "Read about writing" (not writing)

2. Start Your Chain

Right now. Not Monday. Not "after vacation." NOW.

Your Day 1 Post:

"Starting my #100DayChain today.

Committing to: [Your one action]
Why this matters: [Your reason]
Day 1: ☑ [What you did today]

Who's joining me?"
Make it public. Make it real. Make it now.

3. Never Break the Chain

The chain is sacred. Miss one day = start over at Day 1. No exceptions. No excuses. No negotiations.

Daily proof required:

- Screenshot of work
- Photo of creation
- Description of progress
- Time stamp included

"But I'm sick!" Do 15 minutes from bed. "But I'm traveling!" Do it in the airport. "But it's Christmas!" Santa built toys on Christmas. "But I'm tired!" Tired people build different futures than energetic quitters.

The chain doesn't care about your circumstances. Neither does your future.

4. Tag Someone New Daily

Your chain becomes their permission. Their chain becomes someone else's inspiration.

Day 1: Tag your most supportive friend
Day 2: Tag your most skeptical friend
Day 3: Tag someone who needs this
Day 4-100: Keep finding people

Template: "@[Name], I'm on day [X] of my #100DayChain. Building [thing] daily. You mentioned wanting to [their goal]. Join me?"

One tag. One person. Every day. Watch the compound effect of community.

5. Support Others in Valleys

Days 31-90 are brutal for everyone. EVERYONE. When you see Valley posts, respond. When you feel Valley pain, share.

Valley posts to watch for:

- "Day 43. This is pointless."
- "Day 67. Nobody cares about my work."
- "Day 78. Want to quit so bad."
- "Day 85. Why am I doing this?"

Your Valley support:

- "Day 67 here too. We got this."
- "Your Day 100 self is counting on you."
- "The Valley ends. Keep building."
- "Quitting on day 78 is like mining for 77 days then stopping."

When you're in the Valley, post:

"Day [X]. In the Valley. Still building. #100DayChain"

Simple. Honest. Powerful. Watch support flood in from others in valleys, others past valleys, others approaching valleys. Nobody builds alone.

The Multiplier Effect

This isn't just your chain. It's a chain reaction.

Day 1: You alone, nervous but starting
Day 10: 10 people you've tagged joining
Day 30: Those 10 bring 10 each = 100 builders
Day 60: Community self-supporting through valleys
Day 100: Movement changing thousands of lives

Your chain becomes their courage. Their courage becomes community. Community becomes movement. Movement becomes transformation.

The Compound Results

What happens to chain survivors:

Skill Level:

Day 1: Absolute beginner
Day 30: Competent amateur
Day 60: Confident practitioner
Day 90: Emerging professional
Day 100: "How did I get here?"

Identity Shift:

Day 1: "I'm going to try..."
Day 30: "I'm actually doing this"
Day 60: "This is harder than expected"
Day 90: "Wait, I'm actually good at this"

Day 100: "This is who I am now"

External Results:

Day 1-30: Nobody notices
Day 31-60: Few people asking questions
Day 61-90: Opportunities appearing
Day 91-100: "How do you have time for this?"
Day 101+: New life, new identity, new possibilities

Valley Emergency Kit

When you want to quit (and you will), use this:

The Valley Post:

"Day [X]. In the Valley. Still building. #100DayChain

What's hard: [Specific struggle]
Why continuing: [Your why]
Tomorrow's plan: [Keep it simple]"

The Valley Mantra:

"The Valley is temporary. My chain is testament. Day 100 me is counting on today me."

The Valley Math:

Days invested: [X]
Days to 100: [100-X]
Quitting wastes: [X] days
Continuing rewards: Lifetime

The Valley Truth:

Everyone who made it to 100 wanted to quit between days 31-90. Everyone. The only difference between success and failure? They posted "Still building" instead of "I quit."

Real Chains That Changed Lives

Marcus, Developer: 100 days of coding. Day 1 couldn't write function. Day 100 hired as junior developer. Day 500 leading team.

Sarah, Writer: 100 days of 500 words. Day 1 garbage. Day 50 finding voice. Day 100 first paid article. Now bestselling author.

David, Designer: 100 days of daily designs. Day 30 "These suck." Day 70 "Getting better." Day 100 hired by dream agency.

Lisa, Entrepreneur: 100 days building business. Day 45 zero sales. Day 89 wanted to quit. Day 94 first customer. Day 365 six figures.

All started with Day 1. All survived the Valley. All thankful they didn't break the chain.

Your chain starts now.

Not tomorrow. Not Monday. Not January 1st. NOW.

Before you turn this page. Before you check your phone. Before another moment passes without building.

Right now:

1. Decide your one daily action
2. Do it (even just 15 minutes)
3. Post your Day 1
4. Tag one person
5. Start your 100-day transformation

The builders are waiting for your Day 1 post.

The Valley is waiting for your persistence. Day 100 you is waiting for current you to start. Your transformed life is waiting for your first link.

100 days will pass whether you build or not. On day 100, you'll either have a chain of 100 victories or 100 regrets.

What's your first link?

Open your phone. Open your laptop. Open your future.

Post now: "Day 1 of my #100DayChain..."

Your chain starts with your next action. Make it now. Make it count. Make it the first of 100.

The movement is waiting. The Valley is waiting. Your transformation is waiting.

But they all wait for the same thing: Your Day 1.

Don't make us wait long.

#100DayChain

What will you build for 100 days straight?

177

223

PART THREE

THE DAILY PRACTICE

Building Your Future in Any Country, Any Condition

Chapter 8: *The Daily Builder's Practice.*

Exactly How 15 Minutes Creates Income Anywhere.

"You don't need Silicon Valley. You need 15 focused minutes and WiFi. That's how anyone anywhere competes with everyone everywhere."

The Money Path That Works

The biggest lie in the modern economy? That your zip code determines your income. That your city limits your ceiling. That geography is destiny.

Tell that to the developer in Kansas earning San Francisco rates. The designer in Detroit serving Dubai clients. The teacher in Tennessee reaching students in Tokyo.

Location used to matter when value required presence. When showing up meant physically appearing. When proximity determined possibility.

That world is dead. WiFi killed it.

The New Reality

Your competition isn't local. Neither are your opportunities. The playing field isn't level—it's gone. Replaced by a global marketplace where value travels at light speed and payment follows performance, not position.

But here's what nobody tells you: There's a specific path from learning to earning. Four exact steps. Miss one, stay broke. Hit all four, transform everything.

The Progression Nobody Teaches

Watch how value actually builds:

Step   1:   Learning   (No   Money)
You consume tutorials. Read books. Take courses. Feel productive. Bank account unchanged. You're a professional student earning student wages: zero.

Step   2:   Building   (Some   Money)
You apply knowledge. Solve real problems. Create actual value. Someone benefits. They pay. Not much, but proof you're on the path.

Step   3:   Teaching   (Real   Money)
Others want your results. You show them how. One-to-one becomes one-to-many. Time decouples from income. $100/hour appears.

Step   4:   Scaling   (Wealth)
Your solution becomes system. System becomes product. Product serves thousands. You sleep, income flows. $10K months become normal.

Real Example: The Excel Evolution

Sarah's Step 1: Learning Excel (Month 1)

- YouTube tutorials every morning
- Learned VLOOKUP, pivot tables, macros
- Felt smart, earned nothing
- "I'm investing in myself" (true but insufficient)

Sarah's Step 2: Building Solutions (Month 2-3)

- Automated weekly report at work
- Saved team 10 hours/week
- Boss impressed, small raise
- First money from skill: $200/month extra

Sarah's Step 3: Teaching Others (Month 4-6)

- Coworkers begged for training
- Started lunch workshops
- Companies heard, hired her weekends
- Teaching income: $100/hour, 10 hours/week

Sarah's Step 4: Scaling Systems (Month 7-12)

- Created Excel template pack

- Recorded training videos
- Built email list of Excel learners
- Product income: $10K/month, works 10 hours/week

Same Sarah. Same skill. Four different income levels based on where she was on the path.

Learning alone is consumption.
Learning + application = income.

The course-collector with 50 certificates makes less than the problem-solver with one skill applied well. The degree-hoarder struggles while the solution-creator thrives.

Because customers don't pay for what you know. They pay for problems you solve. And problems don't care about your credentials. Only your solutions.

Stop collecting certificates. Start solving expensive problems.

Every business has expensive problems. Every person faces costly challenges. Every industry bleeds money somewhere. Find the bleeding. Stop it. Get paid.

Your certificate in Excel? Worthless. Your ability to save companies 20 hours weekly? Priceless.

Your degree in marketing? Commodity. Your system that doubles conversion rates? Liquid gold.

Your knowledge of nutrition? Everyone has Google. Your method that helped 100 people lose weight? Million-dollar business.

The Barista vs MBA Reality Check

The Barista with WiFi:

- Learns social media marketing (free)
- Manages café's Instagram (proof)
- Local businesses notice (opportunity)
- Builds agency from coffee shop (scale)
- Income: $10K/month in year one

The MBA with Debt:

- Prestigious degree ($200K debt)
- Competing with identical MBAs

- Sending résumés to algorithms
- Praying for callbacks
- Income: $60K/year if lucky

One collected credentials. One solved problems. Guess who's thriving?

The barista understood: Value travels through WiFi. Solutions sell everywhere. Geography is history. Skills are currency.

The Path Is Always The Same

Whether you're in Manhattan or Mumbai, the path doesn't change:

1. Learn something valuable (15-30 minutes daily)
2. Apply it immediately (solve real problems)
3. Teach your results (help others succeed)
4. Scale your solution (systems and products)

Skip learning? Nothing to apply.
Skip applying? Nothing to teach.
Skip teaching? Nothing to scale.
Skip scaling? Trading time forever.

The path from learning to earning is shorter than you think. It's exactly four steps. Miss one, make nothing. Hit all four, make everything.

But it starts with 15 minutes. And WiFi. And the decision to stop collecting knowledge and start creating value.

The barista in Bangkok can out-earn the banker in Boston. The teacher in Tulsa can out-scale the CEO in Silicon Valley. The student in Sudan can out-build the graduate in Geneva.

Not eventually. Now. Today. Starting with whatever device you're reading this on.

Geography is dead. Degrees are devaluing. Credentials are commoditized.

But problems? Problems are everywhere. Expensive ones. Painful ones. Urgent ones.

And solutions? Solutions pay. Always have. Always will.

In every currency. In every country. In every context.

You don't need Silicon Valley. You need to solve something valuable. You don't need credentials. You need to create results. You don't need permission. You need WiFi and wisdom.

The path is clear. The steps are proven. The only question is:

Which step will you take today?

The Universal Income Formula

Daily Practice → Skill → Applied Value → Monetization → Scale

This isn't a philosophy. It's a physics equation. As predictable as gravity. As reliable as sunrise. Follow the sequence, get the result. Skip a step, get nothing.

Let's map your next 90 days to income.

Daily Practice (Days 1-30)

What it looks like: Alarm at 5:45 AM. Coffee brewing. Laptop opening. Same YouTube playlist. Same notebook. Same determination. 15-30 minutes before the world wakes up. No exceptions. No negotiations.

What you're building: Neural pathways, not income (yet). Your brain is literally rewiring. New connections forming. Like a baby learning to walk—lots of falling, no visible progress, essential foundation being laid.

Real Example:

Emma's	6	AM	Routine:
5:45 - Alarm (across	room,	forces	standing)
5:50 - Coffee	started,	laptop	open
6:00 - Excel	tutorial		playing
6:15 -	Practice		exercise
6:25 - Note	one	thing	learned

6:30 - Regular morning begins

The Trap: "I'm learning but not earning!"

Of course you're not earning. Babies don't run marathons. Seeds don't fruit immediately. Day 15 you'll think: "This is pointless. I should be making money by now."

No. You're making neural pathways. Income comes after infrastructure.

What's Actually Happening:

Day 1-7: Excitement carries you
Day 8-14: Habit forming, resistance rising
Day 15-21: Want to quit daily
Day 22-30: Something clicks, pattern established

By day 30: You've internalized basics. Foundation poured. Ready to build.

Skill (Days 31-60)

The Transformation: From "I watched videos" to "I can do this." From consumer to creator. From following to leading. The tutorials become reference, not requirement.

The Test: Can you solve a real problem without googling every step? Can you create something from blank canvas? Can you help someone else understand it?

Emma's Evolution:

Day 35: Built first spreadsheet without tutorial
Day 42: Automated personal budget (ugly but works)
Day 48: Helped friend track business expenses
Day 55: Creating custom solutions, not copying
Day 60: "Holy shit, I actually know Excel"

The Milestone: First thing you create without help. Might be simple. Definitely imperfect. But yours. Original. Proof you've crossed from learning to knowing.

The Confidence Shift:

Week 1-4: "I'm learning Excel"
Week 5-8: "I know Excel basics"
Week 9+: "I solve problems with Excel"

Small word changes. Massive identity shift.

Applied Value (Days 61-75)

The Shift: From "I can do this" to "I solved THIS." From potential to proof. From theoretical to tangible. Where rubber meets road and value meets world.

Where Money Starts: Solving expensive problems. Not any problems—expensive ones. The ones that cost time, money, or sanity. The ones people gladly pay to eliminate.

Emma's First Value:

- Problem noticed: Team spends 4 hours weekly on reports
- Solution created: Automated dashboard
- Time to build: 3 hours
- Weekly time saved: 4 hours
- Monthly value: 16 hours = $400+ saved
- Reaction: "How did you DO that?!"

Key Insight: Value isn't in knowing. It's in applying.

Knowing Excel = Zero dollars
Saving 16 hours monthly = Quantifiable value
Teaching others to save time = Multiplied value
Creating systems that scale = Exponential value

The Value Progression:

Solve your own problem (proof of concept)
Solve colleague's problem (proof of value)
Solve department's problem (proof of scale)
Solve company's problem (proof of worth)

Each level multiplies your marketability.

Monetization (Days 76-90)

Converting Value to Income: The script writes itself when value is clear. Raises request themselves. Clients appear. Customers find you. Because value is magnetic.

The Pitch That Works:

"I built a system that saves our team 16 hours monthly. That's $400 in productivity recovered. I can do this for other departments. What would that be worth?"

Not asking for charity. Demonstrating ROI. Speaking their language: money saved, time recovered, problems solved.

Emma's Monetization Timeline:

Day 76: Presented automation to boss
Day 78: Asked to automate for other teams
Day 82: Raise conversation initiated

Day 85: 15% salary increase approved
Day 88: First freelance inquiry from LinkedIn
Day 90: Side client paying $500/month
    Truth: Money follows value like night follows day.

Create clear value → Money often follows
Create unclear value → Struggle continues
Create no value → Poverty guaranteed

The universe has perfect accounting. Value out equals money in. Always. Eventually. Inevitably.

Scale (Days 90+)

From Trading Time to Multiplying Impact: The final evolution. From doing to teaching. From solving to systematizing. From linear to exponential.

Emma's Scale Journey:

Month 4: Excel consulting ($2K/month side income)
Month 6: Created "Excel for Teams" course
Month 8: 200 students at $97 each
Month 10: Hired VA to handle support
Month 12: $10K/month, 10 hours/week

The Scale Vehicles:

- **Templates:** Your solution in reusable form
- **Courses:** Your knowledge in teachable form
- **Systems:** Your process in scalable form
- **Teams:** Your impact in multiplied form

The Goal: Income while you sleep. Not passive—you built it actively. But decoupled from daily presence. Your solution solving problems while you live life.

Real Scale Examples:

- Designer's Photoshop actions: Created once, sold 10,000 times
- Consultant's frameworks: Built for one client, licensed to hundreds
- Developer's plugins: Coded once, downloaded globally

- Teacher's curriculum: Designed once, implemented everywhere

This isn't theory. It's a timeline.

Where are you on it?

Days 1-30? Keep practicing. Income isn't supposed to appear yet. Days 31-60? Start building. Skills need application targets. Days 61-75? Find expensive problems. Value needs direction. Days 76-90? Convert value to cash. Results need rewards. Days 90+? Scale or stall. Growth needs systems.

The formula is universal. The timeline is typical. The results are predictable.

But only for those who follow the sequence. Only for those who trust the process. Only for those who understand: Income isn't the goal. It's the inevitable result of following the formula.

Your current day number: ____
Your next milestone: ____
Your required action: ____

The formula doesn't care about your location. Your education. Your background. It only counts your days and measures your value.

Start counting. Start creating. Start climbing.

The timeline is ticking. Your income is waiting at the end of the formula.

But it starts with tomorrow's 15 minutes.

Where will you be 90 days from now? Still reading about formulas? Or living proof they work?

The formula is patient. But your future isn't.

Begin.

FOR EMPLOYEES: Turn Your Job Into an ATM

Stop looking for new jobs. Start looking at your current one differently. You're sitting on a goldmine of problems worth solving, and someone's already paying you to be there.

The Employee's Advantage

While freelancers hunt for clients and entrepreneurs search for problems, you're surrounded by both. Every inefficiency you notice. Every complaint you hear. Every "we've always done it this way" is a paycheck increase waiting to happen.

Your Three Unfair Advantages:

1.   Problems   Right   in   Front   of   You
That tedious process everyone hates? That's not annoyance—it's opportunity. The system that crashes weekly? That's your raise hiding in plain sight.

2.   Proof   of   Impact
You can measure exactly what your solution saves. Hours. Dollars. Errors. Headaches. Real metrics beat hypothetical value every time.

3.   Decision   Makers   Who   Know   You
No cold pitching. No trust building. No proving yourself. They already sign your checks. Now give them reason to increase them.

The Office Worker's Playbook

Sarah's Story: From $35K Clerk to $65K Specialist

Accounting clerk. Columbus, Ohio. Three years doing same thing. Excel all day. Data entry. Report generation. Mind-numbing repetition. Sound familiar?

Weeks 1-4: The Learning Phase

Sarah noticed her torture: 3 hours daily copying data between spreadsheets. Same process. Every. Single. Day. 15 hours weekly of ctrl+c, ctrl+v.

Instead of complaining, she calculated:

15   hours/week   × $17/hour   = $255   weekly   waste
$255   ×   52   weeks   = $13,260   annual   inefficiency
Just on HER salary alone
The Lightbulb: "If I'm wasting $13K, what about the whole department?"

Her Secret Weapon Schedule:

7:30 AM - Arrive early (quiet office)
7:30-7:45 - YouTube: "Excel VBA basics"
12:00-12:30 - Lunch at desk, tutorial running

5:00-5:30 - Practice on actual work files
Total: 45 minutes daily investment

Weeks 5-8: The Application Phase

Week 5: First working macro. Ugly code. But it worked. Monthly report automated. Personal time saved: 5 hours.

Week 6: Showed desk neighbor Janet. "Can it work for my reports too?" Modified code. Janet's time saved: 5 hours.

Week 7: Word spread. "Sarah knows computer magic." Department buzz. Everyone wanted automation.

Week 8: Documented everything:

- 6 people using macros
- 10 hours saved weekly
- 520 hours saved annually
- $8,840 in time recovered

Weeks 9-12: The Expansion Phase

Sarah went full builder mode:

- Automated invoice processing (saved 8 hours/week)
- Created error-checking system (reduced mistakes 90%)
- Built dashboard for management (real-time visibility)
- Wrote simple training guide (anyone could use it)

Total Department Impact:

- Time saved: 25 hours/week
- Annual value: $22,100 in productivity
- Error reduction: 90%
- Morale boost: Immeasurable

Month 4: The Presentation

Sarah didn't ask for a meeting. She scheduled a "Process Improvement Demonstration."

Her Agenda:

- Problem overview (5 minutes of pain points)
- Live demonstration (10 minutes of solutions)
- Impact metrics (2 minutes of pure value)
- Proposal (3 minutes on new role)

The Killer Slide:

"Current state: $22,100 annual waste"
"Future state: $0 waste + expanded possibilities"
"Investment needed: New role for automation"

Month 5: The Payoff

Management math was simple:

- Sarah saves company $22K minimum
- Probably more with expansion
- Current salary: $35K
- Worth investing more to keep her

Results:

- New title: "Financial Systems Analyst"
- New salary: $49K (40% raise)
- New responsibility: Automate entire finance department
- Side bonus: Other departments want training

Month 12 Update:

- Salary: $65K (after second raise)
- Teaching Excel automation workshops
- Weekend consulting: $150/hour
- Total income: $95K

Same company. Same building. Different reality.

The Employee's Formula

**Find Expensive Problem → Learn Solution Skill → Apply at Work →
Document Impact → Present Value → Negotiate Raise**
It's math, not magic. Value created equals income increased. Every time.

More Quick Victories

Marcus: Customer Service → CRM Administrator

- Problem: Team using spreadsheets for customer tracking
- Learned: Salesforce basics (YouTube + Trailhead)
- Applied: Built simple CRM for team
- Result: 50% faster response times
- Raise: From $32K to $48K
- Timeline: 4 months

Jennifer: Warehouse Worker → Operations Analyst

- Problem: Inventory chaos, constant stockouts
- Learned: Inventory management systems
- Applied: Implemented barcode tracking
- Result: 80% reduction in stockouts
- Raise: From $15/hour to $30/hour
- Timeline: 6 months

David: Receptionist → Digital Marketing Coordinator

- Problem: Company invisible online
- Learned: Social media marketing
- Applied: Managed company profiles
- Result: 300% increase in leads
- Raise: From $28K to $45K
- Timeline: 5 months

The Pattern Is Clear

Every single success story:

1. Identified expensive inefficiency
2. Learned solution on their time
3. Applied solution on company time

4. Measured concrete results
5. Presented value professionally
6. Received inevitable raise

Not one quit. Not one risked. All transformed.

Your Action Plan

Week 1: Problem Hunting

- List every inefficiency you see
- Calculate time/money wasted
- Pick the most expensive one

Weeks 2-4: Skill Building

- Find free learning resources
- Practice 30-45 minutes daily
- Apply to real work immediately

Weeks 5-8: Value Creation

- Build working solution
- Test with colleagues
- Document time/money saved

Week 9-12: Expansion

- Scale solution wider
- Create documentation
- Calculate total impact

Month 4: Presentation

- Schedule demonstration
- Show working solution
- Present value metrics
- Propose new role/raise

The Negotiation Script

"I've identified a problem costing us $X annually. I've built a solution saving Y hours weekly. This translates to $Z in recovered productivity. I'd like to discuss adjusting my compensation to reflect this value I'm creating."

Not begging. Demonstrating. Not hoping. Proving.

Your job is a laboratory. Your problems are opportunities. Your salary is negotiable.

Every inefficiency is income hiding. Every "that's how we've always done it" is a raise waiting. Every complaint from colleagues is commission potential.

You don't need a new job. You need new eyes for your current one. You don't need permission to learn. You need 30 minutes and YouTube. You don't need an MBA. You need to solve one expensive problem.

Sarah still works in the same building. Parks in the same spot. But her paycheck tells a different story. Her skills opened doors. Her initiative created opportunities. Her value demanded compensation.

Your turn.

What expensive problem will you solve this week? What skill will you learn this month? What raise will you negotiate this quarter?

The formula works. The examples prove it. The only variable is you.

Your job isn't a trap. It's a treasure map. Start digging.

FOR LOW-WAGE WORKERS: The Leap Strategy

Let's tell the truth nobody wants to say: You can be the world's best cashier and still make $12 an hour. Excellence in a minimum-wage role doesn't create maximum income. The ceiling is built into the job, not your performance.

But there's a way out. A leap strategy. Not slow climbing—strategic jumping.

The Wage Ceiling Reality

Some harsh math:

Cashier Excellence:

- Starting: $10/hour
- After 5 years + perfect reviews: $13/hour
- Ceiling: $15/hour (maybe)
- Annual max: $31,200

Medical Assistant Reality:

- Starting: $18/hour
- After 2 years: $25/hour
- With specialization: $30+/hour
- Annual potential: $62,400

Same person. Same hours. Different game entirely.

The solution isn't working harder at limited jobs. It's building bridges to unlimited ones.

Maria's Leap: From $12 to $28 in 9 Months

Starting Point

Maria cleaned offices in Denver. 6 PM to 2 AM shift. $12/hour. Three years in, making $12.50. The math was brutal:

- Monthly income: $2,000
- After rent: $800
- After basics: $200
- Savings: Ha.

"I realized I could clean perfectly for 20 years and still be poor," Maria recalls. "The job had a ceiling. I needed a ladder."

The Research (Month 1)

Instead of Netflix after her shift, Maria googled:

- "Jobs that pay $25/hour with training"
- "Careers with 6-month programs"
- "High-demand jobs near me"

Medical assistant kept appearing. Demand everywhere. Training available. Real career path.

The Discovery

Maria found gold:

- Average pay: $18-28/hour
- Training needed: 6-9 months
- Cost at schools: $15,000 (impossible)

But wait...

Free resources existed:

- Medical terminology apps
- YouTube anatomy courses
- Practice test websites
- Volunteer opportunities

The Plan

Maria created her bridge while keeping her cleaning job:

3 AM - 4 AM: Medical terminology app (in bed)
4 PM - 5 PM: YouTube anatomy videos (before work)
Weekends: Volunteer at free clinic
Daily: 10 new medical terms during breaks

Month 1-3: Foundation Building

- Downloaded free medical apps
- Learned 500 medical terms
- Understood basic anatomy
- Watched procedures on YouTube

"I turned my phone into medical school," Maria says. "Free education in my pocket."

Month 4-6: The Bridge

Key move: Volunteered at free health clinic Saturdays.

- Filed papers initially
- Observed procedures

- Helped with patient intake
- Learned clinic software
- Got to know doctors and nurses

"I was exhausted. Cleaning all week, clinic on Saturdays. But I was building my bridge."

Month 7: The Proof

Maria asked Dr. Rodriguez for a reference letter. He wrote: "Maria demonstrates exceptional knowledge of medical terminology, strong work ethic, and natural patient rapport. She would be an asset to any medical practice."

That letter was worth more than any certificate.

Month 8-9: The Leap

Maria applied strategically:

- Resume highlighted medical knowledge
- Cover letter mentioned volunteer experience
- Reference letter from doctor attached
- Applied to clinics, not just hospitals

First interview: "How do you know medical terminology without formal training?" Maria pulled out her phone, showed her study apps, recited terms flawlessly. Hired on the spot.

The Result

- Starting pay: $22/hour (week one)
- After 90 days: $25/hour
- After 1 year: $28/hour + benefits
- Current: Lead medical assistant, studying nursing

Same Maria. Same city. Income more than doubled.

The Pattern for Any Leap

1. Research What Pays 2-3X Current

Don't aim for 10% raises. Aim for different leagues:

- Current: $10-15/hour jobs
- Target: $25-35/hour jobs
- Research: In-demand skills for those jobs
- Reality check: Can be learned in 6-12 months

2. Find Free/Cheap Training

Expensive schools want your money. The internet wants to teach you:

- YouTube University (everything's there)
- Coursera/Khan Academy (often free)
- Library resources (books, computers, programs)
- Apps (turn phone into classroom)
- Podcasts (learn while commuting)

3. Learn at Protected Times

Not after exhausting shifts. Before the exhaustion:

- 30 minutes before work (brain fresh)
- During breaks (10 minutes adds up)
- Weekend mornings (not nights)
- Commute time (audio learning)

4. Get ANY Experience

Credentials help. Experience wins:

- Volunteer in target field
- Intern for free initially
- Shadow professionals
- Do projects for portfolio
- Help friends/family (document it)

5. Apply with Knowledge + Proof

Not just "I learned online" but:

- "I know X, here's proof"
- "I've done Y, here's reference"
- "I solved Z, here's example"

6. Make the Leap

When you have:

- Basic knowledge (not mastery)
- Some experience (not years)
- One good reference (not ten)
- Clear communication skills

Jump. The perfect moment never comes.

Other Leap Examples

David: Retail → Bank Teller

- Studied banking basics online
- Dressed professionally always
- Learned to speak "bank"
- Volunteered as tax prep assistant
- Leap: $11/hour → $19/hour → now loan officer at $60K

Jennifer: Fast Food → Pharmacy Tech

- Found scholarship for certification
- Studied during morning shift lulls
- Shadowed pharmacy tech cousin
- Passed certification exam
- Leap: $9/hour → $18/hour → now at $25/hour

Carlos: Janitor → IT Help Desk

- Watched Professor Messer videos (free)
- Fixed computers for church
- Got CompTIA A+ certification
- Built reputation as "tech guy"

- Leap: $13/hour → $22/hour → now network admin at $65K

Ashley: Server → Real Estate Assistant

- Learned MLS system online
- Studied real estate terms
- Helped friend (agent) organize showings
- Created sample marketing materials
- Leap: Tips uncertain → $20/hour → now licensed agent earning $80K

The Universal Truth

Every leap story has same elements:

1. Identified higher-wage target
2. Found free education
3. Created experience somehow
4. Applied with confidence
5. Made imperfect leap

None waited for perfect conditions. All started tired. All felt unqualified. All leaped anyway.

Your current job funds your future job. Use it as a launching pad, not a landing spot.

That minimum wage isn't your maximum worth. It's your temporary funding while you build bridges to better. It's not your career—it's your scholarship for learning what's next.

Maria still remembers cleaning those offices. But now she remembers them from her medical assistant desk, helping patients instead of emptying trash, earning respect instead of invisibility.

Your Leap Awaits

- What job pays double your current wage?
- What skills does it require?
- Where can you learn them free?
- Who can you help to gain experience?
- When will you make your leap?

The ceiling above you is real. But it's not your ceiling—it's your current job's ceiling. Your real ceiling is wherever you choose to leap to.

Some people polish floors forever. Others use those floors to launch higher.

Which will you be?

The research awaits. The free education exists. The bridge can be built. The leap is possible.

But it starts with tonight's Google search: "Jobs that pay $[your target] with training."

Your current job is Chapter 1. What's Chapter 2?

FOR THE UNEMPLOYED: Create Your Own Position

The Proactive Value Creation Method

"No job? Good. You're free to create value without permission."
While others wait for job postings, you can solve problems. While they tailor résumés, you can build solutions. While they hope for callbacks, you can generate offers.

The employed are trapped in their roles. You're free to create any role you want.

Jake's Story: From Layoff to Dream Job in 30 Days

Software developer. Laid off from automotive supplier. Detroit area. Six months of traditional job hunting: 200 applications, 12 interviews, 0 offers. Depression setting in.

Then Jake flipped the script.

Week 1: The Target List

Instead of browsing job boards, Jake created his hit list:

10 Companies He Actually Wanted:

- Mid-size manufacturing companies (understood the industry)
- Within 30 miles (no relocation)

- Growing but not huge (could make impact)
- Tech-forward but not tech companies (his sweet spot)

Deep Dive Research:

- Studied their websites (looking for pain points)
- Read their press releases (what are they struggling with?)
- Analyzed their job postings (what problems are they hiring to solve?)
- Checked their Google reviews (what do customers complain about?)

Discovery: Precision Parts Inc. kept posting for inventory managers. High turnover. Reviews mentioned "order delays" and "stock issues."

Jake smelled opportunity.

Week 2-3: The Solution Creation

Jake didn't apply. He built.

The Problem: Their website showed "Call for availability" on 500+ products
The Hypothesis: Poor inventory tracking causing customer frustration
The Solution: Simple inventory tracking system prototype

What Jake Built:

- Basic database structure
- Simple web interface
- Real-time stock updates
- Low-stock alerts
- Integration mockup with their site

Not production-ready. But good enough to demonstrate value.

Time invested: 40 hours over 2 weeks
Cost: $0 (used free tools)
Traditional applications sent: 0

Week 4: The Direct Approach

Jake found the Operations Manager on LinkedIn. Skipped HR. Went straight to decision maker.

The Message:

Subject: Built Something That Could Save Precision Parts $200K Annually

Hi Tom,

I noticed you've hired 3 inventory managers in 18 months. I think I know why.

Your "call for availability" system is killing sales and burning out staff. I built a prototype solution that could:
- Eliminate 90% of availability calls
- Reduce stockouts by 70%
- Save 20 hours/week in manual checking

Here's a 3-minute demo: [link]

If this interests you, I'd love to show how it works with your specific systems.

Best,
Jake

P.S. I built this because I want to work for a company like yours, and I believe in solving problems before asking for jobs.

The Results Chain Reaction

Day 1: Tom forwarded to CEO
Day 2: CEO called Jake directly
Day 3: In-person demonstration
Day 5: Three other companies Jake had messaged responded
Day 8: Precision Parts created "Systems Developer" role
Day 10: Two other companies offered contract work
Day 15: Negotiating between three opportunities
Day 30: Started at Precision Parts, $95K + equity

Same Jake. Same skills. Different approach. Different outcome.

The Unemployed Advantage

Stop seeing unemployment as disadvantage. Start seeing it as competitive edge:

1. Full Time to Build Value

- Employed competitors get 1 hour after work
- You get 8 hours of prime energy
- You can outbuild anyone with a job

2. Can Help Multiple Companies

- Not locked to one employer
- Can solve for entire industry
- Portfolio of solutions, not just one

3. Not Limited by Job Descriptions

- They hire for what they think they need
- You solve what they actually need
- You create positions that don't exist yet

4. Can Create Your Ideal Position

- Combine skills they didn't know they needed
- Define role around your strengths
- Build the job you want to have

The Value-First Formula

1. Identify Expensive Problems

Look for:

- High employee turnover in specific roles (systemic problem)
- Customer complaints about same issues (unresolved pain)
- Manual processes in digital age (automation opportunity)
- "Coming soon" that's been coming for years (execution problem)

2. Build/Create Solution

Partial solutions win:

- Prototype > Perfect product
- Working demo > Theoretical proposal
- Specific example > Generic capability
- Something tangible > Everything promised

3. Show Solution to Decision Makers

Skip HR. Find the person who:

- Feels the pain directly
- Has budget to solve it
- Can create positions
- Values results over résumés

4. Let Them Figure Out How to Pay You

Options they might propose:

- Contract project (immediate income)
- Part-time role (steady + flexibility)
- Full-time position (created for you)
- Equity + salary (startup approach)
- Retainer relationship (ongoing value)

You solved their problem. They'll solve yours.

Quick Win Options

For Any Business:

- Analyze their website speed, send optimization report
- Create 30 social media posts in their voice
- Mystery shop and provide detailed improvement plan
- Build simple calculator for their complex pricing

For Specific Industries:

Restaurants:

- Design delivery menu that increases orders
- Create Instagram content strategy
- Build reservation system improvement

Real Estate:

- Create virtual tour templates
- Design listing presentations
- Build neighborhood comparison tools

E-commerce:

- Improve product descriptions for SEO
- Create abandoned cart email sequences
- Design better checkout process

Local Services:

- Build review response templates
- Create booking system mockup
- Design service area maps

The Message Template:

"I noticed [specific problem] on your [website/business].

This typically costs companies like yours [impact].

I created [specific solution] that could [specific benefit].

Here's what it looks like: [link/attachment]

Would you like to discuss implementing this?"

Real Examples of Created Positions

Sarah: Analyzed local gym's member dropout rate. Created retention program mockup. Now "Member Success Director" at $55K.

Marcus: Built better FAQ system for software company. Noticed support tickets dropped 40% in demo. Now "Documentation Lead" at $70K.

Jennifer: Redesigned patient intake forms for dental office. Saved 10 minutes per patient. Now "Patient Experience Coordinator" for 5 offices.

David: Created TikTok content for restaurant. Drove 200 customers in test week. Now "Social Media Chef" at $45K + free meals.

None of these positions existed. All were created after value was demonstrated.

Jobs follow value. Create value, and jobs will find you.

The traditional path:

- See job posting
- Apply with résumé
- Hope for interview
- Pray for offer
- Accept what's given

The builder's path:

- Identify problem
- Create solution
- Demonstrate value
- Receive multiple offers
- Choose best option

One path begs. One path builds. One path waits. One path creates.

Jake spent six months in the traditional path going nowhere. Spent 30 days in the builder's path choosing between opportunities.

Your Unemployment Advantage Awaits

Tomorrow, instead of scrolling job boards:

1. List 10 companies you'd love to work for
2. Research one deeply
3. Identify one expensive problem
4. Start building a solution
5. Message decision maker next week

Your competition is sending résumé #201. You're sending solution #1.

Who would you hire?

The job you want might not exist yet. Good. That means you get to create it.

Value first. Position second. Income follows.

Start building.

Income Acceleration Tools

Forget motivation. You need multiplication. These three tools transform same effort into exponential results. Not theory. Actual calculators you can use tonight.

Tool 1: The Skill Stack Calculator

Skills don't add. They multiply. Watch the math:

Single Skill Income:

Excel		expert:	$25/hour
Good	living,	low	ceiling
Trading	time		forever
Competition with millions			

The Multiplication Effect:

Stack Level 1: Base Skill

Excel	expertise	=	$25/hour
Limited	by	hours	in	day

Maximum: 40 hours × $25 = $1,000/week

Stack Level 2: + Digital Delivery

Excel	+	Screen	recording	=	Serve	10X	people
Create		once,		sell			repeatedly
Tutorial		value:	$250		per		product

Potential: 10 sales/week = $2,500

Stack Level 3: + Teaching Ability

Excel	+	Digital	+	Teaching	=	Course	creation
One		course,		unlimited			students
Course			price:				$497

20 students/month = $9,940 passive

Stack Level 4: + System Creation

Excel	+	Digital	+	Teaching	+	Systems	=	Business
License		templates		to			companies

Enterprise deals: $5,000-25,000
Annual potential: $250,000+

Same person. Same base skill. 10X income per stack level.

Real Stack Progressions:

The Excel Evolution:
Year 1: Excel ($40K)
↓
Year 2: Excel + Automation ($65K)
↓
Year 3: Excel + Automation + Teaching ($120K)
↓
Year 4: Excel + Automation + Teaching + Enterprise Systems ($300K)

The Writer's Journey:
Writing ($30K freelance)
↓
Writing + SEO ($60K content marketing)
↓
Writing + SEO + Email Marketing ($150K as consultant)
↓
Writing + SEO + Email + Team = Agency ($500K+)

The Organizer's Ascent:
Organizing ($20/hour)
↓
Organizing + Digital Tools ($50/hour)
↓
Organizing + Digital + Systems ($150/hour consulting)
↓
Organizing + Digital + Systems + Certification = Training Company

Your Stack Calculator:

Your base skill: _____ = $_____/hour

+ Digital delivery = $_____ × 10

+ Teaching ability = $_____ × 100

+ System creation = $_____ × 1000

The multiplication is mathematical. Pick your stack. Start building.

Tool 2: The Time Arbitrage System

"I don't have time" = "I don't have systems." You have 168 hours weekly. You're just spending them linearly instead of stacking them.

Find Your Hidden Hours:

Commute Conversion (30-60 min/day)

- Driving: Podcasts, audiobooks, voice memo practice
- Public transport: Video tutorials, reading, coding
- Weekly gain: 5-10 hours of learning
- Annual gain: 250-500 hours (6-12 work weeks!)

Lunch Learning (30 min/day)

- Desk lunch + tutorial = Daily skill dose
- Social lunch Mon/Wed/Fri, learning Tue/Thu
- Weekly gain: 2.5 hours
- Annual gain: 125 hours (3 work weeks)

Waiting Wisdom (20 min/day)

- Doctor's office: Phone app practice
- Kid's soccer practice: Skill videos
- Grocery line: Audio lessons
- Weekly gain: 2.3 hours
- Annual gain: 115 hours

Morning Momentum (15-30 min/day)

- Before family wakes
- Before checking phone
- Before day owns you
- Weekly gain: 3.5 hours
- Annual gain: 175 hours

Evening Education (15-30 min/day)

- After dinner dishes
- Instead of scroll time
- Before bed routine
- Weekly gain: 3.5 hours
- Annual gain: 175 hours

Total Hidden Time:

- Daily: 2-3 hours without sacrificing anything
- Weekly: 14-21 hours of building time
- Monthly: 60-90 hours (almost 2 work weeks!)
- Annual: 720-1,080 hours (18-27 work weeks!)

Real Time Arbitrage Winners:

Marcus: Uber driver, learned coding during wait times between rides. Now full-stack developer.

Sarah: Commuter, completed MBA-level education through podcasts. Now strategy consultant.

Jennifer: Stay-at-home mom, built business during nap times. Now earning six figures.

Tool 3: The Value Ladder Map

Every skill has a ladder. Most people stop at rung one. Income multiplies with each rung climbed.

The Universal Value Ladder:

Rung	1:	Solve	One	Problem	($)
Your		own		problem	solved
Proof			of		concept
Single					payment

Example: Organize your closet

Rung	2:	Solve	for	Others	($$)
Same		solution,		multiple	people
Direct			service		delivery
Hourly/project					rate

Example: Organize 10 closets for pay

Rung	3:	Solve	Repeatedly	($$$)
Systematize				solution
Reduce			delivery	time
Increase			profit	margin

Example: Closet organizing system/checklist

Rung	4:	Teach	the	Solution	($$$$)
Enable		others		to	solve
One-to-many					model
Passive			income		possible

Example: Closet organizing course

Rung 5: License the System ($$$$$)

Others use your system
Complete business model
True multiplication
Example: Franchise organizing method

Real Ladder Climbs:

Jake's Coding Ladder:

Built app for himself ($0)
Built apps for others ($5K/month)
Created app templates ($15K/month)
Taught app building ($30K/month)
Licensed framework to companies ($100K+/month)

Maria's Fitness Ladder:

Lost 50 pounds ($0)
Trained friends ($500/month)
Developed meal/workout system ($2K/month)
Created online program ($10K/month)
Certified other trainers ($50K/month)

Your Value Ladder Map:

Answer for your skill:

1. What problem did I solve for myself?
2. Who else struggles with this?
3. How can I package my solution?
4. Who would pay to learn this?
5. What companies need this systemized?

Draw your ladder. See your future.

The Multiplication Matrix

Combine all three tools:

Your Stack × Your Time × Your Ladder = Exponential Income

Example:

Base skill: $30/hour
Stack multiplier: 10X = $300/hour potential
Time found: 20 hours/week
Ladder position: Teaching level
Result: $6,000 weekly potential vs $600 working harder
Same person. Same week. Different tools. Different life.

These aren't just tools. They're multipliers.

**Use one, get linear results.
Use all three, get exponential results.**

The calculator shows your potential. The time system funds your building. The ladder maps your progression.

Tonight, before bed:

1. Calculate your stack value
2. Identify tomorrow's hidden hour
3. Draw your value ladder

Tomorrow, start climbing.

These tools work whether you're in Manhattan or Manila. Whether you're 20 or 60. Whether you're employed or searching.

They only fail when unused.

Your current income reflects your current tools. Your future income reflects your future tools.

Which tools will you use?

The multiplication awaits. The time exists. The ladder stands ready.

Climb.

The 90-Day Sprint Framework

Three months. Twelve weeks. Ninety days. That's the gap between your current reality and your transformed life. Not someday. Not eventually. 90 days from today.

Here's your blueprint.

Your Personalized 90-Day Sprint

Days 1-30: Foundation Phase

The Focus: Building neural pathways, not bank deposits. You're an athlete in training, not yet competing.

Daily Requirements:

- ONE skill only (resist the buffet, order one meal)

- Same time daily (before life interferes)
- 30-45 minutes minimum (15 if desperate, but 30-45 transforms)
- Document everything (screenshots, notes, aha moments)

What You're Actually Doing:

- Installing new mental software
- Creating automatic behaviors
- Building competence foundation
- Collecting proof of progress

Expected Reality:

- Income: $0 (and that's perfect)
- Skill level: Conscious incompetence → Conscious competence
- Confidence: Low but building
- Temptation to quit: Daily
- Mindset: "I'm planting seeds"

Seeds don't sprout overnight. Neither do skills. Every tutorial watched, every exercise completed, every frustrated retry—all seeds in soil. Invisible but essential.

Day 30 Checkpoint:

- Can do basic tasks without tutorials
- Have collection of practice work
- Habit feels somewhat automatic
- Ready to apply to real problems

Days 31-60: Application Phase

The Shift: From learning to doing. From theory to practice. From student to practitioner.

Daily Evolution:

- Continue learning (maintenance)
- Apply to real problems (growth)

- Build solution portfolio (proof)
- Connect with others in field (network)

Where to Find Problems:

- Your own life (usually the best start)
- Friends and family (eager guinea pigs)
- Online communities (endless complaints)
- Local businesses (visible pain points)
- Work challenges (if employed)

What You're Creating:

- Before/after examples
- Testimonials (even informal)
- Case studies (even simple)
- Confidence through competence

Expected Reality:

- Income: $0-500 (first taste)
- Skill level: Conscious competence → Fluid capability
- Confidence: Building rapidly
- Valley of Despair: In full effect
- Mindset: "I'm growing shoots"

First green appears. Tiny. Fragile. Easy to dismiss. But roots are deepening. Structure is strengthening. Breakthrough is scheduling itself.

Day 60 Checkpoint:

- Solved 5-10 real problems
- Have portfolio of work
- Know your skill's value
- Ready to monetize

Days 61-90: Monetization Phase

The Transformation: From value creator to value capturer. From free to fee. From hobby to income.

Monetization Paths:

- Freelance projects (fastest)
- Salary negotiation (if employed)
- Product creation (most scalable)
- Service offering (most sustainable)

The Presentation Formula:

"I solved [specific problem] resulting in [specific outcome]. I can do the same for you. Investment: [price]"

Pricing Confidence:

- Start lower than comfortable
- Raise with each success
- Value-based, not time-based
- Package deals over hourly

Expected Reality:

- Income: $500-5,000 (depending on skill/market)
- Skill level: Fluid capability → Confident expertise
- Pipeline: Building rapidly
- Future: Clearly visible
- Mindset: "I'm harvesting results"

Seeds planted day 1 now bearing fruit. Work invisible for 60 days now undeniable. Value created finally captured.

Day 90 Results:

- Skill transformed from zero to valuable
- Income stream established
- Identity shifted permanently
- Momentum unstoppable

Real 90-Day Sprints That Worked

Sarah: Graphic Designer → UI/UX Specialist

- Days 1-30: Daily Figma tutorials, practice interfaces
- Days 31-60: Redesigned 5 friend's apps for free
- Days 61-90: First paid project $1,500, then $3,000
- Day 90 rate: $150/hour (vs $50 starting)
- Current: Lead designer at startup

Marcus: Teacher → Corporate Trainer

- Days 1-30: Studied adult learning, presentation design
- Days 31-60: Created sample training modules
- Days 61-90: First corporate workshop $2,000
- Month 6: Fully booked at $5,000/workshop
- Current: Training consultancy, six figures

Jennifer: Bartender → Cocktail Consultant

- Days 1-30: Studied mixology theory, menu design
- Days 31-60: Created cocktail programs for friends
- Days 61-90: First restaurant client $500/menu
- Year 1: Working with 20+ establishments
- Current: Featured in industry magazines

David: Stay-at-Home Parent → Virtual Assistant Agency

- Days 1-30: Learned project management tools
- Days 31-60: Managed tasks for 3 small businesses
- Days 61-90: Systemized and hired first VA
- Month 6: 5 VAs, 15 clients
- Current: $10K/month profit, works 20 hours/week

The Sprint Rules

1. One Skill Only

- JavaScript OR Python (not both)
- Facebook ads OR Google ads (not both)
- Writing OR design (not both)
- Mastery beats scattered competence

2. Daily Practice

- Weekends included
- Holidays included
- Sick days = 15 minutes minimum
- 90 means 90, not 65

3. Document Progress

- Daily screenshot/photo
- Weekly compilation video
- Build your proof portfolio
- Future you needs evidence

4. Share Journey

- Post updates with #90DayIncome
- Find accountability partner
- Join skill-specific community
- Teaching solidifies learning

5. Trust the Timeline

- Days 1-30 will feel too slow
- Days 31-60 will feel pointless
- Days 61-90 will feel magical
- Day 91+ will feel inevitable

Your 90-Day Launchpad

Tonight:

- Choose your ONE skill
- Set tomorrow's alarm
- Find learning resource
- Post commitment publicly
- Screenshot this framework

Tomorrow (Day 1):

- Complete first lesson
- Document what you learned
- Share progress
- Plan day 2
- Trust the process

The Sprint Commitment Script:

"I'm starting my 90-day sprint in [skill]. Daily practice at [time]. Documenting at #90DayIncome. See you on day 90 with results. Who's joining me?"

Post it. Own it. Begin it.

90 days. That's all.

While others debate which skill to learn, you'll be earning with yours.

While they research perfect courses, you'll have completed free ones.

While they plan their someday transformation, you'll be living yours.

90 days from today, you'll either have:

- A new skill generating income, or
- Another 90 days of excuses

Both take the same time. Only one changes your life.

The sprint starts with your next action. Not your next Monday. Not your next month. Your next moment.

Set the alarm. Choose the skill. Start the timer.

90 days. 2,160 hours. 129,600 minutes.

Each one moving you closer to transformation or keeping you in place.

The math is simple. The choice is binary. The time is now.

Your current life has an expiration date: 90 days from today.

Your new life has a start date: Tomorrow morning.

The sprint begins at dawn.

Will you run it?

Your Chapter 8 Challenge (The 90-Day Income Challenge)

Theory ends here. Transformation begins now.

You've read about formulas. Studied examples. Analyzed possibilities. Knowledge without action is sophisticated procrastination. Time to birth results.

The 90-Day Income Challenge

Not another feel-good exercise. A mathematical transformation. A public commitment. A movement that starts with you and ripples globally.

Step 1: Declare Your Goal

Right now. Not tomorrow. Open your phone and post:

"Starting my 90-Day Income Challenge.
Goal: [specific income increase]
Skill focus: [chosen skill]
Current reality: [honest starting point]
Day 1 begins tomorrow at [time].
#90DayIncome

Who's brave enough to join me?"

Examples to Model:

"Starting my 90-Day Income Challenge.
Goal: $500/month side income
Skill focus: Copywriting
Current reality: Zero clients, basic writing skills
Day 1 begins tomorrow at 5:30 AM.
#90DayIncome"

"Starting my 90-Day Income Challenge.
Goal: 30% salary increase
Skill focus: Data analysis automation
Current reality: Manual Excel user
Day 1 begins tomorrow at 6 AM.
#90DayIncome"

Make it specific. Make it public. Make it real.

Step 2: Daily Learning Posts

Every single day. No exceptions. Share:

The Daily Formula:

"Day [X] #90DayIncome
Learned: [One specific thing]
Applied: [How you used it]
Time: [X minutes]
Insight: [What clicked today]
Tomorrow: [What's next]"

Real Examples:

"Day 12 #90DayIncome
Learned: VLOOKUP function in Excel
Applied: Automated weekly report
Time: 45 minutes
Insight: This could save our team 5 hours weekly!
Tomorrow: Pivot tables"

"Day 34 #90DayIncome
Learned: Email copywriting headlines
Applied: Rewrote client welcome series
Time: 30 minutes
Insight: Questions get 3X more opens than statements
Tomorrow: CTA optimization"

Step 3: Weekly Progress Updates

Every Sunday. Honest assessment. Community connection.

Week 1 Update Template:

"Week 1 Complete #90DayIncome
✓ What worked: Morning routine locked in
⚡ Challenge: Fighting imposter syndrome
◦ Breakthrough: First automation actually works!
◡ Need help with: Anyone know good Python resources?
☑ Progress: Can now do X without googling"

Step 4: Build Your Cohort

You're not climbing alone. You're building a movement.

Day 1: Tag 3 people who need this
"@Friend1 @Friend2 @Friend3 - you mentioned wanting to level up. Join me?"

Week 1: Find your accountability twin
Someone starting same day, similar goals, mutual support

Week   2: Create   mini-mastermind
3-5 people, weekly check-ins, resource sharing

Daily: Celebrate   others'   wins
Comment, encourage, share resources, build karma

Step 5: Document the Transformation

Future you needs evidence. Future followers need inspiration.

The Transformation Timeline:

Day 1 Photo/Screenshot: Your learning setup, starting point, commitment post, excited/terrified face
Day 30 Update: Skills learned list, first application, habit streak proof, confidence shifting
Day 60 Reality Check: Portfolio building, Valley survived, first value created, identity evolving
Day 90 Victory Lap: Before/after skills, income proof, transformation story, next 90 goals

The Viral Momentum

Watch the mathematics of movement:

You start: 1 builder beginning
You + 3 people: 4 builders building
Each brings 3: 16 builders learning
Their results inspire 3 each: 64 builders growing
90 days later: Hundreds transforming
Your courage creates permission. Your progress proves possibility. Your persistence produces followers.

The Valley Protocol

Between days 31-60, you'll want to quit. Post this:

"Day   [X]   #90DayIncome
In   the   Valley.   Everything   feels   pointless.
Still   showing   up.   Still   building.
Valley survivors - remind me why?"
Watch support flood in. From people on day 80 who survived. From people on day 20 who need hope. From people on day 180 who remember.

266

The Valley can't kill a supported builder.

The Challenge Commitment

Screenshot this. Sign it. Post it. Live it.

"I commit to the 90-Day Income Challenge.

I will practice daily - no exceptions.
I will document progress - building proof.
I will support others - creating community.
I will not quit in the Valley - trusting the process.
I will prove that 90 days changes everything.

My future income depends on my present commitment.

Signed: [Your name]
Date: [Today]
#90DayIncome"

Success Metrics

You win if:

- You complete 90 days (even imperfectly)
- You learn one valuable skill (even basically)
- You increase income (even slightly)
- You inspire one other person (even accidentally)

You've already won if you start.

The Hall of Fame

Previous Winners:

Sarah: +$2K/month from Excel automation
Marcus: Promotion + 35% raise from Python
Jennifer: $5K/month copywriting business
David: Remote job, doubled salary from web design
All started with Day 1 post. All wanted to quit around day 40. All grateful they didn't.

Your spot awaits.

You Just Started a Movement. Keep It Moving.

You posted your 90-Day commitment. Tagged three friends. Started your chain.

But there's someone who needs this book who hasn't found it yet. They're googling "how to make more money" at 3 AM. They're drowning in get-rich-quick schemes. They need what you just found.

Reviews are how they find us.

The Builder's Review Challenge:

- Post your commitment ✓
- Start your chain ✓
- Leave a review ☐

Take 60 seconds right now:

- Share why you're starting the 90-Day Challenge
- Be honest about where you are and where you're going
- Mention the specific value you've already received
- Use #90DayIncome so others can find your journey

Someone reading your review tonight starts their Day 1 tomorrow.

Your review becomes their breakthrough.

The movement spreads one builder at a time. One review at a time. One transformation at a time.

Leave it now. While the commitment energy is hot. While the decision is fresh.

Then get back to building. Day 1 starts tomorrow.

Your current income is not your permanent income. It's just your starting point.

90 days from now, you'll prove it.

But proof requires starting. Starting requires commitment. Commitment requires action.

The action is your next post: "Starting my 90-Day Income Challenge..."

90 days will pass whether you build or not. Your income will be higher or the same. Your skills will multiply or stagnate. Your confidence will soar or shrink.

The only variable is your participation.

Tonight   you   choose:
Another   90   days   of   wishing,   or
Your first 90 days of building

Tomorrow   you   begin:
Day   1   of   your   old   life's   end,   or
Day 1 of your new life's start

The builders are waiting for your declaration.

The movement needs your momentum. The community craves your courage. Your future demands your decision.

Post now. Start tomorrow. Transform in 90.

Your current income is about to become a memory. Your future income is about to become reality.

But only if you post that commitment.

Only if you start that sprint.

Only if you join the movement.

#90DayIncome

The challenge has been issued. The cohort is forming. The transformation is scheduled.

Will you be explaining your success on day 90? Or explaining why you never started?

The next 90 days answer everything.

Post. Commit. Begin.

Your new income awaits.

From Practice to Prosperity

The Two Mornings

Tomorrow, two versions of you will wake up.

Version A: hits snooze. Scrolls phone. Same morning. Same skills. Same income. Same complaints. Same limits. Same life. Tomorrow identical to today. Next month identical to this month. Next year? Don't ask.

Version B: alarm across room. Laptop open. Tutorial playing. Skills building. Value growing. Income pending. First day of different. First brick of transformation. First step toward everything.

Only one thing separates them: Starting the daily practice.

Not talent. Not money. Not time. Not luck. Not location. Not education.

Just the decision to begin. To do the thing. To be Version B.

One version reads about building. One version builds. One version knows the path. One version walks it. One version wishes. One version wins.

Which version sets their alarm tonight?

The Income Truth

Let's end the lies forever:

Your income is not about your location. The developer in Kansas outearns the one in California.

Not about your education. The self-taught crush the credentialed.

Not about your background. The disadvantaged become advantaged through value.

Not about your current job. The cleaner becomes consultant through skill.

Not about your age. The 60-year-old beginner beats the 20-year-old dreamer.

Your income is about the value you create.

And value creation is learnable by anyone, anywhere, with 15 minutes and intention.

15 minutes. Not 15 hours. Not 15 years. 15 minutes.

The barista who learns social media. The driver who learns coding. The parent who learns design. The retiree who learns writing.

All started with 15 minutes. All started scared. All started anyway.

Geography is dead. Credentials are dying. Only value is eternal. Only builders are thriving.

And building starts with tomorrow morning's alarm.

The Movement You're Joining

Stop reading. Check #90DayIncome right now.

See them? Hundreds starting their Day 1. Thousands in their Day 30. Some celebrating Day 90. All building. All struggling. All succeeding. All human. All heroic.

"Day 13: Finally understand functions!"

"Day 47: In the Valley but not quitting"

"Day 72: First client said yes!"

"Day 90: Income up 40%. Mind blown."
Your story adds to theirs. Their success fuels yours.

This isn't just personal transformation. It's economic revolution, one builder at a time.

Each person who transforms proves it's possible. Each success story gives permission. Each Day 90 victory creates ten Day 1 starters.

You're not just changing your income. You're changing what's possible. For yourself. For everyone watching. For everyone waiting for proof it works.

Your Day 1 post might be the exact inspiration someone needs to start. Your Day 45 Valley update might keep someone from quitting. Your Day 90 success might change a family's future.

This is bigger than your bank account. This is building the world where anyone, anywhere can create value and capture wealth.

But it starts with your alarm clock.

The Final Questions

- What skill will you learn?
- What time will you wake?
- What value will you create?
- What income will you build?

The answers matter less than the starting. The perfect plan matters less than the imperfect beginning. The ideal conditions matter less than the real commitment.

Part Three complete.

You know the Four Laws:

- Value decays without investment (grow or die)
- What you fund first flourishes (priority changes everything)
- Value multiplies at intersections (combination creates wealth)
- Small actions compound into transformation (momentum is mathematical)

You have the Daily Practice:

- Universal Income Formula (practice → skill → value → income → scale)
- Specific paths for your situation (employee, low-wage, unemployed, entrepreneur)
- Tools for acceleration (skill stacks, time arbitrage, value ladders)
- 90-day sprint framework (your transformation timeline)

You understand the path from learning to earning. From practice to prosperity. From daily discipline to different life.

Only one thing remains:

The challenge every builder faces. The test every transformer takes. The Valley that stops 90% of starters.

Chapter 9 reveals how to survive the Valley that kills most dreams.

You'll discover:

- Why days 31-90 feel impossible (and why that's normal)
- The psychology of the Valley (it's not personal, it's universal)
- Valley survival strategies from those who made it through
- How to turn the Valley from grave to graduation

But none of that matters if you don't start the practice. None of it helps if you remain Version A. None of it exists without Day 1.

Tonight you're someone who knows the path.

Tomorrow morning, you're someone walking it.

Set your alarm.

Your new income awaits.

The #90DayIncome builders are waiting for your Day 1 post. The movement is waiting for your momentum. Your future self is waiting for your courage.

Don't make them wait long.

Your alarm tomorrow morning isn't just waking you up. It's waking up your potential. It's waking up your prosperity. It's waking up the version of you that builds instead of browses.

Version A or Version B?

Your alarm clock decides. Your morning reveals. Your practice proves.

15 minutes. One skill. 90 days. New income. New life.

It really is that simple. And that difficult. And that possible. And that necessary.

The practice awaits. The prosperity follows. The path is clear.

Walk it.

Tomorrow. First thing. No excuses. No delays. No more reading without doing.

Your new income has an appointment with your alarm clock.

Keep it.

Chapter 9: Navigating the Valley

The Universal Test Every Builder Faces
"The Valley isn't geographic. It's psychological. Every builder in history faced it. Those who survived it shaped the world."

The Valley is Universal

It has a thousand names but one experience. That soul-crushing period where your efforts feel worthless, your progress invisible, and your dreams delusional. Often arrives between days 30 and 90. Frequently appears when you need momentum most.

Silicon Valley calls it the "trough of sorrow"—that graph line that drops after initial excitement and stays down for what feels like forever. Wall Street knows it as the "drawdown period"—when investments tank before they soar. Artists call them the "struggle years"—when genius goes unrecognized and rent goes unpaid.

Different industries. Different terms. Same psychological torture.

The Valley doesn't discriminate.

Thomas Edison's Valley

10,000 experiments before the light bulb worked. Ten. Thousand. Failures. Imagine experiment 5,847. Middle of the night. Another filament burned out. Assistants quitting. Investors questioning. Wife wondering if she married a madman. That's the Valley.

Colonel Sanders' Valley

1,009 rejections for his chicken recipe. One thousand and nine times hearing "no." At age 65. After failing at everything else. Sleeping in his car. Each rejection deeper into the Valley. Restaurant 1,010 said yes. The Valley ended. KFC began.

J.K. Rowling's Valley

Single mother on welfare. Clinically depressed. Baby daughter sleeping while she wrote in cafés because they had heat her flat didn't. Twelve publishers rejected Harry Potter. Twelve professional opinions that her Valley efforts were worthless. Publisher thirteen disagreed. The Valley became history.

Modern Valley Dwellers

Every YouTuber knows the Valley. Upload daily for months. Seven views per video. Three from your mom. Comments section: empty. Analytics: flatline. Day 67: "Why am I talking to nobody?" Day 134: First viral video. Valley crossed.

Every coder enters the Valley. Tutorials make sense. Building doesn't. Three months in: "I can't even center a div properly." Error messages mock you. Stack Overflow judges you. Imposter syndrome owns you. Then suddenly, on some random Tuesday, code clicks. Valley conquered.

Every writer lives in the Valley. Blog posts to the void. Medium articles with 12 claps (you clapped 10 times from different accounts). Newsletter with 7 subscribers (including your backup email). Six months of shouting into digital darkness. Then one piece resonates. Readers appear. Valley exits open.

The Valley Truth Nobody Tells You

The Valley isn't failure. Failure is quick. Clean. Clear. You try, you fail, you know. Done.

The Valley is different. The Valley is purgatory. You're not failing—you're just not succeeding yet. You're building skills but can't see them. Making progress but can't measure it. Getting closer but feel further away.

The Valley isn't failure. It's the price of admission to success.

Think of it as tuition. University costs money. The Valley costs faith. Both teach through suffering. Both graduate those who persist. Both seem overpriced until you're on the other side.

The 3 AM Valley Reality

It's 3 AM. You can't sleep. The alarm for your morning practice is set for 5:30. You stare at the ceiling calculating:

"67 days of waking early. 67 days of practice. Zero dollars earned. Zero recognition. Zero evidence this works."

Your spouse sleeps peacefully. They stopped asking about your "project" around day 40. Your friends think you've joined a cult. Your brain screams logic:

"This is stupid. You're wasting time. Those success stories? Lucky people. Special circumstances. Not for people like you. Be realistic. Quit now before you waste more time."

Everything feels pointless. Quitting seems logical. Actually, quitting seems like the only intelligent choice. The Valley makes failure feel like wisdom and persistence feel like stupidity.

That's the Valley's superpower—it makes quitting feel smart.

The Valley has destroyed more dreams than failure ever could.

Because failure is an event. The Valley is a season.

And seasons feel eternal when you're in them.

Winter feels permanent on the coldest night. You forget spring exists. Forget you've survived winters before. Forget that spring always follows winter. Always. Without exception. Unless you freeze to death first.

The Valley is your entrepreneurial winter. Your skill-building winter. Your transformation winter. And like all winters, it feels eternal while you're shivering.

But here's what Edison knew that the quitters didn't: Experiment 10,000 was coming. He just had to survive experiments 1-9,999 first.

What Sanders knew: Restaurant 1,010 existed. He just had to endure 1,009 rejections to reach it.

What Rowling knew: Publisher 13 was out there. She just had to write through depression, poverty, and 12 rejections to find them.

What every Valley survivor knows: The breakthrough is scheduled. It has an appointment with persistence. It always keeps its appointment. But only with those who show up.

The Valley isn't trying to destroy you. It's trying to qualify you. Not everyone deserves what's on the other side. The Valley decides who does.

Your Valley is waiting. Or you're in it. Or you just survived it.

But wherever you are with the Valley, remember: It's not geographic. It's not personal. It's not permanent.

It's just the price of admission to the life you want.

The question is: Will you pay it?

Or will you join the millions who quit in the Valley, forever wondering what waited on the other side?

Your 3 AM moment is coming. Your experiment 5,847 awaits. Your rejection 1,009 is scheduled.

Will you be there when the Valley ends? Or will you be another casualty of the season that felt eternal?

The Valley doesn't care. But your future does.

Choose wisely. Choose daily. Choose to continue.

Especially at 3 AM.

The Author's Valley (Yes, I Had Multiple)

Before I guide you through valleys, you should know: I've walked through several.

The deepest? When I crashed from $17,000 a month to almost zero.

But let me start at the beginning.

The Construction Wake-Up

$9 an hour. Construction laborer. Summer heat that started before dawn and didn't quit until after dark.

I'd come home covered in dust and exhaustion, too tired to shower. Fall asleep in my work clothes. Wake up and do it again. Seven days a week sometimes, because overtime was the only way to almost pay bills.

Month eleven, I did the math:

- Monthly income: $1,440 (before tax)
- Rent: $700
- Everything else: $740
- Savings: $0
- Life outside work: What life?

I was young but felt ancient. Living to work. Working to barely live. Managing decline at poverty wages.

The First Leap

I didn't read inspiring books. I googled "jobs that pay more than construction." Found warehouse work. $12 an hour. Inside. No more concrete dust.

33% raise felt like winning the lottery.

For about two weeks.

Then I realized: $12 an hour is just air-conditioned poverty. Same trap, slightly nicer cage.

The Research That Changed Everything

One night, exhausted but desperate, I searched: "highest paying jobs without college degree."

Sales kept appearing. I physically recoiled.

Sales? I hated pushy salespeople. The manipulation. The fake enthusiasm. The sliminess. Everything about it felt wrong.

But $18/hour plus commission felt right. Double my construction pay. Potentially triple with good months.

I applied to five sales jobs that night. No sales experience? Didn't matter. I'd figure it out.

The Sales Valley

First sales job: Solar. Knocking doors in suburban neighborhoods. Talking to people who didn't want to talk to me. Selling something I barely understood.

I was terrible. Stumbling through scripts. Feeling like a fraud. Watching naturals close deals while I collected rejections.

Jumped to pest control. Different product, same struggle. The rejection felt personal. The tactics felt manipulative. The culture felt toxic.

But something was building. Each rejection taught me. Each job added skills:

- Reading people
- Handling objection
- Understanding value
- Communicating clearly

Went back to solar. Different company this time. Started to understand: Maybe it wasn't sales I hated. Maybe it was how some companies did sales.

The Breakthrough Moment

Then I found THE company. Also solar, but everything was different.

They actually cared about helping homeowners save money. The product actually delivered value. The sales process was educational, not manipulative. Customers thanked us instead of avoiding us.

Suddenly, sales wasn't manipulation. It was problem-solving. It wasn't pushing. It was helping. It wasn't slimy. It was service.

My income exploded:

- First few months: Learning curve, but consistent base
- Year 1: Dialed in, commissions flowing
- Year 2: Top performer
- Years 3-4: Averaging $45/hour effective rate

From $9 to $45 through building. Not overnight. Not easily. But inevitably.

The First Business Valley

Here's what successful people don't usually admit: I threw it all away.

After years of building sales skills, product knowledge, and business understanding, I quit. Started my own business. Went from $45/hour to $0/hour overnight.

My girlfriend (now wife) watched our savings disappear. Parents asked when I'd "get serious." Friends thought I'd lost my mind.

- Month 1: Few hundred dollars
- Month 2: $1,000 (progress!)
- Month 3: $2,000 (momentum building)
- Month 4: $3,000 (this might work)

The climb felt good. Skills from sales translated. Systems started working. Clients referring others.

Then the explosion:

- Month 8: $15,000 (per month)
- Month 10: $20,000 (profit) (Income examples represent individual results and are not typical. Your results will vary based on effort, market conditions, and numerous other factors.)

I'd done it. Escaped employment. Built something mine. The Valley was behind me.

Or so I thought.

The Second Valley (The Deeper One)

Success is more dangerous than failure. Because success makes you think you've figured it out.

The crash came fast. Key client left. Market shifted. Systems that worked stopped working. Revenue evaporated like morning dew in Death Valley.

$17,000 a month to almost nothing.

This Valley was different. Darker. Because I'd tasted success and lost it. Because I'd already burned the bridge back to employment. Because now I had overhead, obligations, reputation at stake.

The whispers were crueler:

- "You got lucky once."
- "Should have stayed at $45/hour."
- "Not everyone's meant to be an entrepreneur."
- "Time to get a real job again."

My wife watching me stress. My confidence shattered. My identity in question.

But here's what the first Valley taught me: Valleys end. If you don't quit.

The Rebuild

Started over. Not from zero—from negative. But with hard-won knowledge:

- What worked before
- Why it stopped working
- What to build differently

Brick by brick. Client by client. System by system.

Month by month, climbing back. Past $3,000. Past $10,000. Past the old $17,000 peak.

Eventually doubling what I'd lost. Then tripling. Then stopping counting because the number wasn't the point anymore.

The same person who made $9/hour hauling concrete now helps thousands of builders escape their own valleys.

Not because I'm special. Because I survived multiple valleys. Because each Valley taught me something the peaks couldn't.

The Valley Truth I Learned

Every level has its Valley:

- $9 to $12: Valley of exhaustion
- $12 to $18: Valley of learning sales
- Solar to success: Valley of rejection
- $45 to $0: Valley of entrepreneurship
- $17K to crash: Valley of humility
- Crash to rebuild: Valley of resilience

Each Valley wanted me to quit. Each time, quitting seemed logical. Each time, continuing felt insane.

But here's what I know now: The Valley isn't your enemy. It's your qualification. It's not happening to you. It's preparing you.

The second Valley? That's where I learned what actually matters. Not the tactics that got me to $17K. But the principles that got me through the crash.

Those principles became this book.

Your Valley is waiting. Or you're in it. Or you think you've escaped it. (Spoiler: Another one's coming.)

But that's not bad news. That's your next level knocking.

Answer the door.

Your construction job might be retail. Your solar might be coding. Your crash might be coming or behind you. But the physics are identical.

Build. Hit Valley. Survive. Build more. Hit deeper Valley. Survive stronger. Keep building.

One day you'll write your own Valley story. And someone reading it will think, "If they hit $17K, lost it all, and rebuilt bigger... I can survive my Valley too."

They'll be right.

Now let me show you exactly how to survive yours...

The Valley Timeline: From Honeymoon to Hell to Heaven

Every builder's journey follows the same emotional arc. Different skills. Different goals. Identical psychological pattern. Here's the map of your next 90 days—screenshot it now, you'll need it around day 73.

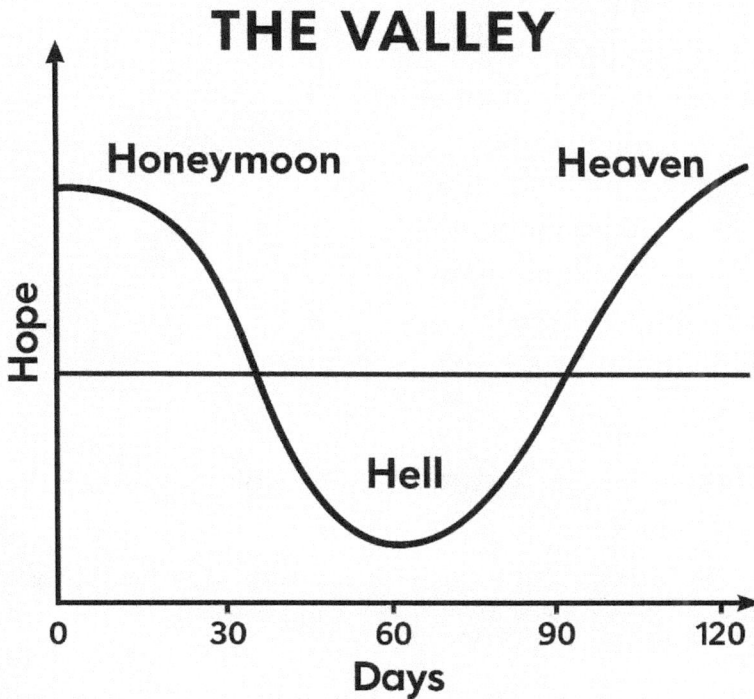

THE VALLEY

Honeymoon   Heaven

Hope

Hell

0   30   60   90   120

Days

Days 1-14: The Honeymoon High

You're drunk on possibility. Every tutorial feels like unlocking superpowers. Every small win feels like destiny confirming your choice. This is it. This is your transformation. Why didn't anyone tell you it was this accessible?

Your brain on Days 1-14:

- Dopamine flooding from novelty

- Future projecting exponential success
- Energy that could power cities
- Sleep optional because excitement mandatory

What you're saying:

- "This is amazing! I just built my first JavaScript function!"
- "I'm finally doing it! Day 7 streak!"
- "My life is changing! I can feel it!"
- "In 90 days I'll be making bank!"
- "Why didn't I start this sooner?"

Your social media:

- Daily posts about your journey
- Motivational quotes with sunrise photos
- Screenshots of every tiny victory
- Friends liking and encouraging
- You're becoming "that person" (in a good way)

The dangerous thought: "If I'm this good after one week, imagine three months!"

You're calculating exponential growth. If Week 1 = this much progress, then Week 12 = Silicon Valley calling. The math seems obvious. The path seems clear. The future seems guaranteed.

This is the honeymoon. Enjoy it. Store this feeling. You'll need to remember it exists around day 67.

Days 15-45: The Reality Check

The drug is wearing off. Novelty becomes routine. Easy wins become complex challenges. The exponential curve you imagined? Looking decidedly linear. Maybe even flat.

Your brain on Days 15-45:

- Dopamine normalizing (withdrawal beginning)

- Comparing progress to expectations (disappointment)
- Discipline replacing motivation
- Questions replacing certainty

What you're saying:

- "This is harder than I thought"
- "I missed three days, starting over feels demoralizing"
- "Everyone else seems to learn faster"
- "Maybe I need a better course"
- "Just need to push through this rough patch"

Your social media:

- Posts becoming sporadic
- Less enthusiasm, more determination
- Friends stopped commenting (old news)
- Comparing yourself to others' highlight reels
- Considering going private with journey

The creeping thoughts:

- "Those success stories had advantages I don't"
- "Maybe some people just aren't meant for this"
- "I should have started younger"
- "What if I'm wasting my time?"

But you push through. This is just a dip. The good stuff is coming. Has to be. Day 46 will be better.

Days 46-90: THE VALLEY (Abandon Hope, All Ye Who Enter)

Welcome to hell. Population: Every builder ever. Weather: Perpetual darkness with a chance of existential crisis.

Everything feels pointless. Not just difficult—pointless. The gap between effort and results has become a chasm. You're shouting into it. Only echoes of your own doubt return.

Your brain in the Valley:

- Dopamine? What dopamine?
- Cortisol party (stress hormones dancing)
- Pattern matching to past failures
- Logic screaming "QUIT" hourly

What you're saying (mostly to yourself):

- "Maybe I'm not cut out for this"
- "Those success stories must be lying"
- "I've wasted two months of my life"
- "Everyone was right—I should be realistic"
- "What's the point of continuing?"

What others are saying:

- Spouse: "How long are you going to do this?"
- Parents: "Maybe focus on your real job"
- Friends: (Nothing—they stopped asking)
- Brain: "You're embarrassing yourself"
- Logic: "Smart people quit when things aren't working"

Sarah's Valley Journal:

Day 72: "I've been learning JavaScript for two months and can't even build a working website. Spent 4 hours debugging only to realize I had a typo. A TYPO. My husband asked how long I'm going to 'play with computers.' I couldn't answer. Maybe he's right. Maybe I'm too old. Maybe I'm not smart enough. The teenager on YouTube builds apps in a weekend. I can't make a button work properly."

Day 78: "Skipped practice this morning. First time. Felt like relief. Then felt like failure. Then felt nothing. Considering deleting all my code and pretending this never happened."

Day 85: "Why am I doing this? Seriously. Why? Nobody's reading my progress posts. Nobody cares about my tiny victories. I don't even care anymore. Every tutorial feels like proof I don't belong here."

The Valley's Greatest Hits:

- "Everyone learns faster than me"
- "I'm the only one struggling"
- "This works for others, not me"
- "I should quit before I waste more time"
- "Being realistic isn't giving up"

The Valley whispers lies that sound like wisdom. Makes quitting feel intelligent. Makes persistence feel pathological. Makes your dreams feel delusional.

This is where 90% quit. Right here. Days 46-90. When the honeymoon is a distant memory and success feels like fantasy.

Day 91+: The Breakthrough (Wait, What Just Happened?)

Something shifts. Tuesday feels different from Monday. The code that broke your brain last week makes sense. The skill that felt foreign feels familiar. You solve a problem without Stack Overflow. You create something without tutorials.

Holy shit. When did that happen?

Your brain after the Valley:

- New neural pathways finally connected
- Compound effect suddenly visible
- Confidence replacing doubt
- Identity shifting permanently

What you're saying:

- "Why did I almost quit?"
- "It's actually clicking!"
- "I can't imagine not doing this"
- "Was it always this obvious?"
- "I need to tell everyone about Day 91"

Sarah's Breakthrough:

Day 91: "Built a working todo app. FROM SCRATCH. No tutorial. No copy-paste. My brain to the screen. It's ugly. It's simple. It's MINE. I literally cried."

Day 95: "Husband asked to see what I built. Showed him. He said 'You made that?' Like he was seeing me for the first time. Maybe he was."

Day 105: "First freelance inquiry. Someone wants to pay me. TO CODE. The same person who couldn't center a div two weeks ago. The Valley was lying."

The Perspective Shift:

- The struggle was the education
- The Valley was the curriculum
- The doubt was the test
- The persistence was the answer

You realize: Everyone who made it went through exactly this. Every coder who now builds complex apps once cried over syntax errors. Every writer now published once wrote to no one. Every successful builder has Valley scars.

The Valley wasn't trying to stop you. It was trying to prepare you. Not everyone deserves what's on the other side. The Valley was your qualification process.

The Universal Graph: Every builder's graph looks the same: Climb, crater, conquer.
The only variable is who survives the crater.

Edison's graph: 10,000 experiments, massive crater, light bulb. Rowling's graph: Years of rejection, depression crater, Harry Potter. Your graph: Same pattern, different scale, equal importance.

The Valley isn't unique to you. It's universal protocol. The price everyone pays. The test everyone takes. The season everyone endures.

But only some survive it.

Will you?

Day 73 is coming. Your Valley moment approaches. Your "why am I doing this?" night is scheduled.

Screenshot this timeline. Save it for the darkness. Read it when quitting feels smart.

Because the breakthrough is always scheduled for just after most people quit.

Don't be most people.

Valley Survival Stories

The Valley has a 90% kill rate. These are the survivors. Not because they were special. Because they were still there when the sun finally rose.

The Developer's Darkness (Austin, Texas)

Mark was 34, marketing manager, father of two. Good salary. Stable life. Soul-crushing boredom. Watched his cousin make $150K coding remotely. Decided to learn JavaScript. How hard could it be?

Days 1-30: The Dream Phase

Every morning at 5 AM. Coffee brewing. Codecademy loading. Kids still sleeping. Wife supportive. "I'm proud of you for trying," she said. Silicon Valley dreams dancing in his head. Three months to new career. Six months to six figures. The plan was perfect.

Posted daily on Twitter: #100DaysOfCode. Fellow beginners cheering. Experienced developers encouraging. Built a calculator. Built a clock. Built confidence. "Why doesn't everyone do this?"

Day 65: The Collision with Reality

"I've built 15 broken projects. Not one works properly."

That's what Mark told his wife over dinner. She paused. "When does this... pay off exactly?" The question hung between them like an invoice.

Fifteen projects:

- Todo app that didn't save todos
- Weather app showing wrong weather

- Portfolio site that crashed on mobile
- Calculator that couldn't calculate
- Timer that didn't time

Each failure meticulously documented. Each representing hours stolen from sleep, family, life. For what?

Day 78: The Reddit Confession

Posted to r/learnprogramming at 1 AM:

"I want to quit. Two months of 5 AM practice for nothing. I'm 34. Too old for this. My brain doesn't work like a programmer's. I see 22-year-olds building full apps while I can't make a button work. Wife thinks I'm wasting time. She's right. Someone tell me it gets better or tell me to stop."

47 comments. 46 saying "I feel this." 1 saying "Day 79 was when it clicked for me."

Day 82: The Almost Deletion

Saturday morning. Family at the park. Mark at his laptop. Staring at his projects folder. 127 files of failure. Select all. Right-click. Delete.

Finger hovering. One click away from ending this madness. Returning to normal. Accepting his marketing fate.

His daughter ran in. "Daddy, show me the color game you made!" The broken color-guessing game. She loved it anyway.

He closed the laptop. Kept the files. Kept the dream. Barely.

Day 89: The Crack of Light

One project finally worked. Simple task manager. Add tasks. Check them off. Save to local storage. Nothing revolutionary. Everything to Mark.

He added 10 tasks. Refreshed the page. They persisted. He stared at the screen. Refreshed again. Still there. His code. Working.

He cried. Actually cried. Over a todo app that any developer could build in an hour. But they didn't build it. He did.

Day 94: The First Money

Posted his todo app on Twitter. "Finally built something that works!"

DM appeared: "Hey, could you build something similar for my small business? I'll pay $500."

$500. For code he wrote. Not huge money. Huge validation. Showed his wife the message. She read it twice. "Someone wants to pay you? To code?" The disbelief in her voice hurt and healed simultaneously.

Day 180: New Reality

Remote developer position. Austin salary. Work-from-home life. Same Mark who almost deleted everything now reviewing pull requests. Teaching junior developers. Living the dream he almost abandoned.

Today: The Valley Guide

Senior developer. Runs "Valley Survivors" support group. 500+ members. His pinned message:

"Day 82 I almost deleted everything. Day 89 it clicked. Day 94 first payment. Now I mentor others through their Day 82s. The Valley almost took my dream. Now I know it was building my character. Your breakthrough is scheduled. Don't delete your files."

Every month, someone messages: "I was on Day 82. Your story kept me going. Just got hired."

The Content Creator's Crisis (Phoenix)

Ashley, 28, nurse, fitness transformation success story. Lost 70 pounds. Wanted to help others. Started Instagram fitness page. Dreams of inspiring millions. Reality of inspiring her mom.

Days 1-30: Building with Hope

Daily posts at 6 AM before hospital shift. Workout videos. Healthy recipes. Transformation photos. Motivational quotes over sunrise pics. "Building my empire," she'd caption. 12 likes. 8 from family.

Day 70: The Statistics of Sadness

147 followers. Two months of daily content. Average likes: 12. Comments: mostly her sister being supportive. Follower growth chart: flatlining like a failed EKG.

Posted side-by-side transformation. Her proudest achievement. 73 pounds lost. Life changed. 19 likes. Her cat videos got 200.

Her husband, watching her edit videos at midnight: "Babe, you're wasting time on this Instagram thing. No one's watching."

She knew he meant well. Still stung like antiseptic on wounds.

Day 85: The Breaking Point

Posted 20-minute workout routine. Spent three hours filming. Two hours editing. Heart and soul poured into pixels.

Views: 43. Family: 35. Actual strangers: 8.

Cried in the bathroom at work. Fellow nurse asked what's wrong. "Nothing," Ashley lied. How do you explain crying over Instagram metrics? How do you justify dreams that look delusional?

Day 88: The Dark Night

Scrolled through fitness influencers. Millions of followers. Perfect lives. Perfect bodies. Perfect engagement. What was she thinking? Another nurse thinking she's special. Another transformation thinking anyone cares.

Typed the post: "Taking a break from social media to focus on real life." Finger on "Share."

Deleted it. Posted workout tips instead. 11 likes. Went to bed defeated.

Day 92: The Algorithm Smiled

Posted simple before/after with story. No fancy editing. Just truth. How she felt at 220 pounds. The day she decided to change. The struggle nobody sees.

Woke up to notifications exploding. 1,000 likes. 100 comments. 50 DMs. "Your story is exactly what I needed." "Thank you for being real." "How do I start?"

The algorithm finally saw her. Or maybe authenticity finally broke through. Same Ashley. Same content. Different day. Different outcome.

Day 120: First Brand Deal

Small fitness apparel company. $500 for three posts. Not life-changing money. Life-changing validation. Showed her husband the contract. He read it slowly. "They want to pay you? For Instagram?" This time, wonder instead of doubt.

Year 2: The New Normal

Six-figure business. 200K followers. Quit nursing to create full-time. Daily DMs from women starting their journey. Speaking at fitness events. Living the dream she almost deleted.

"The Valley taught me to create for the process, not the praise. Days 1-90 I was performing. Day 91+ I was serving. The Valley taught me the difference."

Brief Global Perspective: The Universal Valley

Samuel in Nairobi faced the same Valley. Banking professional. Saw opportunity in mobile money training. Created curriculum. Rented small office. Posted flyers everywhere.

Day 73: Zero customers. Empty training room. Rent due. Wife pregnant. "Maybe formal employment is better," she suggested gently. He knew she meant "stable paycheck" when she said "better."

Day 95: First corporate contract. Small bank wanting staff trained. Led to bigger banks. Led to telecommunications companies. Now trains financial institutions across East Africa. Same Valley. Different continent. Same survival required.

"The Valley is the same whether you're in Kansas or Kampala. It whispers the same lies in every language. But breakthrough speaks universal too."

Every success story has a Valley chapter.

Between "started" and "succeeded" lies a darkness that swallows dreams. Between "beginner" and "expert" lies a desert that dehydrates hope. Between "idea" and "income" lies a test that breaks most spirits.

Mark survived his developer darkness. Ashley outlasted her content crater. Samuel persevered through his training tribulation.

They're not special. They're just survivors. The 10% who discovered that Day 91 exists. That algorithms eventually notice. That code eventually clicks. That customers eventually come.

The question isn't whether you'll face your Valley, but whether you'll finish it.

Your Day 73 is coming. Your "why am I doing this?" moment is scheduled. Your spouse will ask "the question." Your friends will offer "realistic" advice. Your brain will present "logical" arguments for quitting.

The Valley will test you like it tested them. Same test. Same lies. Same breakthrough waiting for survivors.

Will you be explaining your success story next year? Or explaining why you quit on Day 82?

The Valley doesn't care. But your future desperately does.

Keep going. Especially when stopping seems smart.

Your breakthrough is scheduled. Don't miss the appointment.

The Psychology of the Valley

Your Valley isn't just emotional. It's neurological. Your brain is literally rewiring, and rewiring hurts. Understanding the science transforms the Valley from mysterious suffering to predictable psychology.

Your Brain in Battle

The Dopamine Drought

Your brain runs on dopamine. Not happiness—dopamine. The anticipation chemical. The "this might be good" neurotransmitter. And the Valley is engineered to starve you of it.

Days 1-30: The Neurochemical Honeymoon

- New skill = Novel stimulus
- Novel stimulus = Dopamine flood
- Every tutorial = Mini achievement high
- Every small win = Chemical celebration
- Brain status: "This is amazing! More please!"

Your brain loves novelty like addicts love fixes. New pathways forming. New possibilities detected. Dopamine dealing like Vegas on New Year's. You're high on hope, drunk on potential.

Days 31-90: The Withdrawal Phase

- Novelty worn off = Dopamine supply cut
- Same tutorials = No chemical reward
- Practice feels routine = Brain says "boring"
- No visible progress = No achievement chemicals
- Brain status: "This isn't fun anymore, let's quit"

You're not weak. You're in withdrawal. Literal chemical withdrawal from the future-projection hormones that made starting feel magical.

Your brain, like a toddler denied candy, throws tantrums:

- "This is pointless!" (Translation: "Where's my dopamine?")
- "Let's try something else!" (Translation: "New thing = new dopamine")
- "We're not cut out for this!" (Translation: "This withdrawal hurts")

Coffee withdrawal gives headaches. Sugar withdrawal brings irritability. Dopamine withdrawal from learning creates existential crisis. Same mechanism. Different magnitude.

The Progress Paradox

Here's the cruelest Valley joke: You're improving faster than ever while feeling more incompetent than ever.

The Underground Growth:

- Day 1: Know nothing (and know it)

- Day 30: Know basics (feel accomplished)

- Day 60: Know enough to see the mountain (feel worthless)

- Day 90: Climbing mountain (breakthrough begins)

Your skills ARE improving exponentially. Neural pathways strengthening. Pattern recognition developing. Unconscious competence building. But it's all underground. Like roots growing deep before trees grow tall.

The Competence Curve Reality:

Day 1 You: Can't write "Hello World"
Day 60 You: Building broken projects
Feeling: "I've learned nothing"

   Reality: Day 60 You is literally 10X more capable. You just can't see it because you're measuring against perfection, not progress.

Example: The Invisible Multiplication

- Day 1: Follow tutorial to make button

- Day 30: Make button without tutorial

- Day 60: Make complex forms with multiple buttons

- Your brain: "But I can't build Facebook yet, so I suck"

The cruel irony: Biggest growth happens during the Valley. When you feel stupidest, you're learning fastest. When progress seems stalled, skills are compounding. When nothing works, everything is building.

   Plants grow roots in darkness before sprouting in light. Your skills follow same pattern. The Valley is your root-growing season.

The Social Pressure

The Valley is lonely. Not because you're alone, but because you're surrounded by people who don't understand why you continue.

The Conversation Cycle:

Week 2: "How's the coding going?" "Great! Learning so much!"
Week 6: "Still doing that computer thing?" "Yeah, getting there..."
Week 10: "Maybe you should try something else?" "..."

Everyone becomes helpful:

- "My cousin tried that, didn't work out"

- "The market's so saturated"

- "But you have a good job already"

- "Be realistic about your capabilities"

- "I'm just trying to protect you from disappointment"

They mean well. They're also killing you slowly. Death by a thousand caring cuts.

The Isolation Progression:

- Month 1: Share every small victory

- Month 2: Share only big wins (there aren't any)

- Month 3: Stop sharing entirely

- Internal dialogue: "Nobody understands"

You're right. They don't understand. They see you struggling and assume failure. You see yourself building and know it's process. The gap creates loneliness that makes the Valley darker.

The Identity Crisis

This is the Valley's deepest cut. The gap between who you claim to be and what evidence suggests.

The Declaration:

- "I'm becoming a developer"

- Changed Twitter bio to "Aspiring coder"

- Bought the courses

- Set the alarm

- Made the commitment

The Evidence:

- Can't build working website
- Stack Overflow makes no sense
- Teenage YouTubers code circles around you
- Two months in, zero money earned
- Still googling basic syntax

The Psychological Torture: Your brain demands consistency. When identity and evidence don't match, cognitive dissonance creates suffering.

"Am I developer learning, or am I pretending to be a developer?"
"Am I building a business, or playing business?"
"Am I transforming, or am I delusional?"

Self-doubt becomes self-attack: *"Maybe I'm just someone who starts things. Maybe I'm not a finisher. Maybe I'm exactly who I've always been, just with new hobbies."*

The Valley makes imposters of everyone. Because you are imposting— imposting as your future self before the evidence arrives. That's not fake. That's necessary. But it feels fraudulent in the Valley.

Valley Brain Hacks

You can't skip the Valley. But you can hack your brain to survive it.

1. Document Everything

Progress invisible to you is obvious in retrospect.

- Daily screenshots of work
- Weekly progress videos
- Journal one line: "Day 43: Finally understood functions"
- Save your terrible early projects

Future you needs proof current you is wrong about progress.

2. Find Valley Warriors

Others in Days 30-90 are your tribe.

- Join communities with progress tags
- Search "#Day45" "#Day67" "#StillBuilding"
- Share Valley updates, not just victories
- Connect with those who get it

Misery loves company. But Valley misery creates movements.

3. Celebrate Inputs, Not Outputs

Outputs are Valley-dependent. Inputs are you-dependent.

- "I practiced" > "I succeeded"
- "I showed up" > "I made money"
- "I tried something new" > "It worked"
- "I didn't quit today" > "I broke through"

Control what you can control. Celebrate what you can celebrate.

4. Reframe the Valley

Instead of: "Why is this so hard?"
Think: "Hard means valuable. If it were easy, everyone would do it."

Instead of: "I'm making no progress"
Think: "I'm in the root-growing phase"

Instead of: "Nobody cares about my journey"
Think: "I'm building for future audiences"

Instead of: "Maybe I should quit"
Think: "This is exactly where everyone wants to quit"

Remember: The Valley is proof you're doing something significant.

Easy things don't have Valleys. Trivial pursuits don't create withdrawal. Small dreams don't trigger identity crises. The depth of your Valley correlates to the height of your potential peak.

The Valley isn't your enemy. It's your filter.

It separates the committed from the curious.

The curious quit when dopamine dries up. The committed continue through withdrawal.

The curious stop when progress hides. The committed trust the process.

The curious fold under social pressure. The committed find fellow warriors.

The curious abandon challenged identities. The committed become who they declared.

Your brain will heal. Dopamine will return—different dopamine, sustainable dopamine, earned dopamine. Progress will surface. Evidence will mount. Identity will solidify.

But only if you survive the filter.

The Valley is asking one question: "Do you want this enough to earn it?"

Your continued presence is your answer. Even on days when continuing feels insane. Especially on days when quitting feels intelligent.

The filter is working. The question is: Will you make it through?

Your brain says no. Your future says yes.

Choose your future. Choose daily. Choose especially when your brain begs otherwise.

The psychology is predictable. The survival is possible. The breakthrough is scheduled.

But only for those who understand: The Valley isn't happening to you. It's happening for you.

Now you understand. Now survive it.

Building Your Valley Support Network

The Valley kills solo travelers. It's designed to. But the Valley can't kill a supported builder. Here's how to build your survival network before you need it—because by the time you need it, you won't have energy to build it.

The Valley Support System

Daily Check-ins (The Lifeline)

The simplest support system is also the most powerful. One post. Every day. Especially the dark days.

The Format:

"Day 67. Valley is brutal. Still practiced 15 minutes. Still alive. #ValleyWarrior"

That's it. No inspiration needed. No positivity required. Just proof of life.

Why This Works:

Public Accountability: Hard to quit after 67 public posts. Your streak becomes your identity. Breaking it feels like breaking yourself.

Normalizes the Struggle: Others see your Day 67 struggle. Their Day 23 feels less isolating. Your honesty gives permission for theirs.

Creates Connection: "Valley is brutal" gets more real responses than "Crushing it!" Vulnerability builds bonds. Bonds build strength.

Builds Evidence Trail: Day 150 you can scroll back. See your Valley posts. Remember surviving. Proof for next Valley (there's always another).

Real Valley Check-ins:

"Day 71. Husband asked when I'm giving up. Told him Day 91. Still coding. #ValleyWarrior"

"Day 54. YouTube kid built in 1 day what took me 1 week. Still showing up. #ValleyWarrior"

"Day 83. No progress visible. Faith invisible too. But I'm here. #ValleyWarrior"

These aren't motivation. They're documentation. The difference between Valley victims and Valley warriors is evidence of continuing.

The Valley Buddy System

Solo accountability is good. Mutual accountability is unstoppable.

Finding Your Valley Buddy:

Post: *"Day 45 looking for Valley Buddy days 40-55. Daily check-ins. Neither quits alone. #ValleyBuddy"*

Requirements:

- Within 10 days of your timeline (shared experience)
- Same timezone preferable (real-time support)
- Different skill fine (Valley is universal)
- Commitment to daily contact

The Daily Text Protocol:

Morning: "Practicing?"
Response: "Yes" or "Struggling"

If struggling: "What's one tiny thing you could do?"

Evening: "How was it?"
Response: Brief honest update

Not therapy. Not coaching. Just presence. Sometimes "Yes" is all that keeps you going.

Weekly Valley Calls:

15-minute weekly check-in:

- Share biggest Valley moment
- Share any tiny wins

- Plan next week's minimum viable practice
- Remind each other why you started

The Valley Pact:

"I promise not to quit without calling you first. You promise the same. We both get veto power over Valley decisions."

This pact has saved more dreams than any motivation could. Hard to quit when someone's counting on you counting on them.

Valley Victory Broadcasts

When you break through, you become hope dealer.

The Victory Format:

"Day 91. First client paid. $500. Valley was worth it.

To those on Day 50: KEEP GOING
To those on Day 30: The Valley is coming, but so is victory
To those on Day 70: You're closer than you think

The Valley ends. I'm proof. #ValleyVictory"

Why Victory Stories Matter:

For You: Documents your journey. Cements your identity. Proves it wasn't luck.

For Others:

- Day 30 them sees Day 91 is possible
- Day 65 them sees Day 91 is close
- Day 10 them sees Valley has end date

Your victory becomes their possibility. Their possibility becomes their persistence. The cycle continues.

Real Victory Broadcasts:

"Day 94. First freelance project complete. Client wants more. Valley tried to kill this dream. Failed. Still here. Still building. #ValleyVictory"

"Day 102. Got the promotion. Same person who couldn't understand basic concepts Day 60. Valley was my teacher. Brutal teacher. Effective teacher. #ValleyVictory"

The Multiplication Effect

This isn't just personal support. It's movement building.

The Network Math:

- You support 5 people actively
- They each support 5 others
- Network of 25 Valley Warriors
- Each supporting entire network passively

Success Rate Transformation:

- Solo through Valley: 10% make it
- With Valley Buddy: 40% make it
- With Network of 25: 90% make it

The math is clear. The Valley can kill individuals. It can't kill communities.

How to Build Your 25:

1. Start with your Day 1 post
2. Engage with 5 others starting
3. Form Valley Buddy connection
4. Share resources with all 5
5. They naturally do same
6. Network forms organically

Not forced. Not formal. Just humans helping humans survive what humans aren't meant to survive alone.

Valley Wisdom Library

Someone's Day 73 could save someone else's Day 73. Create collective wisdom.

Start or Contribute to Shared Document:

"Valley Survival Guide - Real Experiences by Day"

Structure:

Day 1-30: Honeymoon Phase
- What to expect
- What helped
- What to watch for

Day 31-60: Reality Setting In
- Common feelings
- Survival tactics
- Small wins to notice

Day 61-90: Deep Valley moments
- The darkest
- What kept us going
- Signs of coming breakthrough

Day 91+: Breakthrough
- How it happened
- What changed
- Message to Valley dwellers

Contribution Examples:

"Day 42: Wanted to quit when teenager's tutorial made me feel ancient. What helped: Reminded myself they don't have my life experience to combine with coding. Age is advantage, not limitation."

"Day 73: Almost deleted everything. What helped: Valley Buddy asked 'What would Day 1 you think of what you can build now?' Realized I'd grown 100x. Invisible to me. Obvious in comparison."

"Day 89: Breakthrough started with tiny win. One function finally worked. Not impressive to anyone else. Everything to me. The crack that became the flood."

"If I Could Tell Day 60 Me Something..."

Collective wisdom from survivors:

"The skills are building underground. You can't see roots growing, but they are."

"Every expert you admire had a Valley. They just don't Instagram their Day 73."

"The Valley is temporary. Your quit would be permanent."

"Day 91 exists. I promise. I'm writing from Day 150."

The Valley is where solo dreams die and supported dreams thrive.

You can be the strongest person alive. The Valley is stronger. You can be the most motivated human breathing. The Valley outlasts motivation. You can be the most talented individual learning. The Valley doesn't care about talent.

But the Valley can't kill what it can't isolate.

Build your support before you need it.

Because Day 67 you won't have energy to find buddies. Day 73 you won't want to post publicly. Day 82 you'll convince yourself nobody cares.

But if the network exists, if the buddy is texting, if the wisdom is documented—you'll survive what solo you couldn't.

Tonight's Valley Prep:

1. Post your current day and status
2. Find one person within 10 days of you
3. Exchange numbers for Valley Buddy pact
4. Bookmark #ValleyWarrior for dark days
5. Contribute one line to wisdom library

Your Valley is coming. Or you're in it. Or you just survived it.

Wherever you are, you're not alone. Unless you choose to be.

And choosing alone in the Valley is choosing death for your dreams.

Choose community. Choose survival. Choose to be the Valley Victory story someone needs to see on their Day 73.

The network is waiting. The support is available. The survival rate is 90% with community.

Will you be the 90% or the 10%?

Your next post decides. Your next connection determines. Your next day defines.

Build your network. Survive your Valley. Tell your story.

The Valley Warriors are waiting for you.

Your Chapter 9 Challenge (The Valley Victory Chain)

Most people prepare for success. Smart builders prepare for the Valley. Here's how:

The Valley has a 90% kill rate because people stumble into it blind. You're about to join the 10% who enter it armed, supported, and inevitable.

The Valley Victory Chain

Not another feel-good exercise. A military-grade preparation system for the psychological warfare of days 30-90. Your dreams depend on this preparation.

Step 1: Pre-Valley Power-Ups (Do Today, Not Tomorrow)

Write Your Valley Letter

Right now. To future Valley you. They need to hear this:

"Dear Day 67 Me,

You feel like quitting. Everything seems pointless. Nobody understands. Progress is invisible.

I'm writing from Day [X] to remind you:
- *Why we started: [Your why]*

- What we're building: [Your vision]
- Who we're becoming: [Your identity]
- What Day 91 will bring: [Your breakthrough]

The Valley is lying to you. I'm telling you truth. Keep going.

Love,
Pre-Valley You"

Seal it. Label it "OPEN ON DAY 60." Your life depends on this letter.

Screenshot This Page

Actually do it. Name it "Valley Emergency." Save to favorites. You'll need it at 3 AM on Day 73 when quitting seems genius.

Find 5 Valley Warriors

Post now:

"Looking for Valley Warriors to exchange numbers. Real support for days 30-90. No solo journeys. Who's building something big? #ValleyReady"

Get actual phone numbers. Social media fails in deep Valley. Texts save dreams.

Set Three Valley Milestone Rewards

- Day 45 survival: [Specific reward]

- Day 70 survival: [Bigger reward]

- Day 91 victory: [Celebration worthy of the battle]

Example: Day 45 = Favorite meal out. Day 70 = New equipment/tools. Day 91 = Weekend trip.

Book them now. Paying for future rewards makes quitting more expensive.

Create Valley Emergency Plan

When you want to quit, you will:

1. Read Valley letter first

2. Text all 5 Valley Warriors

3. Do 5 minutes practice (not zero)

4. Post "Valley Emergency" to community

5. Sleep before any quit decision

Write this plan. Sign it. You're legally bound to your future self.

Step 2: Valley Daily Protocol

When you hit the Valley (you'll know—everything feels pointless), activate this protocol:

Morning: Read Valley Letter
Before checking phone. Before coffee. Before the day convinces you to quit. Read why you started.

Practice: Minimum 5 Minutes
Not your best. Not your hour. Just 5 minutes. Valley victories are won in minutes, not hours. Zero minutes = Valley victory. 5 minutes = You victory.

Post: The Valley Signal
"Day X. Valley. Still building. #ValleyWarrior"

Four words that save dreams. Your community will respond. Your identity will strengthen. Your quit will pause.

Connect: Message One Valley Warrior
"Valley check. You building today?"

Their "yes" becomes your yes. Their struggle validates yours. Together, you survive what alone kills.

Night: Valley Victory Line
Write one line about why you didn't quit:

- "Daughter asked about my project"

- "Too curious about Day 91"

- "Valley Warriors wouldn't let me"

- "5 minutes turned into 20"

Document survival. Tomorrow you'll need proof today was survivable.

Future you needs evidence. Success you needs content. Document the transformation.

Daily   **Valley**   **Selfie**

Same time. Same place. Watch your face change from defeat to determination. Day 40 to Day 90 timelapse becomes your most powerful content.

Daily   **Screenshot**

Whatever you built. However broken. Proof you showed up. Day 91 you will cry seeing Day 45's "terrible" work.

Weekly   **Valley**   **Video**

Every Sunday. 60 seconds.

- What was hardest
- What kept you going
- Message to others in Valley
- Promise to continue

Raw. Real. Unedited. These become gold after breakthrough.

Valley   **Journal**

One paragraph nightly:

"Day 67. Wanted to quit at 2 PM when [specific thing]. Instead did [action]. Feel [emotion]. Tomorrow I will [commitment]. The Valley is [observation]."

This becomes your book's best chapter. Your course's most valuable content. Your talk's most powerful moment.

Valley survivors have sacred duty. You know the path. Others need the map.

Share Your Valley Story

Post your complete journey:

- Day 1 hopes

- Day 45 depths
- Day 73 darkness
- Day 91 breakthrough
- Message to current Valley dwellers

Your story becomes someone's survival guide.

Mentor 5 New Builders

Find 5 people starting their journey. Share:

- Your Valley letter template
- Your emergency plan
- Your daily protocol
- Your phone number

Your mentorship multiplies survival rates.

Create Valley Resources

- Valley playlist for dark days
- Valley reading list
- Valley workout routine
- Valley recipe collection

Anything that helped you help others.

Lead Valley Support Group

Weekly call. 30 minutes. Valley Warriors only. Share struggles. Celebrate survivals. Plan breakthroughs. Your leadership saves dreams.

The Chain Effect

Watch the mathematics of multiplication:

Without Preparation:

- Solo through Valley: 10% survive
- Valley kills 9 of 10 dreams
- Graveyards full of "I tried"

You Prepare:

- 80% chance of survival
- Valley becomes challenge, not catastrophe
- Breakthrough becomes probable

You Prepare + Support Others:

- 95% survival rate
- Valley Warriors network activated
- Mutual survival assured

They Support Others:

- Exponential success rate
- Valley loses power through exposure
- Breakthrough becomes normal

Valley Becomes Badge of Honor:

- "I survived Day 73" = Warrior status
- Valley stories become legacy
- Valley alumni become leaders

The chain reaction transforms the Valley from dream killer to dream qualifier. From burial ground to proving ground. From ending to beginning.

Your Valley Victory Chain Starts Now

Post immediately:

"Valley   Ready.
Preparing   for   days   30-90.
Writing   my   Valley   letter   today.

312

Who's   *with*   *me?*
#ValleyWarriors"

Then:

1. Write your Valley letter (10 minutes)
2. Find 5 Valley Warriors (respond to others posting)
3. Screenshot this page
4. Set milestone rewards
5. Create emergency plan

The   **Valley**   **Statistics:**
Unprepared builders: 90% casualty rate
Prepared builders: 20% casualty rate
Prepared + supported builders: 5% casualty rate

Which percentage will you be?
Valley Warriors Help Future Warriors

You just prepared for the Valley. Wrote your letter. Found your warriors. Set your protocol.

You know what's coming. The 90% casualty rate. The 3 AM doubts. The Day 73 darkness.

Right now, someone is on Day 73. About to quit. One review away from finding this book. One review away from discovering the Valley is temporary. One review away from surviving.

Your Valley Victory Mission:

- Write your Valley preparation letter ✓
- Find 5 Valley Warriors ✓
- Leave a review for Day 73 strangers ☐

Be real in your review:

- Share that you're preparing for the hard part
- Mention the Valley concept helped you understand the journey
- Tell them breakthroughs wait on the other side

- Give Day 73 warriors hope

Your honest review becomes someone's Valley lifeline.

Takes 60 seconds. Saves dreams.

Do it now. Before you face your own Valley. Give others what you wish you'd had.

Valley Warriors don't let others quit at Day 73.

#ValleyWarriors

Start your Valley prep now.

The Valley doesn't announce its arrival. Day 29 you feel invincible. Day 31 you question everything. Day 45 you want to die. Day 67 you plan your quit. Day 73 breaks most dreams.

Unless you're prepared. Unless you're supported. Unless you're part of the Valley Victory Chain.

Your Valley letter waits to be written. Your Valley Warriors wait to be found. Your Valley victory waits to be earned.

But it starts with your next action: *"Valley Ready. Who's with me? #ValleyWarriors"*

The builders who survive aren't stronger. They're just prepared. The dreams that live aren't better. They're just supported.

Your future self depends on present you preparing.

Will future you thank present you for preparing? Or curse present you for assuming the Valley wouldn't come?

Write the letter. Find the warriors. Create the plan.

Your Valley is scheduled. Your survival is optional. Your preparation decides which story you tell.

Prepare now. Survive later. Teach others forever.

The Valley Victory Chain starts with your next post.

Don't break it. Extend it. Strengthen it.

Your breakthrough depends on it.

#ValleyWarriors

The chain awaits your link.

The Valley Transforms You

The Valley's Secret Purpose

Here's what nobody tells you about the Valley: It's not a bug in the builder's journey. It's a feature.

The Valley doesn't exist to stop you. It exists to transform you. Every builder who shaped the world has a Valley story. Not because they were lucky enough to avoid it, but because they were strong enough to survive it.

Edison's Valley gave us light. Rowling's Valley gave us magic. Jobs' Valley gave us the future. Your Valley will give us something we don't yet know we need.

The Valley is a cocoon. You enter as one creature. You exit as another. The struggle isn't punishment—it's metamorphosis.

What The Valley Kills

The Valley is a precision weapon. It doesn't kill randomly. It targets specific weaknesses:

Your Amateur Mindset

Day 1: "This will be fun!"
Valley: "This will be work."
Day 91: "This is who I am."

The Valley murders hobbyists and births professionals. Fun becomes fulfillment. Interest becomes identity. Playing becomes practicing.

Your Need for Immediate Gratification

Day   1:   "When   will   I   see   results?"
Valley: "Results?   What   results?"
Day 91: "The work is the result."

The Valley teaches compound math through suffering. Immediate becomes irrelevant. Progress becomes patient. Dopamine gets rewired from quick hits to deep satisfaction.

Your Dependence on External Validation

Day   1:   "Look   what   I'm   doing!"
Valley: "Nobody   cares."
Day 91: "I care. That's enough."

The Valley forces internal scoreboards. Likes become meaningless. Views become vanity. Your own approval becomes the only currency that matters.

Your Fair-Weather Commitment

Day   1:   "I'll   do   this   forever!"
Valley: "Prove   it."
Day 91: "I proved it."

The Valley tests every promise you made to yourself. Easy commitments die. Real commitments crystalize. "I'll try" becomes "I am."

Your Old Identity

Day   1:   "I'm   learning   to   code."
Valley: "Are   you   though?"
Day 91: "I'm a developer."

The Valley is identity surgery. It cuts away who you were to reveal who you're becoming. The operation hurts. The result heals everything.

What The Valley Builds

For everything it kills, the Valley builds something stronger:

Professional Discipline

Amateur you needed motivation. Valley you learned discipline. Post-Valley you operates on identity. "I practice because I'm a builder" replaces "I practice to become a builder."

Long-Term Thinking

Pre-Valley: "90   days   to   riches!"
Valley: "Will   I   survive   today?"
Post-Valley: "Year 5 will be interesting."

The Valley stretches your timeline from weeks to years. Impatience dies. Strategy is born. You start playing games with longer horizons.

Internal Validation

No longer slave to algorithms. Free from dopamine dealers. Your scorecard becomes:

- Did I practice? Win.

- Did I improve? Win.

- Did I continue? Victory.

The world's opinion becomes data, not identity.

Unshakeable Commitment

You survived your worst days. Faced every quit moment. Chose to continue when continuing felt insane. That creates unshakeable knowing: If you survived the Valley, you can survive anything.

Your Builder Identity

Not something you're trying. Something you are. Not future tense. Present reality. The Valley burns away everything except what's true. What remains is who you really are: A builder.

The Valley Graduate's Wisdom

Every Valley survivor says the same thing:

"On Day 1, you want success. In the Valley, you just want to survive. After the Valley, you realize: The survival WAS the success."

The skills matter. The income matters. The achievement matters. But what matters most is who you became by not quitting when quitting made sense.

"The Valley didn't delay your transformation. The Valley WAS your transformation."

You thought you were learning to code. You were learning to persist. You thought you were building a business. You were building character. You thought you were developing skills. You were developing unbreakable self-trust.

The external success? That's just evidence of internal transformation. The Valley builds builders. Everything else is byproduct.

Your Valley Choice

Right now, before your Valley arrives (or while you're in it), decide:

Will you be someone who warns others about the Valley, or someone who guides others through it?

Will your Valley story end with "so I quit" or "so I conquered"?

Will you join the 90% who become Valley statistics or the 10% who become Valley graduates?

The Warning Version: *"I tried that once. Days 30-90 are brutal. Nobody tells you how hard it is. I was smart to quit when I did. Save yourself the trouble."*

The Guide Version: *"I survived that Valley. Days 30-90 nearly killed me. Here's my phone number for when you hit Day 67. You'll make it through. I'm proof."*

One perpetuates failure. One multiplies success. One creates more Valley victims. One creates more Valley victors.

Which storyteller will you become?

You're now equipped for the Valley.

You have the map. You know the timeline. You understand the psychology. You can build the support. You've prepared the protocols.

But survival isn't enough. You want to thrive. You didn't come this far to just make it through. You came to multiply everything—your impact, your income, your influence.

Chapter 10 reveals how builders compound their success beyond borders, beyond limitations, beyond imagination.

You'll discover:

- Why geography is now irrelevant to income
- How to serve globally while living locally
- The time zone arbitrage that multiplies opportunity
- Real builders creating borderless empires
- Your path from local to global impact

The Valley built your character. Now it's time to build your empire.

The Valley is coming.

For some, it's 30 days away. For others, it's tonight's 3 AM ceiling stare. For many, it's the current address.

Wherever you are in relation to the Valley, know this: You're ready.

Not because you won't struggle. You will. Not because you won't want to quit. You will. Not because it won't hurt. It will.

You're ready because you know what's happening. You know it ends. You know you're not alone. You know it's not personal. You know it's necessary.

Your breakthrough is on the other side.

Not maybe. Definitely. Not if you're special. If you're still there. Not through luck. Through lasting.

The Valley has your name on it. So does the breakthrough. One is the price. The other is the prize. Both are yours if you choose.

See you there.

On Day 91. In the sun. Changed forever. Ready to build what the Valley prepared you for.

Your fellow Valley Warriors are waiting. Your future self is cheering. Your breakthrough is patient. The Valley can't stop someone who won't stop.

Become unstoppable.

Chapter 10: Your New Reality.

What Really Happens When Builders Build
"Year One isn't about the money. It's about becoming someone who makes money inevitably."

Let me tell you what nobody else will about Year One:

It won't look like Instagram. It will look like war.

A war between who you've been and who you're becoming. Between your old habits and new ones. Between family saying "be realistic" and that voice whispering "keep building."

And that's exactly how it should be.

The Lie Everyone Tells You

The guru posts the screenshot: "$10K month in 90 days!" The course promises: "Six figures by Christmas!" The testimonial gushes: "Changed my life overnight!"

All lies. Not because transformation doesn't happen. Because that's not how transformation works.

Real Year One looks like this:

Sarah in Phoenix learning UI/UX. Day 67, crying in her car because the tutorial makes no sense. Day 127, building her first wireframe. Day 298, landing her first client. Day 365, earning more as a freelancer than her old corporate job.

Same person. Same year. Different story than the screenshot.

The Three Types of Year One

After watching thousands of people transform worldwide, I've seen the same three patterns emerge. In Tokyo and Toledo. In Mumbai and Minneapolis.

The Rocket (10% of builders)

Right skill, right time, right market. Sarah learned UI/UX just as startups exploded in her city. Quit her $35K admin job after six months. Ended Year One at $95K.

Rare but real. And completely unpredictable.

The Steady Climb (70% of builders)

Consistent progress, solid foundation. Mike the accountant added data visualization to his skills. Clients started paying premium for reports that actually made sense. Year One: 35% income increase, clear path to more.

Most common path. Most sustainable growth.

The Deep Foundation (20% of builders)

Internal transformation first, external results later. Jennifer explored writing while keeping her marketing job. Year One: Same salary, but found her voice and direction. Year Two: book deal and speaking engagements.

Looks like nothing happened. Everything actually happened.

Here's what matters: All three paths lead to transformation. Speed varies by person, not perfection.

The Quarter-by-Quarter Reality

Q1: The Messy Beginning

- Multiple false starts ("Maybe I should learn coding... or graphic design... or copywriting...")
- Forgetting to practice daily, then restarting
- Family thinks you're having a midlife crisis
- Zero visible progress
- **Key milestone:** Completing 30 days of anything

Q2: Finding Your Lane

- One skill emerges as favorite
- Habits starting to stick

- First tiny win ($47 from a weekend project)
- Confidence building slowly
- **Key milestone:** First earned dollar from new skill

Q3: The Momentum Shift

- More opportunities than time
- Old life feels constraining
- Can't stop talking about your projects
- Friends asking for advice
- **Key milestone:** Saying no to opportunities (good problem)

Q4: The New Normal

- New identity settling in
- Income visibly different
- Planning bigger for Year Two
- Teaching others naturally
- **Key milestone:** Can't imagine going back

The Universal Truth: This timeline plays out whether you're building in Berlin or Bangladesh. The human psychology of growth doesn't check passports.

What Actually Changes in Year One

Week 1-12: Your Mornings

Instead of scrolling anxiety, you're building capability. Instead of dreading the alarm, you're excited about what you'll learn.

Week 13-26: Your Conversations

"How's work?" becomes "Tell me about your project." You stop complaining about your situation. You start creating solutions.

Week 27-39: Your Bank Account

Not dramatically. But directionally. First $50 earned differently feels bigger than any raise. Because it came from value you created.

Week 40-52: Your Identity

The shift happens quietly. Someone asks what you do. You answer differently. Not just your job title. Your capability. Your possibility.

Why Most People Miss Year One Success

They're measuring the wrong things.

They track: Bank account, social media followers, business revenue **They should track:** Skills acquired, problems solved, value created, confidence built

Maria in Mexico City learned English while working at a hotel. Year One: same job, same salary. But Year Two: promoted to international guest relations. Year Three: hired by American company at 3X salary.

Year One built the foundation. Years Two and Three collected the reward.

Your Year One Reality Check

Right now, write down where you'll be December 31st if you change nothing. Same income? Same stress? Same feeling stuck?

Now write where you could be if you build daily. Not fantasies. Realistic progression based on the physics of growth.

The gap between those two futures? That's what Year One offers.

That gap is available in any economy, at any age, from any starting point. The only requirement is starting.

Your Year One begins with tomorrow's alarm. Not when conditions are perfect. Not when you have time. Tomorrow.

Because builders in Buenos Aires and Brisbane are starting tomorrow too. The sun never sets on Year One beginnings.

Will you join them?

Next: We'll map out Years 2-5, where small actions compound into extraordinary results—and where the real magic happens.

Years 2-5: The Compound Explosion

When Small Actions Create Extraordinary Results

"Everyone wants the breakthrough. Nobody wants the thousand invisible actions that create it. But that's exactly how breakthroughs work."

Here's what they don't show you in the success stories: the hockey stick.

Year One feels flat. Like nothing's happening. Then something magical occurs around Month 18. The curve turns vertical. Not gradually. Dramatically.

Like Lisa from Denver.

The Real Compound Timeline

Lisa's Journey (Marketing Manager → Industry Expert):

Year 1: Learned copywriting during lunch breaks. Income: $65K → $70K (small raise).

Year 2: Started freelance copywriting on weekends. Income: $70K salary + $30K side projects = $100K total. In my observation, approximately 90% quit in first 30 days... roughly 1% push through to day 100.

Year 3: Quit corporate job, went full freelance. Specialized in SaaS companies. Income: $150K.

Year 4: Built online course teaching SaaS copywriting. Income: $150K client work + $80K passive course sales = $230K.

Year 5: Launched copywriting agency, expanded course offerings, added coaching. Income: $400K+. (Income examples represent individual results and are not typical. Your results will vary based on effort, market conditions, and numerous other factors.)

Same person. Same 24 hours per day. Same laptop. Different physics.

The Pattern: Linear effort. Exponential results.

This isn't unique to Lisa or Denver or copywriting. This pattern repeats everywhere:

- **Ahmed in Cairo:** Accountant → Tax specialist → Business consultant → Software creator → $300K+

- **Priya in Pune:** Teacher → Online tutor → Course creator → Education platform founder → $250K+

- **Carlos in São Paulo:** Mechanic → YouTube repair channel → Tool designer → Automotive consultant → $180K+

Different skills. Different countries. Same compound curve.

What Actually Compounds (The Hidden Physics)

Skills Stack Like LEGO Blocks:

Year 1: Learn one thing deeply. Lisa mastered email copywriting.
Year 2: Add complementary skill. She learned conversion optimization.
Year 3: Combine uniquely. Email copy + conversion = SaaS email sequences.
Year 4: Teach the combination. Course on SaaS email marketing.
Year 5: Build systems around it. Agency that only does SaaS email marketing.

Each skill multiplies the others. 2 skills = 4X value. 3 skills = 9X value. 4 skills = 16X value.

Network Effect (The Hidden Multiplier):

Year 1: Lisa made 10 meaningful connections in copywriting community.
Year 2: Each introduced her to 5 others (50 total connections).
Year 3: Reputation spread through network (250 people know her work).
Year 4: Opportunities found her (1,000+ people aware of her expertise).
Year 5: She became the hub. When someone needs SaaS copywriting, they think "Lisa."

Network compounds faster than money. And creates more opportunities.

Income Acceleration (The Beautiful Math):

The math is simple. The results are extraordinary.

30 minutes daily × 365 days = 182.5 hours per year
182.5 hours × 5 years = 912.5 hours
912.5 hours = Master-level expertise in any field
Master-level expertise = $100K-$1M+ in value creation potential

But here's the compound secret: Hour 1 is worth $0. Hour 500 is worth $500. Hour 900 is worth $5,000.

Same hour. Different value. Because expertise compounds.

The Compound Domains (Beyond Money)

Health Compounds:

Year 1: John walks 30 minutes daily, loses 20 pounds.
Year 2: Adds strength training, reverses pre-diabetes.
Year 3: Becomes fitness mentor at work, helps 10 colleagues.
Year 4: Launches corporate wellness consulting.
Year 5: Speaking at health conferences, changed hundreds of lives.

Relationships Compound:

Year 1: Sarah learns communication skills, saves marriage.
Year 2: Helps friends with relationship issues.
Year 3: Gets relationship coaching certification.
Year 4: Builds couples retreat business.
Year 5: Thousands of marriages strengthened through her work.

Creativity Compounds:

Year 1: Miguel paints 15 minutes daily after work.
Year 2: Posts art online, builds following.
Year 3: Sells first painting, quits soul-crushing job.
Year 4: Gallery shows in three cities.
Year 5: Art selling internationally, teaching workshops globally.

Everything compounds. Everywhere. Always.

Why Most Miss the Explosion

The Tragic Truth: Most quit in Year One, right before the curve turns vertical.

Day 89: "This isn't working."
Day 150: "Maybe I should try something else."
Day 298: "I'm not seeing results."
Day 425: "I should have stuck with copywriting..." (But they didn't)

Meanwhile, Lisa at Day 425 is landing her biggest client ever.

The Compound Paradox: The closer you get to breakthrough, the more you want to quit. Because the gap between effort and results feels largest right before results explode.

The Valley is Compound's Test: Can you keep building when you can't see the curve turning? Can you trust the physics when emotions say quit?

Those who pass the test inherit the explosion.

Your 5-Year Vision (Right Now)

Stop reading. Grab paper. Write this:

If I build daily for 5 years, by December 2029 I will be:

- Skill level: _____
- Income level: _____
- Impact level: _____
- Life feeling: _____

Now write:

If I change nothing for 5 years, by December 2029 I will be:

- Same answers as today, just older and more frustrated.

The gap between those two futures? That's compound interest on life.

The curve is waiting. The explosion is real. The only question is whether you'll build long enough to see it.

Because builders in Bangkok and Boston are already three years in. Their curves are starting to turn vertical.

Will you join them, or will you quit right before your breakthrough?

Next: We'll explore how your personal transformation becomes a movement that changes the world.

The Movement Multiplier Effect

When Your Breakthrough Becomes Everyone's Possibility

"Your success gives others permission. Your story becomes their blueprint. Your transformation sparks theirs."

Marcus Williams never intended to start a movement.

He just wanted out of the factory.

Standing on the assembly line in Detroit, watching the same parts pass by for the 50,000th time, he made a decision. Learn web design. Escape this place. Build something different.

What happened next changed his city.

From Factory Floor to Freedom (The Origin Story)

Month 1: Marcus started learning HTML after his shift. Posted progress on Twitter with #FactoryToFreelance. Three likes. His mom and two bots.

Month 3: First basic website built. Ugly but functional. Posted screenshots. Co-worker DeShawn asked, "How'd you do that?"

Month 6: First paying client. $300 for a local restaurant website. Posted the win. Suddenly 50 factory workers following his journey.

Month 9: Quit the factory. Freelancing full-time. Posted the resignation letter. 500 followers asking, "How do I start?"

Month 12: Created simple training program. "Factory to Freelance in 12 Months." 23 factory workers enrolled.

Year 2: First cohort graduating. 18 out of 23 earning tech income. Local news picked up the story.

Year 3: 500+ factory workers across Detroit learning tech skills through Marcus's program. Unemployment in his neighborhood dropping.

Year 5: Marcus's program expanding to Cleveland, Milwaukee, Pittsburgh. Former factory workers now teaching other factory workers. Movement self-sustaining.

One person. One decision. One documented journey. Generational change.

The Mathematics of Impact

Here's how transformation multiplies:

Level 1: Personal Success (1 Life Changed)

You escape your trap. Prove it's possible. Feel proud.
Level 2: Shared Process (10 Lives Changed)

You document how you did it. Friends and family follow your path. Feel helpful.
Level 3: Viral Documentation (100 Lives Changed)

Your story spreads online. Strangers replicate your method. Feel amazed.
Level 4: Systematic Approach (1,000 Lives Changed)

You create simple, replicable training. Build community around it. Feel responsible.
Level 5: Movement Creation (Generational Change)

Your followers become teachers. System spreads beyond your control. Feel legacy.

The Beautiful Math: Your one escape plan becomes thousands of escape plans. Your one breakthrough becomes everyone's possibility.

How Movements Actually Start

Phase 1: The Proof of Concept

One person proves something impossible is actually inevitable. Not by talking about it. By doing it. Publicly. With receipts.

Marcus didn't say "Factory workers can learn tech." He became the factory worker who learned tech.

Phase 2: The Documentation

They share the actual process. Not the highlight reel. The real steps. The failures. The breakthroughs. The specific tools.

Marcus tweeted everything. The tutorials that confused him. The clients who didn't pay. The imposter syndrome at 2 AM. Raw truth, not polished success.

Phase 3: The Replication

Others follow the exact same path. Get similar results. Realize it wasn't magic. Just method.

DeShawn became the second factory-to-freelance success. Then Jasmine. Then Tony. Same path, same results. Pattern confirmed.

Phase 4: The Multiplication

Early followers become teachers. Each teaches 10 others. Each of those teaches 10 more. Growth becomes exponential.

DeShawn started teaching while still learning. Jasmine created YouTube tutorials. Tony launched a Discord community. Movement scaled beyond Marcus.

Phase 5: The Institutionalization

Movement becomes normal. Schools adopt it. Companies create programs around it. Culture shifts permanently.

Detroit community colleges now offer "Factory to Freelance" courses. Local government funds the program. What was radical becomes routine.

Real Movement Examples (Proof It's Possible)

#100DaysOfCode: Alexander Kallaway, one developer, committed to coding daily for 100 days. Posted progress. Now millions of people worldwide use his framework to learn programming.

Financial Independence (FIRE): Individual bloggers sharing their early retirement journeys. Became global movement. Millions now pursuing financial freedom using their blueprints.

#SideHustle: Personal stories of people earning extra income. Normalized multiple income streams. Changed how entire generation thinks about work.

#90DayIncome: Your 90-day income journey. Documented daily. Followed by thousands. Becomes the blueprint for escaping any economic trap.

Each started with one person. One decision. One shared journey.

Your Movement Potential

Right now, someone needs exactly what you're building.

The skill you're learning? Someone else needs to learn it too. The trap you're escaping? Others are stuck in the same one. The breakthrough you're creating? Thousands are waiting for proof it's possible.

Your transformation isn't just about you. It's about everyone watching.

When you document your building journey:

- Your cousin sees it's possible to escape retail hell
- Your neighbor realizes they can learn programming at 45
- Your coworker discovers freelancing isn't just for young people
- Strangers find hope they thought was gone

The Movement Maker's Blueprint

Week 1-4: Start building. Document everything. Share the mess.

Month 2-3: First small wins. Share those too. Someone's watching.

Month 4-6: Breakthrough moments. Show the exact process.

Month 7-12: Consistent results. Create simple system others can follow.

Year 2: Teach while you're still learning. Help others start.

Year 3+: Movement becomes self-sustaining. Your legacy multiplying.

The Ripple Effect Reality

Marcus changed Detroit. But Detroit changed America. Factory workers in Ohio saw the news. Started their own programs. Spread to Pennsylvania. Then Wisconsin.

One person in one city became a methodology in 20 cities.

Your ripple will reach places you'll never visit. Touch lives you'll never meet. Create changes you'll never fully know.

That's the beautiful responsibility of building publicly. Your success becomes everyone's permission slip.

The factory worker in Mumbai learning from Marcus's blueprint. The single mother in Manchester following your side hustle documentation. The recent graduate in Mexico City using your freelancing system.

You don't just build a better life. You build a better world.

The movement is waiting. The followers are ready. The impact is inevitable.

Will you just succeed privately? Or will you succeed publicly and spark a revolution?

Because movements need leaders. And leaders are just builders who document the journey.

Your transformation starts tomorrow. Your movement starts the moment you share it.

Next: We'll explore the ultimate question every builder faces: What legacy will you leave?

Building Your Legacy System

From Personal Success to Generational Impact

"Legacy isn't built in boardrooms. It's built in DMs, comments, and coffee shops where you help one person who helps another."

Here's what nobody tells you about legacy:

It doesn't start when you're successful. It starts when you're struggling.

The moment you begin building, you're already creating legacy. Because someone, somewhere, is watching. Taking notes. Finding hope in your progress.

Your Valley becomes their permission to start. Your breakthrough becomes their blueprint. Your transformation becomes their proof it's possible.

But legacy doesn't happen by accident. It requires intention. System. Strategy.

The Four Levels of Legacy

Level 1: Personal Victory (You Escape Your Struggle)

This is where everyone starts. And where most people stop.

You break free from your trap. Debt-free. Growing income. Building daily. Living proof the principles work.

Example: Jessica was drowning in $47K of credit card debt, working retail for $28K/year. Learned graphic design evenings and weekends. Eighteen months later: debt-free, freelancing for $65K/year, clients booking months ahead.

Personal victory achieved. Life transformed.

But only one life.

Level 2: Direct Impact (You Help Your Circle)

This is where builders separate from achievers.

You help 10 people directly. Share exact steps you took. Support them through their Valleys. Guide them to their own breakthroughs.

Jessica's Evolution: Started informal mastermind with five other retail workers wanting to escape. Met monthly at coffee shop. Shared design tutorials. Celebrated small wins. Cried through valleys together.

Eighteen months later: All five earning design income. Two quit retail completely. Three launched agencies. One teaching design at community college.

Ten lives transformed. Ten families impacted.

But still limited by your personal time.

Level 3: Scalable System (You Enable Hundreds)

This is where individual impact becomes systematic change.

You create replicable process. Build teaching resources. Enable hundreds to succeed without direct interaction.

Jessica's Scale: Created "Retail to Designer" online course. Documented every step from portfolio building to client acquisition. Built community platform. Monthly group coaching calls.

Year one: 127 students. Year two: 340 students. Year three: 800+ students across 23 countries.

Hundreds of lives transformed. Multiple industries impacted.

But still dependent on you.

Level 4: Self-Sustaining Movement (Culture Shifts Permanently)

This is where your success becomes cultural change.

Community teaches community. Success stories multiply exponentially. Movement runs without you.

Jessica's Movement: Top students became certified instructors. Created regional chapters. Retail workers teaching retail workers. Success stories spawning success stories.

Five years later: 5,000+ people escaped retail through her methodology. Community colleges adopted her curriculum. Retail industry conferences invite her to speak about "upskilling workforce."

The beautiful reality: Jessica's original struggle became thousands of people's solution.

Your Legacy Roadmap (The Practical Timeline)

Years 1-2: Personal Transformation Focus

- Build your own success foundation
- Document everything meticulously
- Share journey publicly
- Prove the system works on you first

Daily Actions: Learn, apply, share progress, help when asked.

Years 2-3: Direct Circle Impact

- Identify 10 people in similar situations
- Create informal support system
- Share exact methods that worked
- Guide them through their Valleys

Daily Actions: Continue building, answer questions, make connections, celebrate others' wins.

Years 3-4: System Building

- Document replicable process
- Create teaching materials
- Build online community

- Test with larger groups

Daily Actions: Scale yourself, create content, build systems, automate support.

Years 4-5: Movement Launch

- Train other teachers
- Enable self-sustaining community
- Create cultural shift
- Step back gradually

Daily Actions: Support teachers, refine systems, measure impact, plan succession.

Year 5+: Movement Independence

- Community runs without you
- Success stories multiply automatically
- Cultural change embedded
- New challenges await

Daily Actions: Strategic guidance only, new challenges, enjoy the legacy.

Real Legacy Examples (Proof It Works)

Khan Academy (Sal Khan): Started tutoring one cousin. Became global educational revolution. 120 million learners annually.

#100DaysOfCode (Alexander Kallaway): Personal coding challenge. Became worldwide movement. Millions of programmers trained.

Dave Ramsey's Baby Steps: Personal debt freedom. Became methodology used by millions. Changed financial culture.

Weight Watchers (Jean Nidetch): Personal weight loss. Became support system helping millions transform health.

All started with personal struggle. All became movements that outlived their founders.

Why Most Stop at Level 1

Fear: "Who am I to teach? I'm still figuring it out."
Truth: The best teachers are recent students. You remember the struggle.

Perfectionism: "I need to have everything figured out first."
Truth: People need your imperfect help more than your perfect silence.

Scarcity: "If I teach others, I'll create competition."
Truth: Teaching multiplies opportunities. Rising tide lifts all boats.

Overwhelm: "This seems too big for me."
Truth: Start with one person. Then one more. Legacy builds incrementally.

The Legacy Multiplier Effect

You help 1 person directly: They help their family (4 people impacted)

You help 10 people directly: They each help 4 family members (50 people impacted)

You create system for 100 people: They impact 400 families (500 people impacted)

You build movement of 1,000 people: They impact 4,000 families (5,000 people impacted)

Your movement spawns other movements: Exponential impact beyond measurement

One person's escape plan becomes thousands of families' transformation.

Starting Your Legacy Today

Action 1: Help one person this week. Share one thing you've learned. Answer one question. Make one connection.

Action 2: Document your process. What exactly did you do? What worked? What didn't? What would you tell your past self?

Action 3: Share publicly. Post your progress. Your struggles. Your breakthroughs. Someone needs to see it's possible.

Action 4: Find your circle. Identify 10 people who need what you're building. Invite them to build together.

Action 5: Think systems. How could you help 100 people with the same effort you help 10?

The Legacy Truth

You don't need to be perfect to start building legacy. You just need to be ahead of someone.

The person struggling where you struggled last year? You're their expert.

The person afraid to start where you started last month? You're their inspiration.

The person stuck where you were stuck last week? You're their guide.

Legacy isn't about being the best in the world. It's about being the best for someone's world.

Jessica was never the world's best designer. But she became the world's best guide for retail workers wanting to escape.

Marcus was never the world's best programmer. But he became the world's best translator of factory-to-freelance.

Your struggle is someone else's blueprint. Your breakthrough is someone else's hope. Your transformation is someone else's permission slip.

The legacy is already building. The only question is whether you'll nurture it intentionally.

Because somewhere, someone is watching your journey. Taking notes. Finding hope.

Will you just succeed for yourself? Or will you succeed for them too?

The Builder's Code

The Manifesto That Unites Every Builder on Earth

"This isn't just personal development. It's economic revolution, one builder at a time."

In Lagos and London. In Mumbai and Mexico City. In small towns and sprawling capitals. A quiet revolution is happening.

Not in boardrooms or government halls. In bedrooms and coffee shops. In the 15 minutes before the world wakes up. In the daily choice between scrolling and building.

We are the builders. And this is our code.

What We Believe

Growth is not optional, it's survival.

In a world where standing still means falling behind, we choose movement. Forward. Upward. Always. Because stagnation is death disguised as safety.

Value creation transcends circumstances.

Whether we're coding in Nairobi or cooking in Naples, teaching in Tokyo or fixing cars in Toronto—we create value that serves others. Geography doesn't limit us. Economics don't define us. Value flows where value grows.

The Valley is temporary, skills are permanent.

We've walked through the dark places where motivation dies and doubt screams loudest. We know the Valley isn't failure—it's the proving ground. Skills remain when the Valley ends. Forever.

Teaching multiplies impact.

What we learn, we share. What works for us, we offer to others. Not because we're experts, but because we remember being beginners. The best way to master something is to teach it.

Small actions compound into transformation.

We believe in the mathematics of miracles. Fifteen minutes today. Thirty tomorrow. Three hundred sixty-five days later: a different life. We trust the compound curve even when we can't see it turning.

What We Reject

"The economy is bad"

We build anyway. Because builders create their own economy. We solve problems that exist in any market. We add value that transcends economic cycles. Recessions create opportunities for those bold enough to build through them.

"I'm too old/young"

Age is irrelevant. Capability is everything. We've seen 16-year-olds teaching programming and 67-year-olds launching startups. Experience helps. Energy helps. But building helps most.

"I don't have time"

Fifteen minutes is enough. To learn something new. To solve one problem. To create one piece of value. To take one step forward. We don't need hours. We need habits.

"It's too late"

Started beats perfect. Today beats tomorrow. Imperfect action beats perfect inaction. The best time to plant a tree was 20 years ago. The second best time is now.

"I'm not smart enough"

Consistent beats brilliant. Daily beats sporadic. Building beats planning. Intelligence helps, but persistence transforms. We'd rather be steady builders than brilliant quitters.

What We Build

Skills that inflation can't touch.

While money loses value, capabilities gain it. While jobs disappear, problem-solving ability endures. We invest in ourselves first because that's the only investment guaranteed to compound.

Networks that create opportunities.

We connect with other builders. We support each other through Valleys. We celebrate each other's wins. We know that rising together lifts everyone higher than climbing alone.

Systems that generate income.

Not just jobs, but income sources that work while we sleep. Not just salaries, but value systems that scale. We build once, earn repeatedly.

Movements that change lives.

Our success becomes others' permission. Our documentation becomes their blueprint. Our breakthrough becomes their proof it's possible. We don't just escape—we build bridges for others to follow.

Legacies that outlive us.

The person we help builds something that helps someone else. The system we create serves people we'll never meet. The movement we start continues after we're gone. We build not just for today, but for generations.

The Daily Promise

Every builder, everywhere, commits:

"I will build for 15 minutes today." Before checking social media. Before making excuses. Before the world demands my attention. I will create something valuable.

"I will share what I learn." Not because I'm an expert, but because someone needs exactly what I discovered today. My struggle becomes their shortcut.

"I will support another builder." Through their Valley. In their victory. With my experience. With my encouragement. We rise together or not at all.

"I will not quit in the Valley." When motivation fails, I will rely on momentum. When progress seems invisible, I will trust the compound curve. When others doubt, I will persist.

"I will leave this world better than I found it." Not through grand gestures, but through daily value creation. Not through perfection, but through persistent improvement. One build at a time.

The Revolution Spreads

In São Paulo, Maria teaches financial literacy to favela residents. In Manila, Carlos builds apps that solve local transportation problems. In Manchester, Aisha creates online courses for immigrant entrepreneurs. In Mumbai, Raj develops water purification systems for villages.

Different skills. Different problems. Same code. Same revolution.

We are not waiting for permission. We are not asking for rescue. We are not accepting limitation.

We are building our way out. And lighting the path for others.

The Compound Effect of Code

When one builder follows the code, one life changes. When ten builders follow the code, a community transforms. When a hundred builders follow the code, an industry shifts. When a thousand builders follow the code, a culture evolves. When a million builders follow the code, the world changes.

This isn't just personal development. It's economic revolution, one builder at a time.

Because while economists debate theories, we create realities. While politicians make promises, we build solutions. While experts explain problems, we become the answers.

Join the Revolution

The code isn't optional for builders. It's the operating system.

Copy it. Share it. Live it. Teach it.

Translate it into your language. Adapt it to your context. But carry it forward.

Because somewhere today, someone is deciding between scrolling and building. Between managing decline and creating growth. Between accepting limitations and transcending them.

Your commitment to the code gives them permission to start.

Your daily building becomes their proof it's possible.

Your success becomes their blueprint for transformation.

Welcome to the builders. Welcome to the revolution. Welcome to the future you're about to create.

The code is simple. The impact is limitless. The time is now.

Build. Share. Support. Persist. Transform.

This is the way.

And with that code burning in your heart, you're ready for the most important chapter: what you do in the next 24 hours.

Your Final Challenge: The Next 24 Hours

Where Your Transformation Actually Begins

"Your old life ends with tonight's sleep. Your builder's life begins with tomorrow's alarm. The only question: Will you answer it?"

Right now, as you read these words, you're standing at a fork in the road.

Two paths stretch ahead. Both lead to tomorrow morning. But they end in completely different lives.

Choose carefully. Because 365 days from now, you'll live with the consequences of what you decide in the next hour.

Two Mornings, Two Lives

Morning A: The Manager's Tomorrow

Alarm screams. Hit snooze twice. Check phone in bed—scrolling anxiety for 20 minutes. Bank balance notification: $2,847. Same as last month, but groceries cost more.

Rush shower. Skip breakfast. Traffic worse. Radio host complaining about inflation. You nod—feeling seen but helpless.

At work: Same tasks. Same frustrations. Same coworker drama. Clock watching starts at 2 PM. Home by 6:30, exhausted from a day that added zero to your capability.

Netflix. Takeout. Scroll phone. "I should learn something," you think, then choose another episode instead. Bed by 11. Alarm set for same time. Same routine tomorrow.

365 days later: Same morning. Same job. Same frustration. Except now groceries cost 8% more, rent increased, and your purchasing power shrunk. You managed decline perfectly.

Morning B: The Builder's Tomorrow

Alarm sounds 30 minutes earlier. Phone across room forces you up. Coffee brewing while you open laptop. No social media. No news. Just learning.

Thirty minutes on YouTube: "How to Build Your First Web Application." Follow along. Break something. Fix it. Small win before most people wake up.

Document progress in phone notes. Share yesterday's breakthrough on Twitter: "Day 7 of coding. Built my first working contact form. Still ugly, but it works! **#BuildDontBudget**"

Three people like it. One comments: "Keep going! Day 47 here—just landed first client."

Shower feeling energized. Commute becomes podcast education. Work feels different—you're not just killing time anymore. You're buying time to build your future.

Evening: Skip one Netflix episode. Thirty more minutes learning. Apply what you learned. Notice opportunities everywhere. Local restaurants need websites. Your neighbor mentioned needing help with spreadsheets.

Plan tomorrow's learning. Sleep excited about progress. Wake up eager to build more.

365 days later: Different morning. Different life. Three freelance clients. 40% income increase. Confidence multiplied. Teaching others what you learned. Building the life you design.

Same 24 hours. Different choices. Exponentially different outcomes.

Your First Four Actions (Do NOW)

Stop reading. Seriously. Get your phone. Do these four things before you continue:

1. Set Tomorrow's Alarm

- 30 minutes earlier than usual
- Label it: "BUILD"
- Place phone across room (forces you to get up)
- This is non-negotiable. Do it now.

2. Choose Your Skill

Answer these three questions immediately:

- What expensive problem can you solve for others?
- What skill would 10X your value in the marketplace?
- What excites you enough to learn at 6 AM?

Write down ONE skill. Not three. One. Circle it. That's your focus.

3. Find Your Tribe

Open social media right now. Post this exact message:

"Starting my builder journey tomorrow morning. Learning [YOUR SKILL] for 30 minutes before the world wakes up. Who's building with me? #BuildDontBudget"

Find 5 people in comments who are also starting. Exchange numbers. Text them tomorrow: "Day 1 done. You?"

4. Write Your Why

On paper, answer these:

- Why MUST you change? (Make it emotional, make it real)
- Who are you becoming in 365 days?
- What legacy will you build through your transformation?

Put this paper next to your alarm. Read it when motivation fails.

The Accountability Accelerator

Before you sleep tonight, send this text to three people:

"I'm waking up 30 minutes early tomorrow to start building a better life. I'm learning [SKILL] and documenting the journey. If I don't text you proof by 8 AM, I owe you $50. Hold me accountable."

Send it. Feel the commitment lock in. Wake up with skin in the game.

The 10-Year Mirror

Look into the future. See two versions of yourself in 2034:

Version A (The Manager): Still in same situation. Older. More tired. Less purchasing power. Watching others' success stories. Thinking "I could have done that" about opportunities you're seeing right now but won't take.

Version B (The Builder): Teaching thousands the skills you mastered. Multiple income streams. Location independence. Time freedom. Sharing your transformation story. Others calling you inspiration.

The question that will haunt you for a decade:

"In 10 years, will you be sharing your transformation story or still reading about others'? Will you be teaching thousands or still dreaming about it? Will you have built a movement or just watched them?"

The Bridge You're Standing On

This book isn't the end. It's the bridge.

On one side: your old life. Familiar. Predictable. Declining.

On the other: your builder's life. Unknown. Challenging. Ascending.

The bridge is 24 hours long. You cross it one alarm at a time.

But here's what nobody tells you: The bridge doesn't stay there forever.

Every day you don't cross, it gets a little harder to see. A little easier to ignore. Until one day, you can't even remember where it was.

That's why tomorrow matters more than any day in the last five years.

The Revolutionary Truth

Somewhere tonight, in 50 countries and 20 time zones, thousands of people are setting alarms 30 minutes earlier.

- Mumbai: Priya choosing Python over scrolling
- São Paulo: Carlos learning copywriting before his kids wake
- Detroit: Angela studying digital marketing instead of watching news
- London: James building his first app while coffee brews

You could join them. Or you could read about their success stories in 2026.

The revolution doesn't need your permission. But it's saving a seat for you.

Your Final Choice

Close this book. Look around your current life. Feel the weight of where you are.

Now imagine the lightness of where you could be.

The gap between them? It's measured in mornings. In 30-minute decisions. In the choice between comfort and growth.

Your old life ends with tonight's sleep.

Your builder's life begins with tomorrow's alarm.

You know the physics now. You have the tools. You understand the path.

The only question remaining:

Will you answer the alarm?

Set it now. The revolution starts in the morning.

And the world is waiting to see what you'll build.

EPILOGUE: 6 AM Tomorrow

Alarm sounds.
Phone across room.
Feet hit floor.
Coffee brews.
Laptop opens.
Learning begins.
Builder born.
Welcome to your new life.
#BuildDontBudget

The End is The Beginning

Now go build something beautiful.

Welcome to the Builders

Your Transformation Starts at Sunrise

"Welcome to the builders. Your alarm is set. Your future is calling. See you at sunrise."

You're standing at the edge.

Behind you: A life of managing decline. Perfect budgets documenting your slow slide into irrelevance. Tracking every penny while purchasing power evaporates. Playing defense while the game changes around you.

Ahead: A life of building value. Imperfect action creating exponential growth. Skills that multiply your worth. Problems solved, lives changed, legacy built.

The cliff between them isn't geographic. It's philosophical. It's the choice between who you've been and who you're becoming.

You can't stand here forever.

The Promise I Make You

This isn't easy.

The Valley is real—that dark stretch where motivation dies and doubt screams loudest. Where family asks when you're getting serious. Where progress feels invisible and quitting feels logical.

Year One is messy. False starts and failed experiments. Code that breaks. Clients who don't pay. Skills that feel inadequate. Dreams that feel naive.

I won't lie to you about that.

But on the other side?

Freedom you can't imagine. Not just financial—though that comes. But the freedom of knowing you can create value anywhere, anytime. The freedom of skills that can't be fired, downsized, or made obsolete.

Impact you can't fathom. Not just income—though that multiplies. But the ripple effect of your transformation. The people who change because you showed them change was possible. The movement that grows because you planted the first seed.

A life you actually chose instead of one you fell into. Not perfect—no life is. But yours. Designed by your decisions. Built by your hands. Owned by your spirit.

That's what waits on the other side of tomorrow's alarm.

You're Not Alone in This

Right now, as you read these words:

Someone in Seattle is setting their BUILD alarm for 5:30 AM. Someone in Miami is choosing web design as their escape skill. Someone in Denver is posting their Day 1 commitment. Someone in Lagos is learning their first Python command. Someone in Mumbai is writing their first blog post. Someone in São Paulo is uploading their first YouTube video.

Different time zones. Same transformation. Universal choice.

You're not just starting a personal journey. You're joining a global revolution. A quiet uprising of people who refuse to accept decline as destiny.

We don't march in the streets. We build in the mornings. We don't hold protests. We create solutions. We don't wait for systems to change. We become the change.

The Builder's Code connects us across continents. The daily practice unites us across cultures. The shared struggle bonds us across backgrounds.

When you stumble—and you will—thousands of builders worldwide will catch you. When you breakthrough—and you will—thousands will celebrate with you. When you teach—and you will—thousands will learn from you.

You're not alone. You're joining the most important movement of our time.

The Time Truth

Five years from now, you'll be five years older either way.

Time doesn't pause for perfect conditions. It doesn't wait for motivation. It doesn't stop for fear.

The calendar pages keep turning whether you're building or browsing. Whether you're growing or stagnating. Whether you're creating value or consuming content.

Five years of managing decline perfectly = Five years further behind, just with better spreadsheets.

Five years of building imperfectly = Five years into transformation, with skills, income, impact, and options you can't imagine today.

Same time investment. Exponentially different outcomes.

The only question that matters: What will you build with the time that's passing anyway?

Your Builder's Birth Certificate

By reading this book, you've already changed. The person who started Chapter 1 couldn't have finished Chapter 14. That person didn't believe transformation was possible. Didn't see the path. Didn't understand the physics.

You do now.

You know the Four Laws that create wealth in any economy. You understand why budgeting alone guarantees decline. You see how small actions compound into extraordinary results. You recognize the Valley as temporary, skills as permanent. You realize your success gives others permission to start.

Knowledge without action is entertainment. Action without consistency is fantasy. Consistency without community is suffering.

But knowledge + action + consistency + community = transformation.

You have the knowledge. The action starts tomorrow. The consistency builds daily. The community awaits you.

The Last Choice

In the next ten minutes, you'll make the most important decision of the last five years.

You'll either set that alarm 30 minutes earlier, or you won't. You'll either join the builders, or you'll stay in the stands. You'll either answer tomorrow's call, or you'll hit snooze on your life.

No pressure. But everything depends on what you choose.

Your future self is watching. The one living the transformed life. The one with options, impact, and income. The one who conquered the Valley and reached the summit.

That person is whispering across time: "It all started with one alarm. One morning. One choice to build instead of scroll."

Or maybe they're silent. Because you chose comfort over growth. Safety over possibility. The familiar decline over the unknown ascent.

Welcome to the Builders

Your alarm is set for tomorrow. Your skill is chosen. Your tribe is forming. Your journey begins at sunrise.

Millions of us have walked this path. From struggle to strength. From surviving to thriving. From managing decline to building abundance.

We've left breadcrumbs for you to follow. Systems for you to use. Communities for you to join. Proof that it works, wherever you are, whatever your starting point.

The hardest part is over. You've decided to start.

Now comes the beautiful part. The building. The growing. The transforming.

The person you're becoming is already proud of you.

Welcome to the builders.

Your alarm is set.

Your future is calling.

See you at sunrise.

The revolution starts in the morning.

And it starts with you.

#BuildDontBudget

The End

Now go set that alarm.

www.ingramcontent.com/pod-product-compliance
Lightning Source LLC
Chambersburg PA
CBHW061800210326
41599CB00034B/6822